James Brown

BLACK
AND
PROUD

Facebook: **facebook.com/idwpublishing**
Twitter: **@idwpublishing**
YouTube: **youtube.com/idwpublishing**
Tumblr: **tumblr.idwpublishing.com**
Instagram: **instagram.com/idwpublishing**

ISBN: 978-1-68405-338-4   21 20 19 18   1 2 3 4

TRANSLATED BY
JEREMY MELLOUL AND
EDWARD GAUVIN

LETTERED BY
FRANK CVETKOVIC

COLLECTION EDITS BY
JUSTIN EISINGER AND
ALONZO SIMON

COLLECTION DESIGN BY
RON ESTEVEZ

PUBLISHER:
GREG GOLDSTEIN

Originally published by Marabulles as Black and Proud James Brown.

Greg Goldstein, President and Publisher
John Barber, Editor-In-Chief
Robbie Robbins, EVP/Sr. Art Director
Cara Morrison, Chief Financial Officer
Matt Ruzicka, Chief Accounting Officer
Anita Frazier, SVP of Sales and Marketing
David Hedgecock, Associate Publisher
Jerry Bennington, VP of New Product Development
Lorelei Bunjes, VP of Digital Services
Justin Eisinger, Editorial Director, Graphic Novels & Collections
Eric Moss, Senior Director, Licensing and Business Development

Ted Adams, IDW Founder

XAVIER FAUTHOUX

James Brown

BLACK AND PROUD

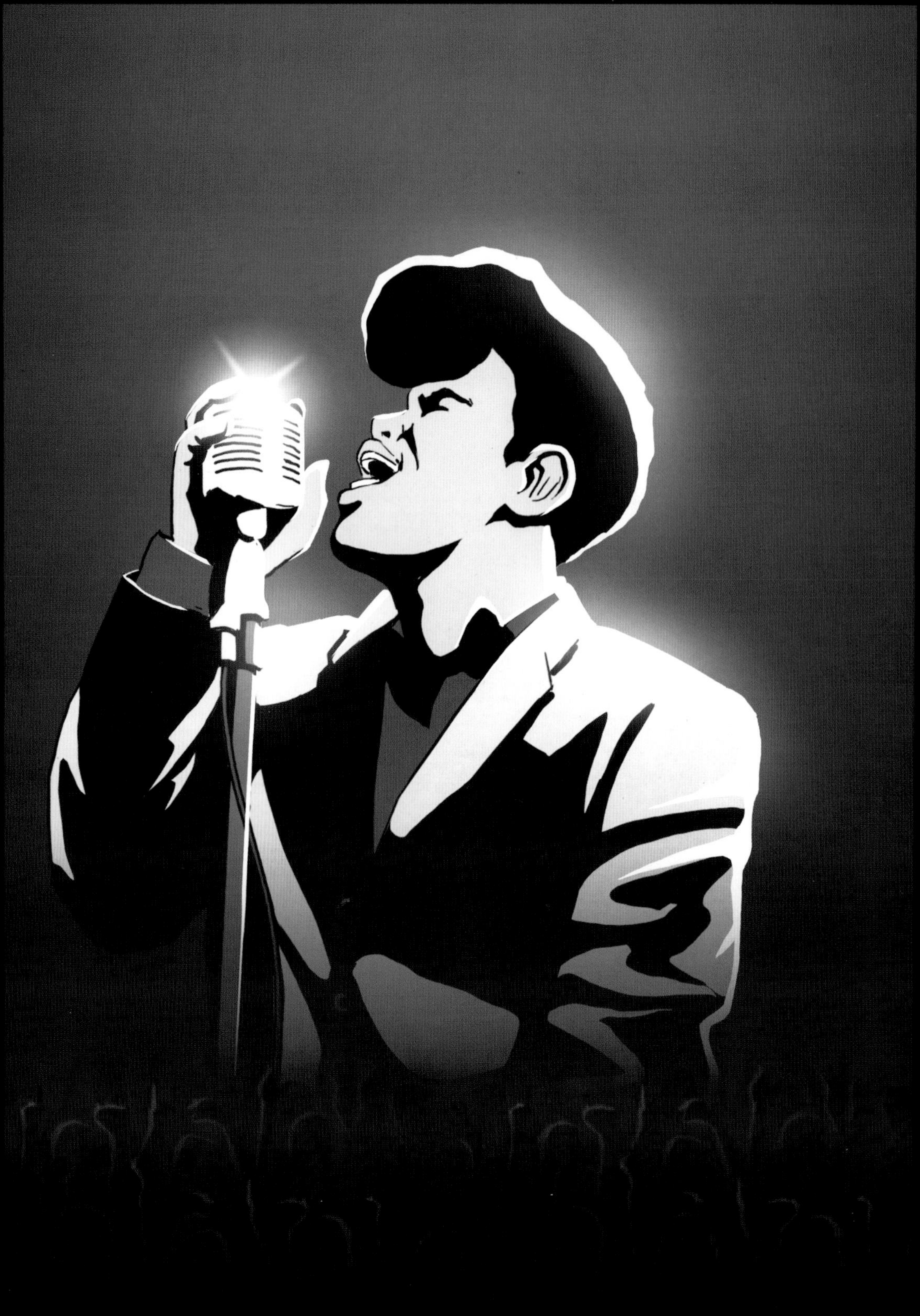

12.24
2006
AUGUSTA
When James Brown came to give presents to the underprivileged kids in the city, like he did every Christmas, it was a special event.
JAMES BROWN!
JAMES BROWN!
KING OF SOUL!
JAMES BROWN!
JAMES BROWN!
SOUL BROTHER NUMBER ONE!
Living legend and benevolent grandfather figure, he was adored by everyone. Accompanied by his wife, Tomi Rae, James was happy to sign a few autographs and spread the good word.

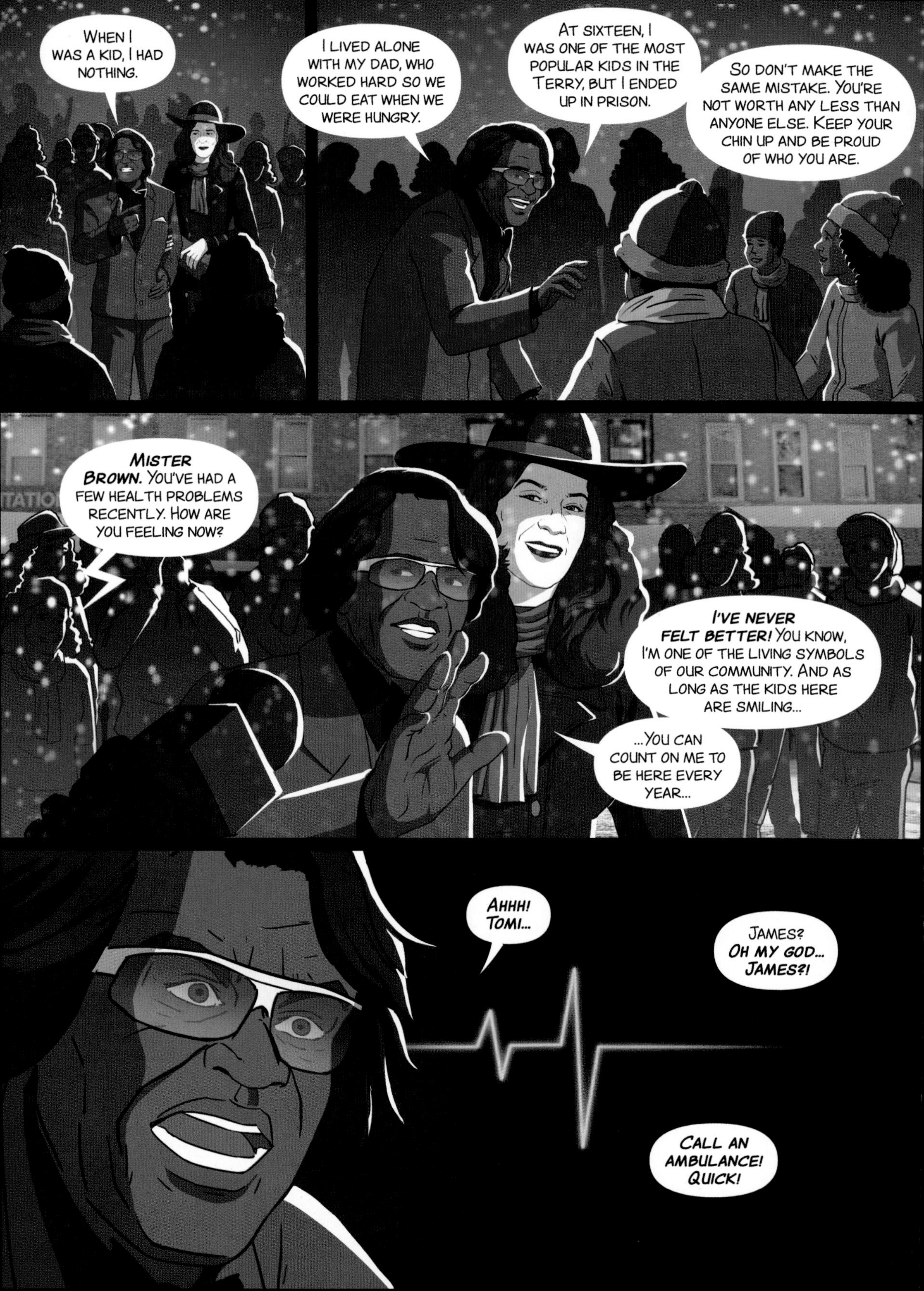
WHEN I WAS A KID, I HAD NOTHING.
I LIVED ALONE WITH MY DAD, WHO WORKED HARD SO WE COULD EAT WHEN WE WERE HUNGRY.
AT SIXTEEN, I WAS ONE OF THE MOST POPULAR KIDS IN THE TERRY, BUT I ENDED UP IN PRISON.
SO DON'T MAKE THE SAME MISTAKE. YOU'RE NOT WORTH ANY LESS THAN ANYONE ELSE. KEEP YOUR CHIN UP AND BE PROUD OF WHO YOU ARE.
MISTER BROWN. YOU'VE HAD A FEW HEALTH PROBLEMS RECENTLY. HOW ARE YOU FEELING NOW?
I'VE NEVER FELT BETTER! YOU KNOW, I'M ONE OF THE LIVING SYMBOLS OF OUR COMMUNITY. AND AS LONG AS THE KIDS HERE ARE SMILING...
...YOU CAN COUNT ON ME TO BE HERE EVERY YEAR...
AHHH! TOMI...
JAMES? OH MY GOD... JAMES?!
CALL AN AMBULANCE! QUICK!

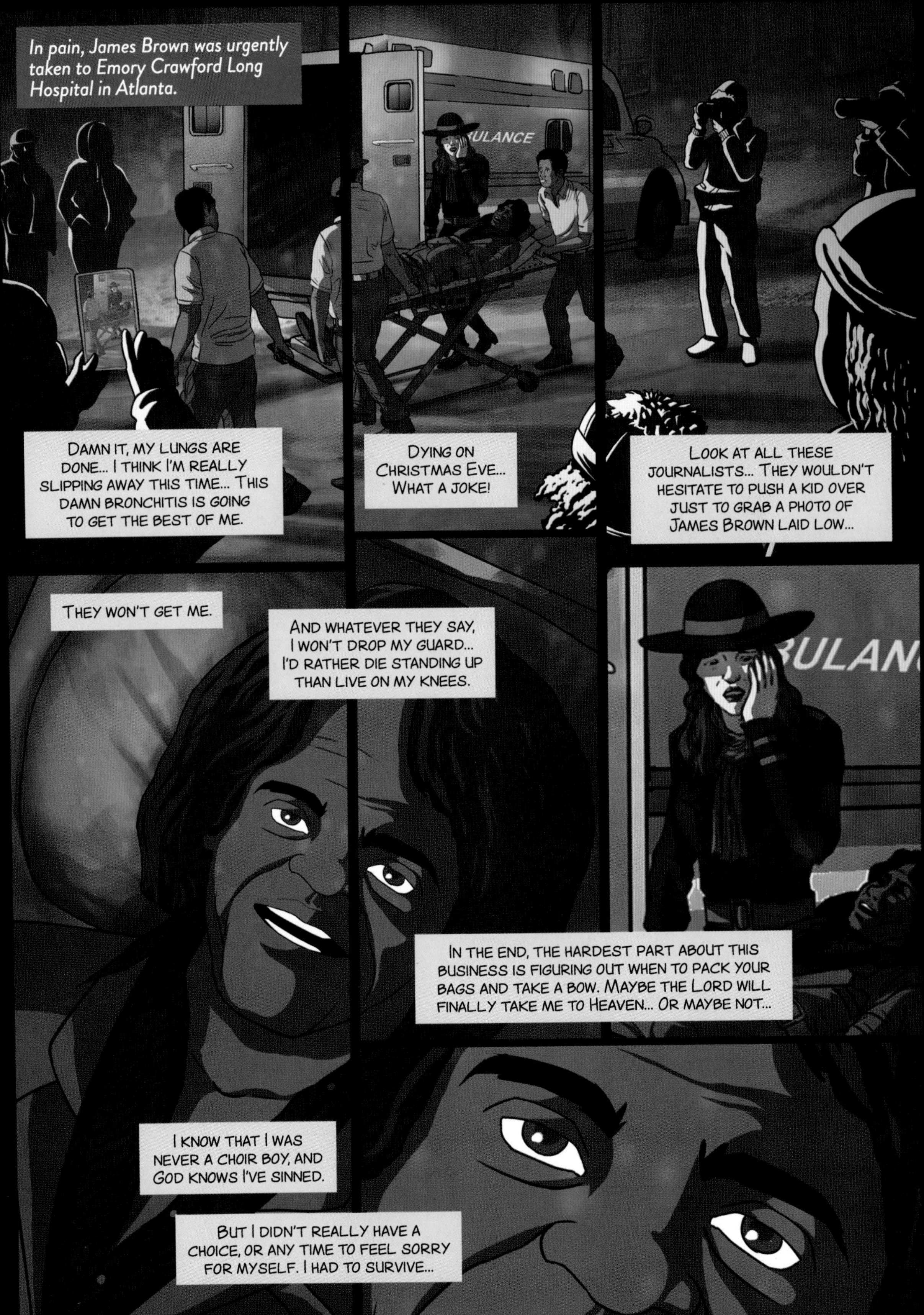
In pain, James Brown was urgently taken to Emory Crawford Long Hospital in Atlanta.
ULANCE
DAMN IT, MY LUNGS ARE DONE... I THINK I'M REALLY SLIPPING AWAY THIS TIME... THIS DAMN BRONCHITIS IS GOING TO GET THE BEST OF ME.
DYING ON CHRISTMAS EVE... WHAT A JOKE!
LOOK AT ALL THESE JOURNALISTS... THEY WOULDN'T HESITATE TO PUSH A KID OVER JUST TO GRAB A PHOTO OF JAMES BROWN LAID LOW...
THEY WON'T GET ME.
AND WHATEVER THEY SAY, I WON'T DROP MY GUARD... I'D RATHER DIE STANDING UP THAN LIVE ON MY KNEES.
BULAN
IN THE END, THE HARDEST PART ABOUT THIS BUSINESS IS FIGURING OUT WHEN TO PACK YOUR BAGS AND TAKE A BOW. MAYBE THE LORD WILL FINALLY TAKE ME TO HEAVEN... OR MAYBE NOT...
I KNOW THAT I WAS NEVER A CHOIR BOY, AND GOD KNOWS I'VE SINNED.
BUT I DIDN'T REALLY HAVE A CHOICE, OR ANY TIME TO FEEL SORRY FOR MYSELF. I HAD TO SURVIVE...

When you can see
the sky through the
roof of your house,
when you can see the
Earth through the
boards of your floor,
if you don't know
where your next meal
is coming from, then
you, my friend,
are poor.

-1-
NO FAMILY

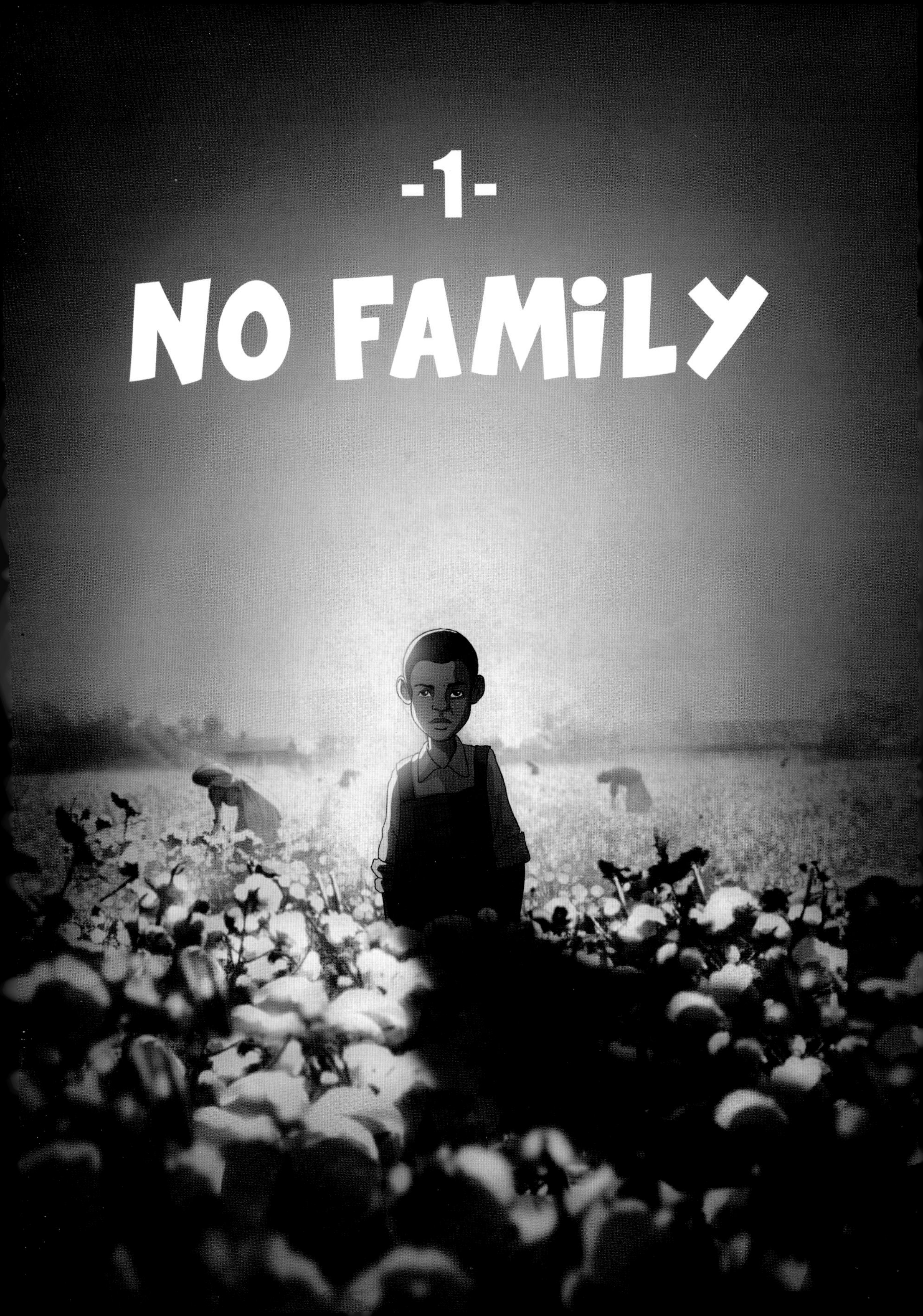

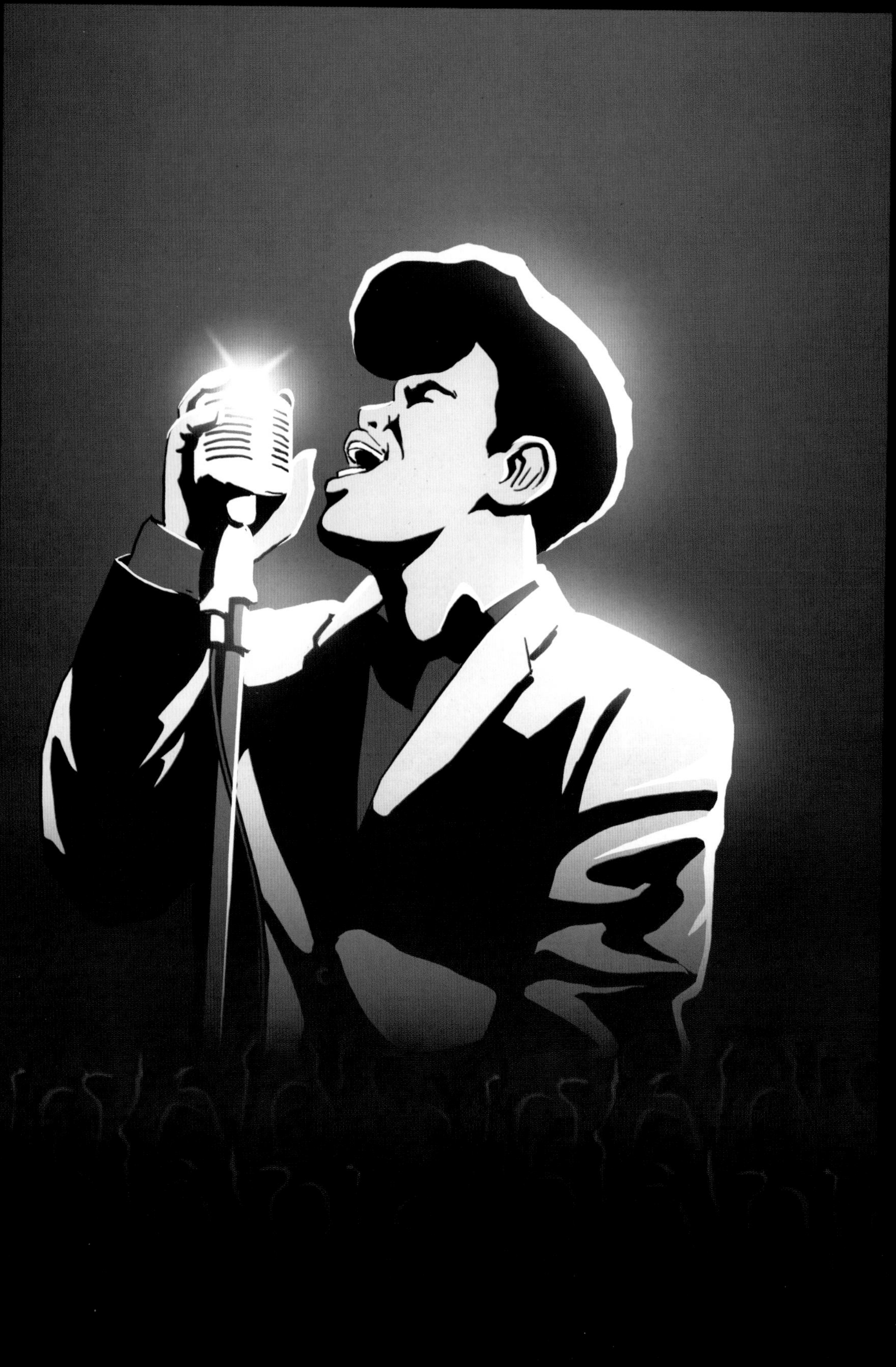

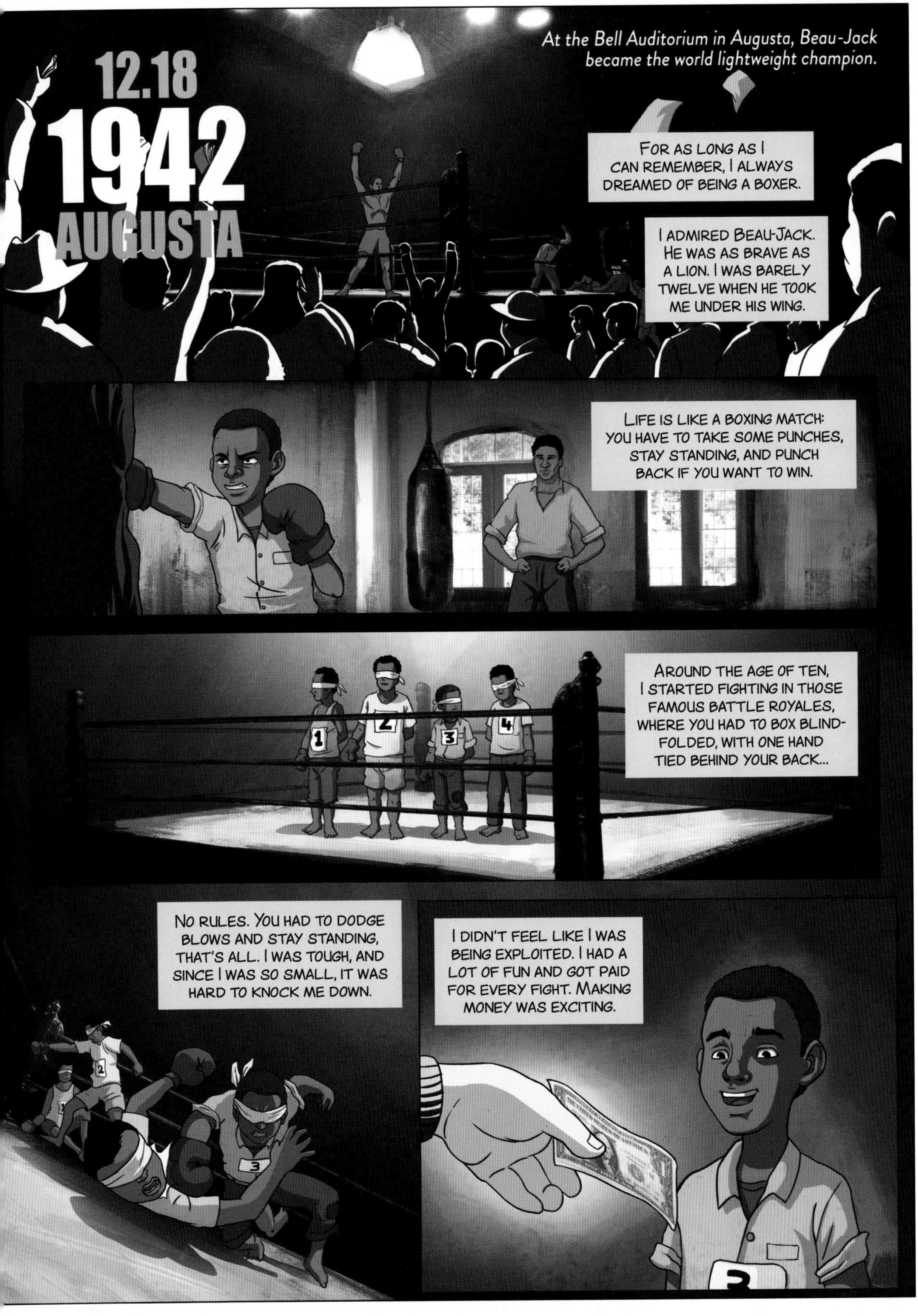
12.18
1942
AUGUSTA
At the Bell Auditorium in Augusta, Beau-Jack became the world lightweight champion.
FOR AS LONG AS I CAN REMEMBER, I ALWAYS DREAMED OF BEING A BOXER.
I ADMIRED BEAU-JACK. HE WAS AS BRAVE AS A LION. I WAS BARELY TWELVE WHEN HE TOOK ME UNDER HIS WING.
LIFE IS LIKE A BOXING MATCH: YOU HAVE TO TAKE SOME PUNCHES, STAY STANDING, AND PUNCH BACK IF YOU WANT TO WIN.
AROUND THE AGE OF TEN, I STARTED FIGHTING IN THOSE FAMOUS BATTLE ROYALES, WHERE YOU HAD TO BOX BLIND-FOLDED, WITH ONE HAND TIED BEHIND YOUR BACK...
1
2
3
4
NO RULES. YOU HAD TO DODGE BLOWS AND STAY STANDING, THAT'S ALL. I WAS TOUGH, AND SINCE I WAS SO SMALL, IT WAS HARD TO KNOCK ME DOWN.
2
1
3
I DIDN'T FEEL LIKE I WAS BEING EXPLOITED. I HAD A LOT OF FUN AND GOT PAID FOR EVERY FIGHT. MAKING MONEY WAS EXCITING.
3

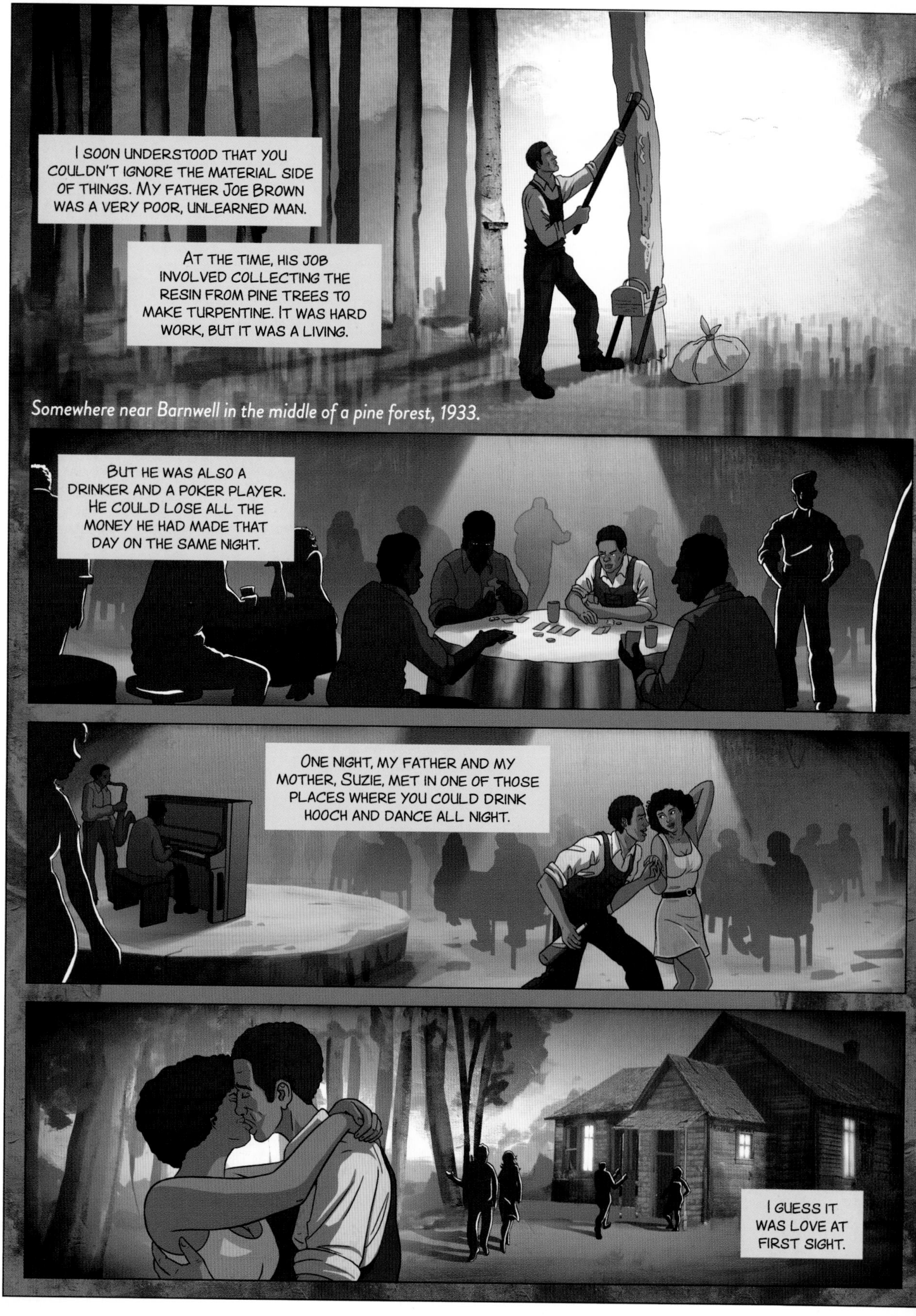
I SOON UNDERSTOOD THAT YOU COULDN'T IGNORE THE MATERIAL SIDE OF THINGS. MY FATHER JOE BROWN WAS A VERY POOR, UNLEARNED MAN.
AT THE TIME, HIS JOB INVOLVED COLLECTING THE RESIN FROM PINE TREES TO MAKE TURPENTINE. IT WAS HARD WORK, BUT IT WAS A LIVING.
Somewhere near Barnwell in the middle of a pine forest, 1933.
BUT HE WAS ALSO A DRINKER AND A POKER PLAYER. HE COULD LOSE ALL THE MONEY HE HAD MADE THAT DAY ON THE SAME NIGHT.
ONE NIGHT, MY FATHER AND MY MOTHER, SUZIE, MET IN ONE OF THOSE PLACES WHERE YOU COULD DRINK HOOCH AND DANCE ALL NIGHT.
I GUESS IT WAS LOVE AT FIRST SIGHT.

05.03
1933
AUGUSTA

In a barn somewhere, James Brown was born during the Great Depression, while the world was in crisis. His mother Suzie gave birth alone with the help of an aunt, Minnie Waler.

IT DIDN'T TAKE LONG FOR MY MOTHER TO GET PREGNANT. SHE WASN'T EVEN 18 YEARS OLD.

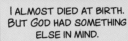

I ALMOST DIED AT BIRTH. BUT GOD HAD SOMETHING ELSE IN MIND.

IT WAS MY AUNT MINNIE WHO SAVED MY LIFE BEFORE I SUFFOCATED.

I THINK THEY WERE HAPPY THEN, THOUGH IT DIDN'T LAST VERY LONG.

James was thought to be stillborn - it was a miracle that he lived. He must have already understood that to survive in this world, he would have to fight.

MY FATHER TRAVELED ALMOST TEN MILES IN ORDER TO DECLARE MY BIRTH.

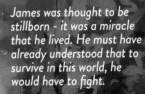

BARNWELL 10KM

MY NAME IS "JAMES JOSEPH BROWN JUNIOR." BROWN IS A NAME THAT THEY GAVE TO MY GRANDFATHER, THE SON OF A SLAVE, BUT MY ANCESTORS WERE CHEROKEE INDIANS.

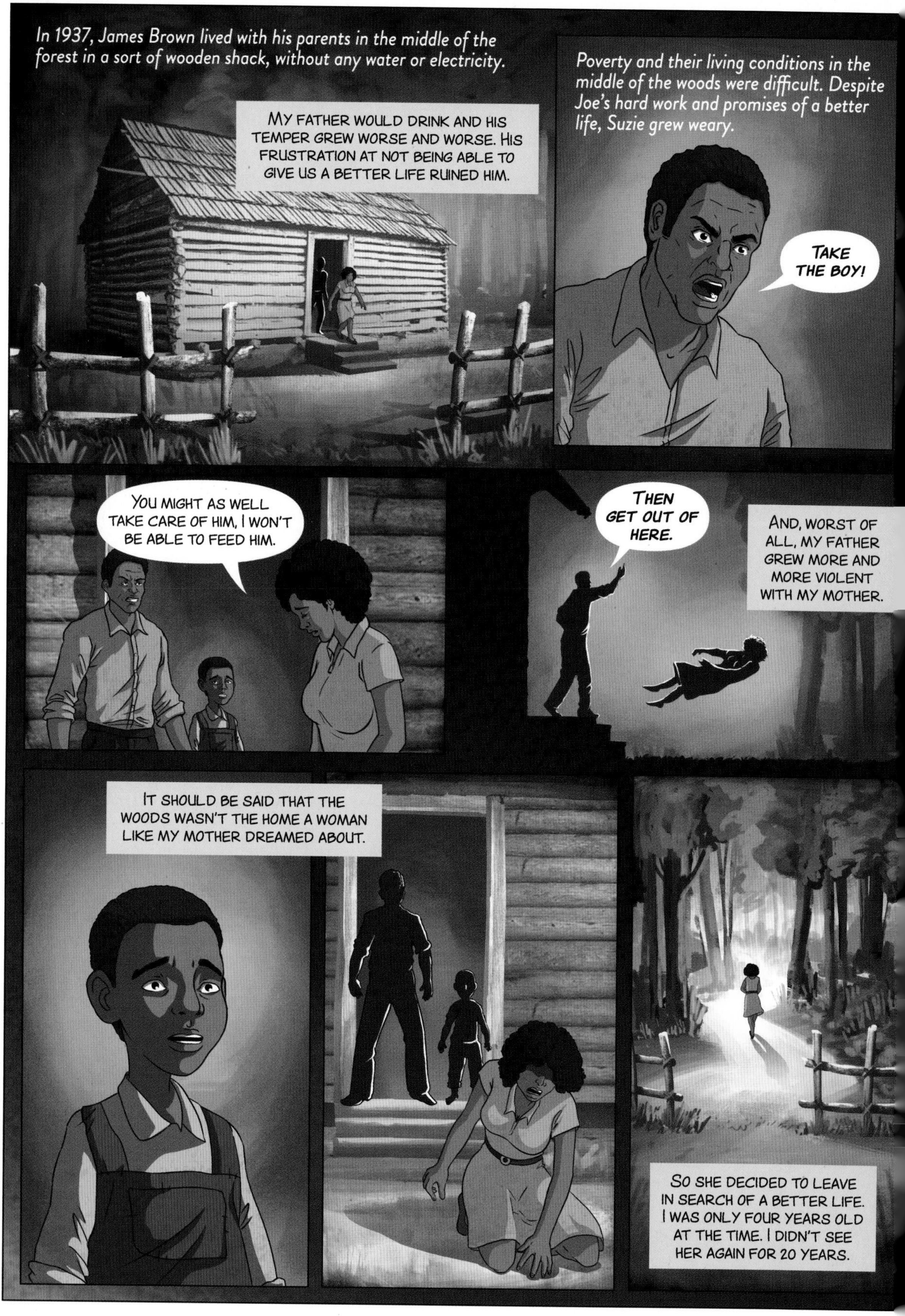
In 1937, James Brown lived with his parents in the middle of the forest in a sort of wooden shack, without any water or electricity.
MY FATHER WOULD DRINK AND HIS TEMPER GREW WORSE AND WORSE. HIS FRUSTRATION AT NOT BEING ABLE TO GIVE US A BETTER LIFE RUINED HIM.
Poverty and their living conditions in the middle of the woods were difficult. Despite Joe's hard work and promises of a better life, Suzie grew weary.
TAKE THE BOY!
YOU MIGHT AS WELL TAKE CARE OF HIM, I WON'T BE ABLE TO FEED HIM.
THEN GET OUT OF HERE.
AND, WORST OF ALL, MY FATHER GREW MORE AND MORE VIOLENT WITH MY MOTHER.
IT SHOULD BE SAID THAT THE WOODS WASN'T THE HOME A WOMAN LIKE MY MOTHER DREAMED ABOUT.
SO SHE DECIDED TO LEAVE IN SEARCH OF A BETTER LIFE. I WAS ONLY FOUR YEARS OLD AT THE TIME. I DIDN'T SEE HER AGAIN FOR 20 YEARS.

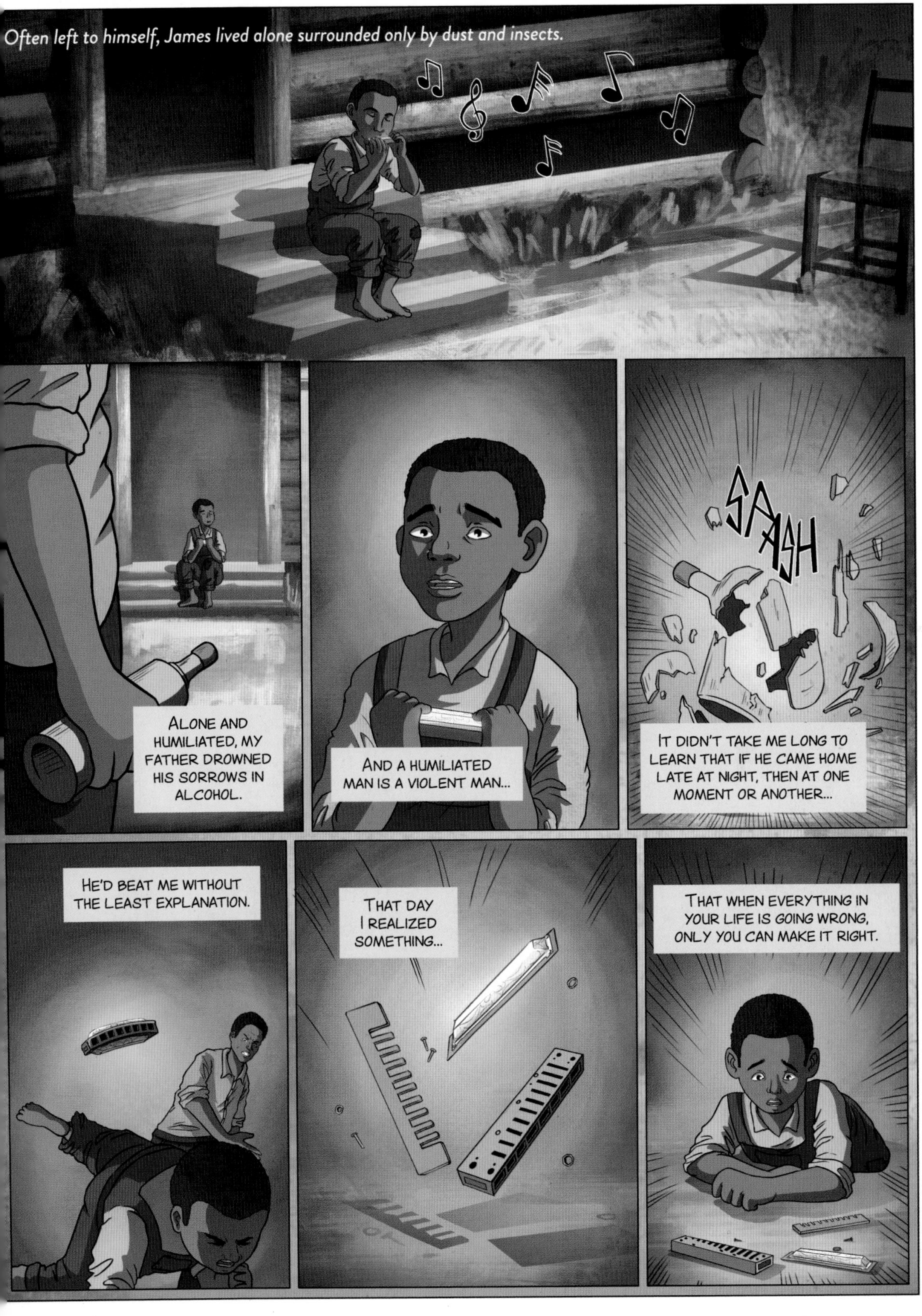

Often left to himself, James lived alone surrounded only by dust and insects.
ALONE AND HUMILIATED, MY FATHER DROWNED HIS SORROWS IN ALCOHOL.
AND A HUMILIATED MAN IS A VIOLENT MAN...
SMASH
IT DIDN'T TAKE ME LONG TO LEARN THAT IF HE CAME HOME LATE AT NIGHT, THEN AT ONE MOMENT OR ANOTHER...
HE'D BEAT ME WITHOUT THE LEAST EXPLANATION.
THAT DAY I REALIZED SOMETHING...
THAT WHEN EVERYTHING IN YOUR LIFE IS GOING WRONG, ONLY YOU CAN MAKE IT RIGHT.

If all those years of solitude with only the forest animals for companions taught him one thing, it was an instinct for survival.

SO, ONE NIGHT, WHILE MY FATHER SLEPT, I DECIDED TO RUN AWAY. TO RUN AWAY AS FAR AS I COULD.

IT DIDN'T MATTER WHERE.

WHEN YOU'RE ALONE, IT ALL COMES DOWN TO WHETHER YOU'LL KEEP FIGHTING IF YOU WANT TO SURVIVE.

BUT WHAT HAPPENED THAT NIGHT TURNED MY LIFE UPSIDE DOWN, AND I'LL NEVER FORGET IT.

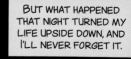

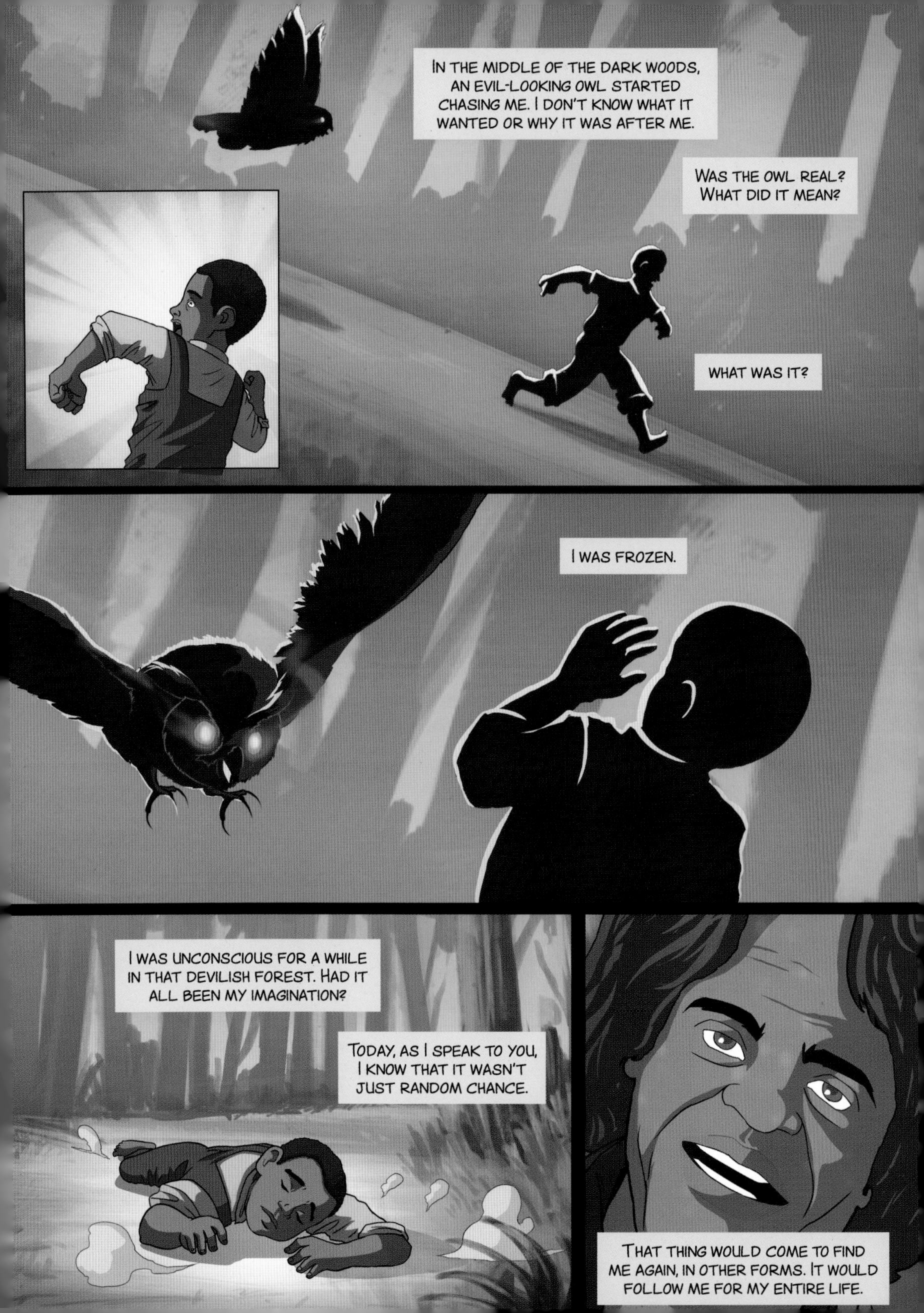

IN THE MIDDLE OF THE DARK WOODS, AN EVIL-LOOKING OWL STARTED CHASING ME. I DON'T KNOW WHAT IT WANTED OR WHY IT WAS AFTER ME.
WAS THE OWL REAL? WHAT DID IT MEAN?
WHAT WAS IT?
I WAS FROZEN.
I WAS UNCONSCIOUS FOR A WHILE IN THAT DEVILISH FOREST. HAD IT ALL BEEN MY IMAGINATION?
TODAY, AS I SPEAK TO YOU, I KNOW THAT IT WASN'T JUST RANDOM CHANCE.
THAT THING WOULD COME TO FIND ME AGAIN, IN OTHER FORMS. IT WOULD FOLLOW ME FOR MY ENTIRE LIFE.

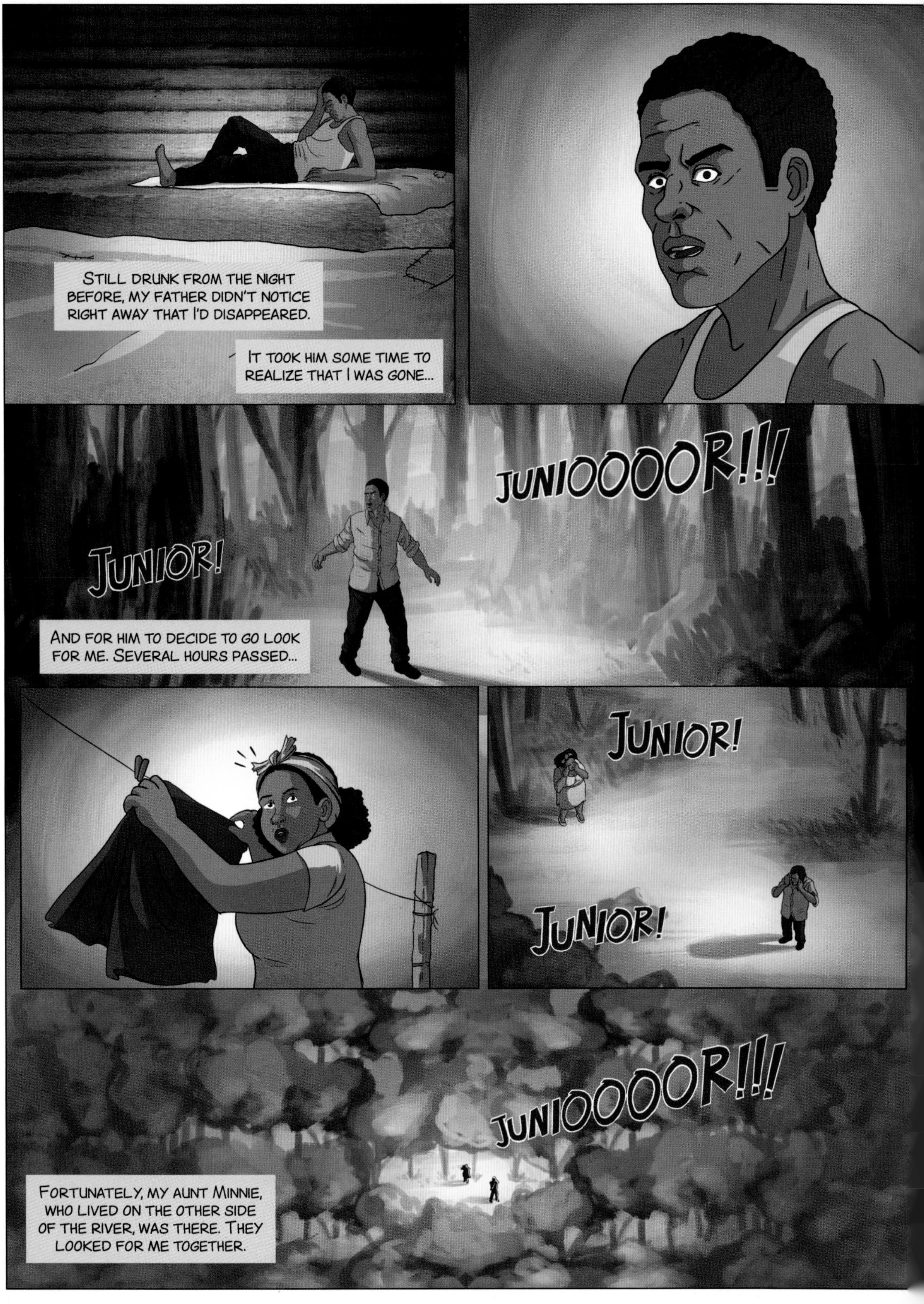
STILL DRUNK FROM THE NIGHT BEFORE, MY FATHER DIDN'T NOTICE RIGHT AWAY THAT I'D DISAPPEARED.
IT TOOK HIM SOME TIME TO REALIZE THAT I WAS GONE...
JUNIOOOOR!!!
JUNIOR!
AND FOR HIM TO DECIDE TO GO LOOK FOR ME. SEVERAL HOURS PASSED...
JUNIOR!
JUNIOR!
JUNIOOOOR!!!
FORTUNATELY, MY AUNT MINNIE, WHO LIVED ON THE OTHER SIDE OF THE RIVER, WAS THERE. THEY LOOKED FOR ME TOGETHER.

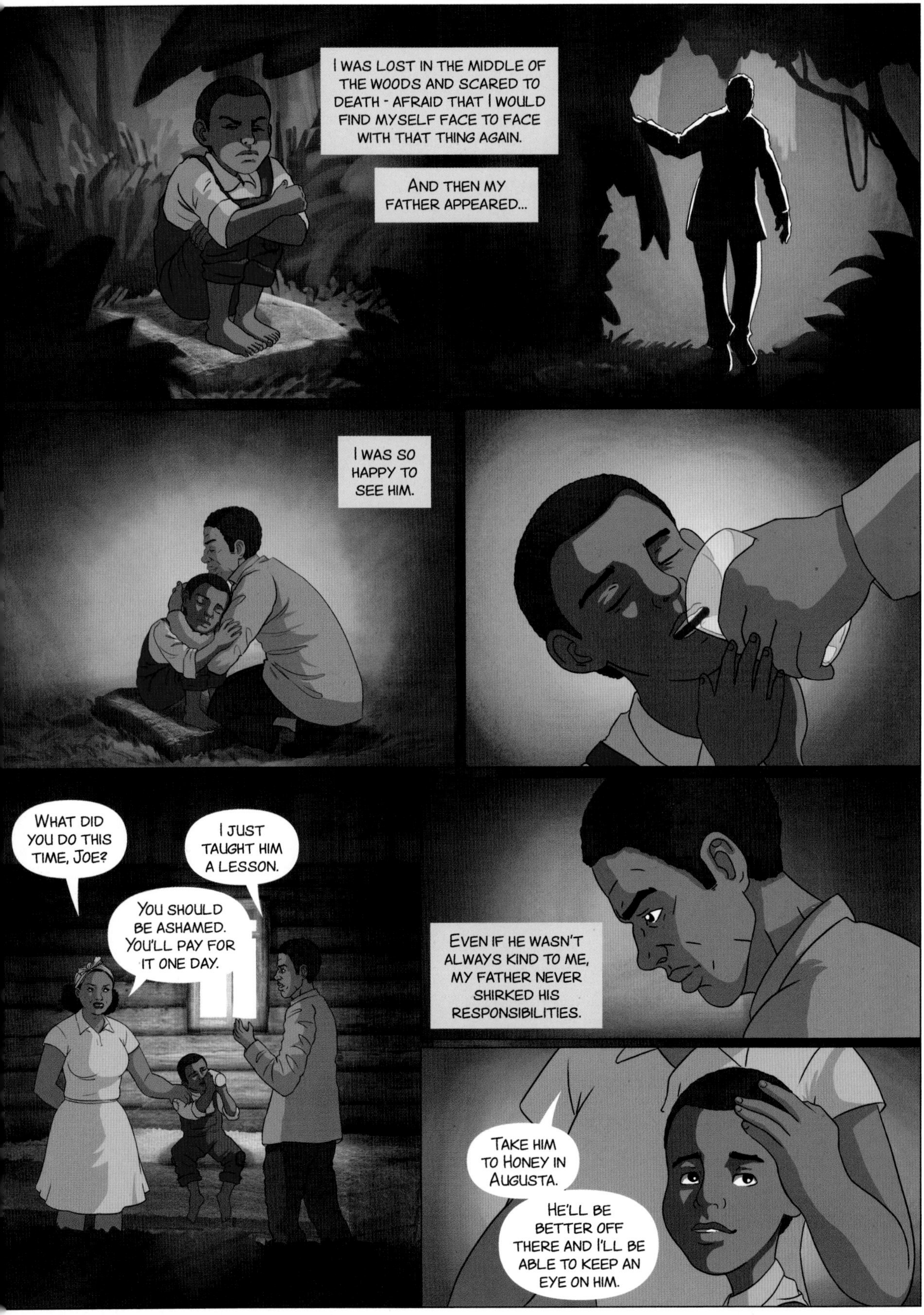
I WAS LOST IN THE MIDDLE OF THE WOODS AND SCARED TO DEATH - AFRAID THAT I WOULD FIND MYSELF FACE TO FACE WITH THAT THING AGAIN.
AND THEN MY FATHER APPEARED...
I WAS SO HAPPY TO SEE HIM.
WHAT DID YOU DO THIS TIME, JOE?
I JUST TAUGHT HIM A LESSON.
YOU SHOULD BE ASHAMED. YOU'LL PAY FOR IT ONE DAY.
EVEN IF HE WASN'T ALWAYS KIND TO ME, MY FATHER NEVER SHIRKED HIS RESPONSIBILITIES.
TAKE HIM TO HONEY IN AUGUSTA.
HE'LL BE BETTER OFF THERE AND I'LL BE ABLE TO KEEP AN EYE ON HIM.

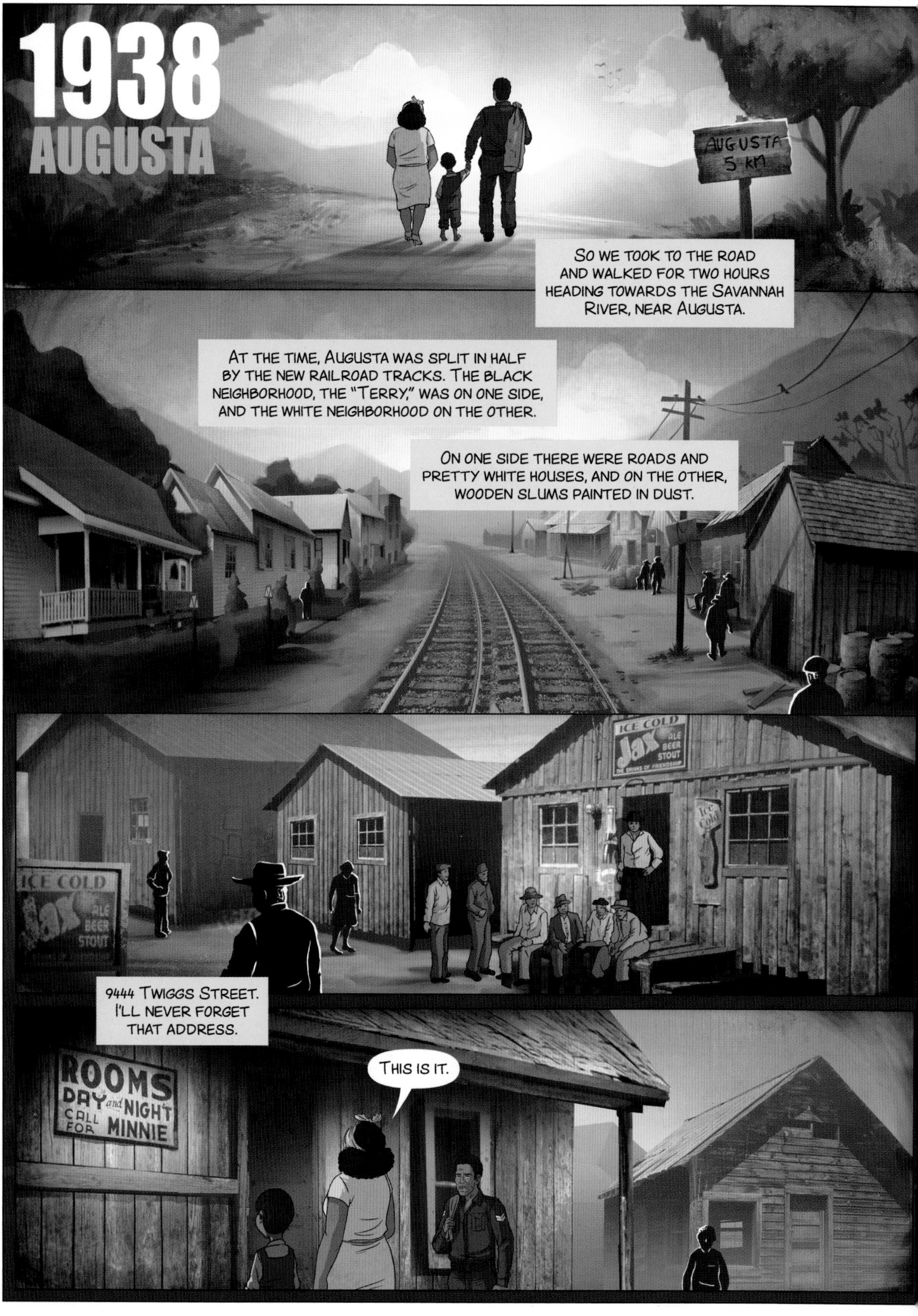
1938
AUGUSTA
AUGUSTA 5 km
SO WE TOOK TO THE ROAD AND WALKED FOR TWO HOURS HEADING TOWARDS THE SAVANNAH RIVER, NEAR AUGUSTA.
AT THE TIME, AUGUSTA WAS SPLIT IN HALF BY THE NEW RAILROAD TRACKS. THE BLACK NEIGHBORHOOD, THE "TERRY," WAS ON ONE SIDE, AND THE WHITE NEIGHBORHOOD ON THE OTHER.
ON ONE SIDE THERE WERE ROADS AND PRETTY WHITE HOUSES, AND ON THE OTHER, WOODEN SLUMS PAINTED IN DUST.
ICE COLD Jax ALE BEER STOUT
ICE COLD Jax ALE BEER STOUT
9444 TWIGGS STREET. I'LL NEVER FORGET THAT ADDRESS.
ROOMS DAY and NIGHT CALL FOR MINNIE
THIS IS IT.

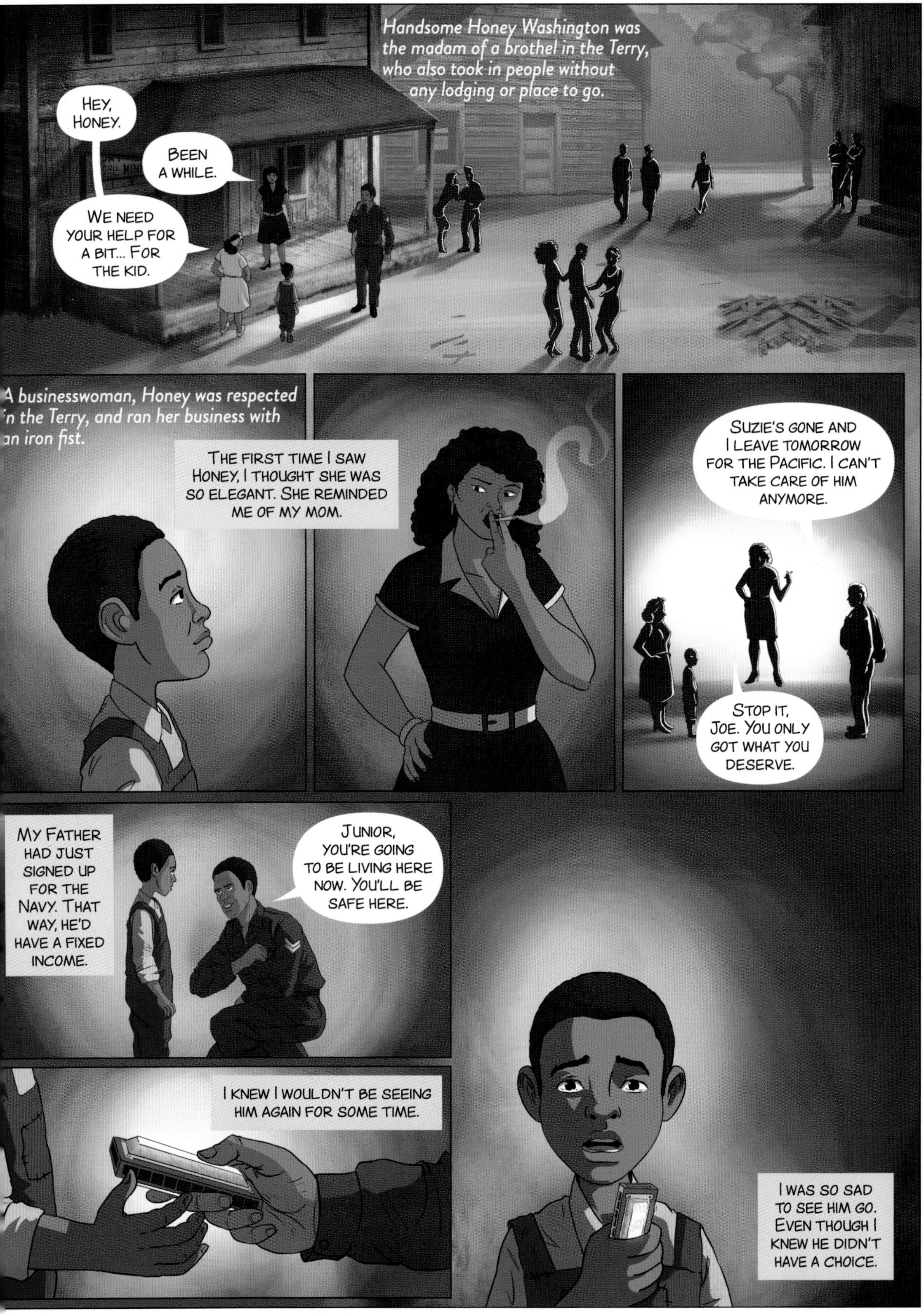
Handsome Honey Washington was the madam of a brothel in the Terry, who also took in people without any lodging or place to go.
HEY, HONEY.
BEEN A WHILE.
WE NEED YOUR HELP FOR A BIT... FOR THE KID.
A businesswoman, Honey was respected in the Terry, and ran her business with an iron fist.
THE FIRST TIME I SAW HONEY, I THOUGHT SHE WAS SO ELEGANT. SHE REMINDED ME OF MY MOM.
SUZIE'S GONE AND I LEAVE TOMORROW FOR THE PACIFIC. I CAN'T TAKE CARE OF HIM ANYMORE.
STOP IT, JOE. YOU ONLY GOT WHAT YOU DESERVE.
MY FATHER HAD JUST SIGNED UP FOR THE NAVY. THAT WAY, HE'D HAVE A FIXED INCOME.
JUNIOR, YOU'RE GOING TO BE LIVING HERE NOW. YOU'LL BE SAFE HERE.
I KNEW I WOULDN'T BE SEEING HIM AGAIN FOR SOME TIME.
I WAS SO SAD TO SEE HIM GO. EVEN THOUGH I KNEW HE DIDN'T HAVE A CHOICE.

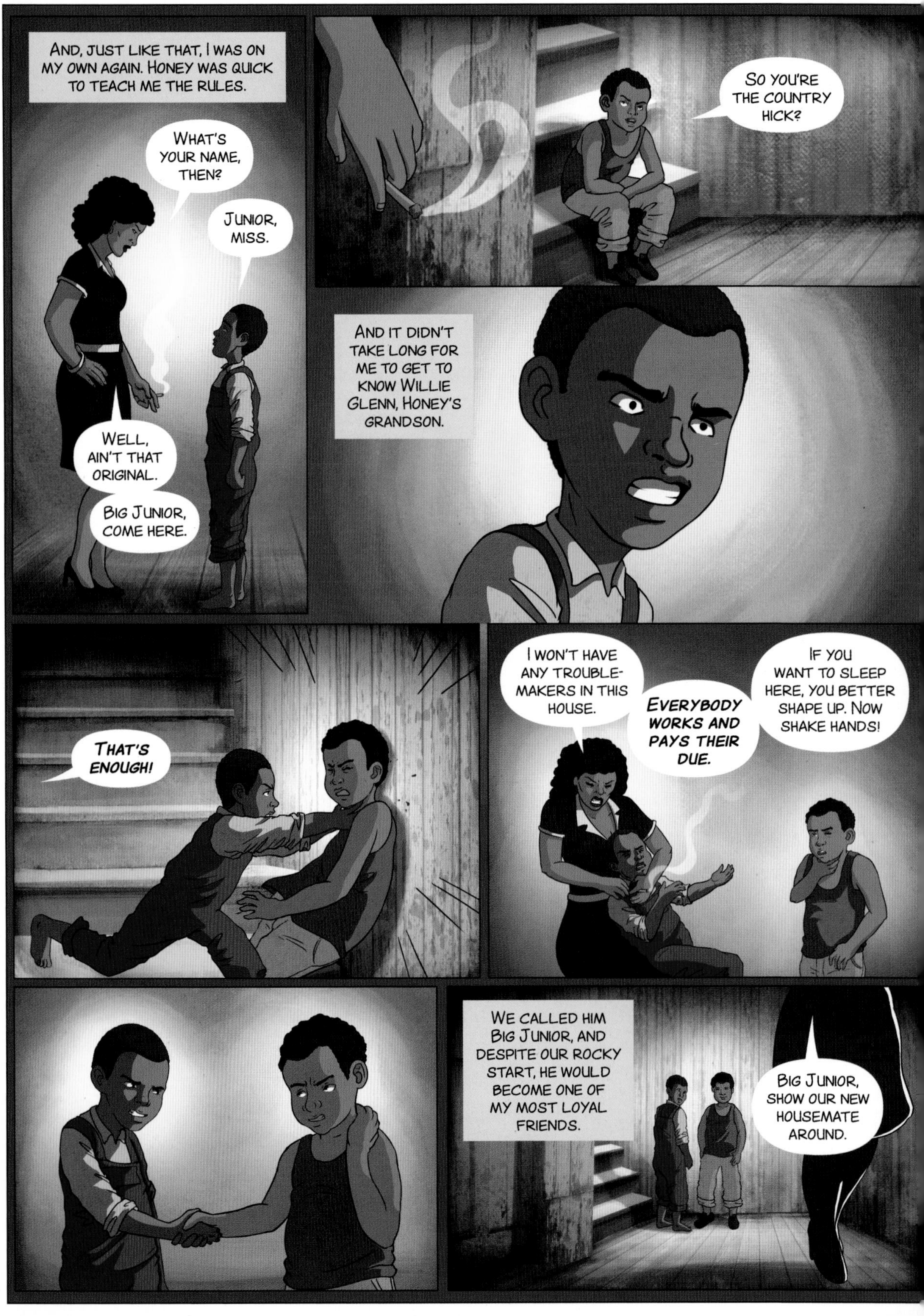
AND, JUST LIKE THAT, I WAS ON MY OWN AGAIN. HONEY WAS QUICK TO TEACH ME THE RULES.
WHAT'S YOUR NAME, THEN?
JUNIOR, MISS.
WELL, AIN'T THAT ORIGINAL.
BIG JUNIOR, COME HERE.
SO YOU'RE THE COUNTRY HICK?
AND IT DIDN'T TAKE LONG FOR ME TO GET TO KNOW WILLIE GLENN, HONEY'S GRANDSON.
THAT'S ENOUGH!
I WON'T HAVE ANY TROUBLE-MAKERS IN THIS HOUSE.
EVERYBODY WORKS AND PAYS THEIR DUE.
IF YOU WANT TO SLEEP HERE, YOU BETTER SHAPE UP. NOW SHAKE HANDS!
WE CALLED HIM BIG JUNIOR, AND DESPITE OUR ROCKY START, HE WOULD BECOME ONE OF MY MOST LOYAL FRIENDS.
BIG JUNIOR, SHOW OUR NEW HOUSEMATE AROUND.

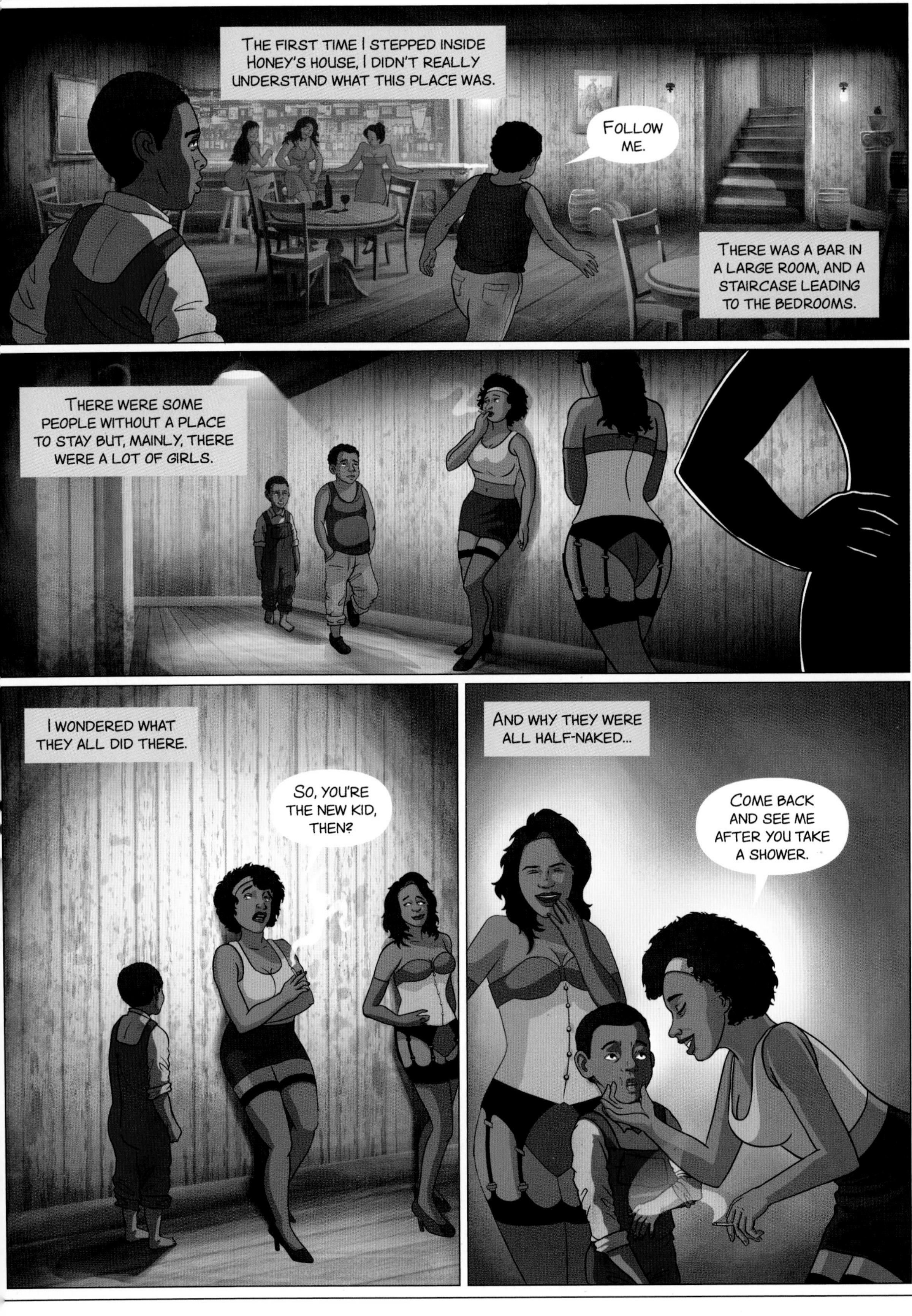

THE FIRST TIME I STEPPED INSIDE HONEY'S HOUSE, I DIDN'T REALLY UNDERSTAND WHAT THIS PLACE WAS.
FOLLOW ME.
THERE WAS A BAR IN A LARGE ROOM, AND A STAIRCASE LEADING TO THE BEDROOMS.
THERE WERE SOME PEOPLE WITHOUT A PLACE TO STAY BUT, MAINLY, THERE WERE A LOT OF GIRLS.
I WONDERED WHAT THEY ALL DID THERE.
SO, YOU'RE THE NEW KID, THEN?
AND WHY THEY WERE ALL HALF-NAKED...
COME BACK AND SEE ME AFTER YOU TAKE A SHOWER.

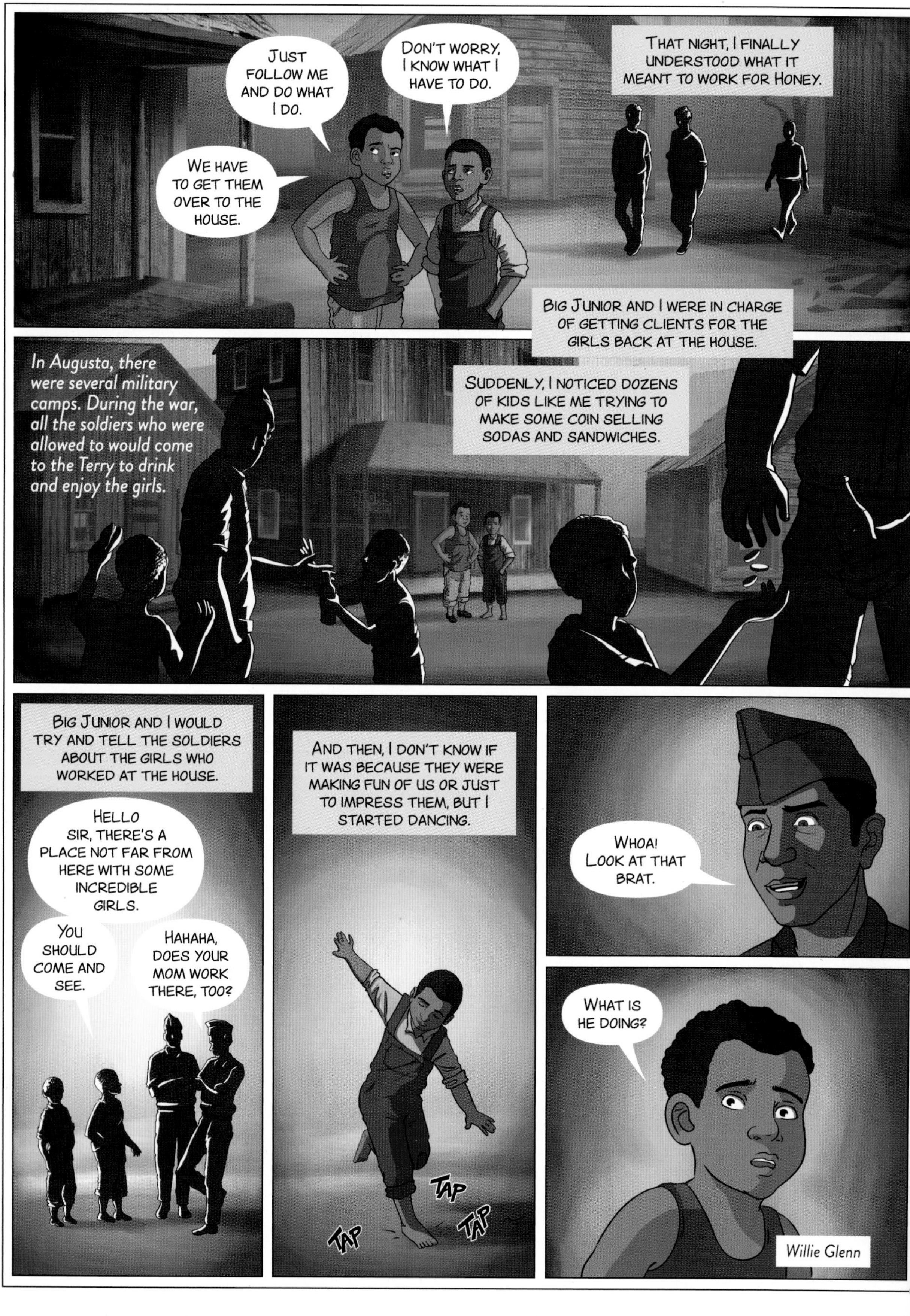

We have to get them over to the house.
Just follow me and do what I do.
Don't worry, I know what I have to do.
That night, I finally understood what it meant to work for Honey.
Big Junior and I were in charge of getting clients for the girls back at the house.
In Augusta, there were several military camps. During the war, all the soldiers who were allowed to would come to the Terry to drink and enjoy the girls.
Suddenly, I noticed dozens of kids like me trying to make some coin selling sodas and sandwiches.
Big Junior and I would try and tell the soldiers about the girls who worked at the house.
Hello sir, there's a place not far from here with some incredible girls.
You should come and see.
Hahaha, does your mom work there, too?
And then, I don't know if it was because they were making fun of us or just to impress them, but I started dancing.
TAP
TAP
TAP
Whoa! Look at that brat.
What is he doing?
Willie Glenn

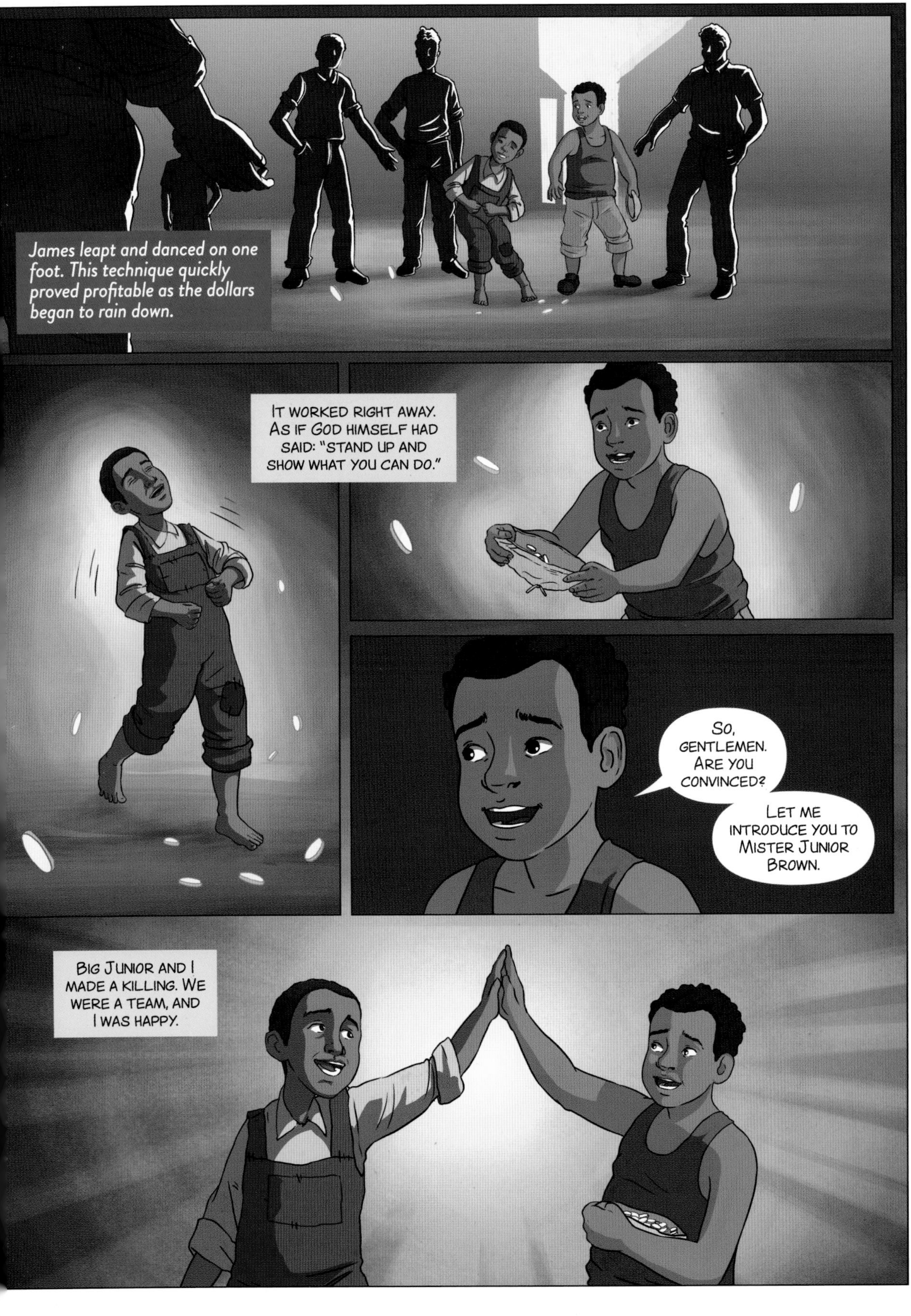
James leapt and danced on one foot. This technique quickly proved profitable as the dollars began to rain down.
IT WORKED RIGHT AWAY. AS IF GOD HIMSELF HAD SAID: "STAND UP AND SHOW WHAT YOU CAN DO."
SO, GENTLEMEN. ARE YOU CONVINCED?
LET ME INTRODUCE YOU TO MISTER JUNIOR BROWN.
BIG JUNIOR AND I MADE A KILLING. WE WERE A TEAM, AND I WAS HAPPY.

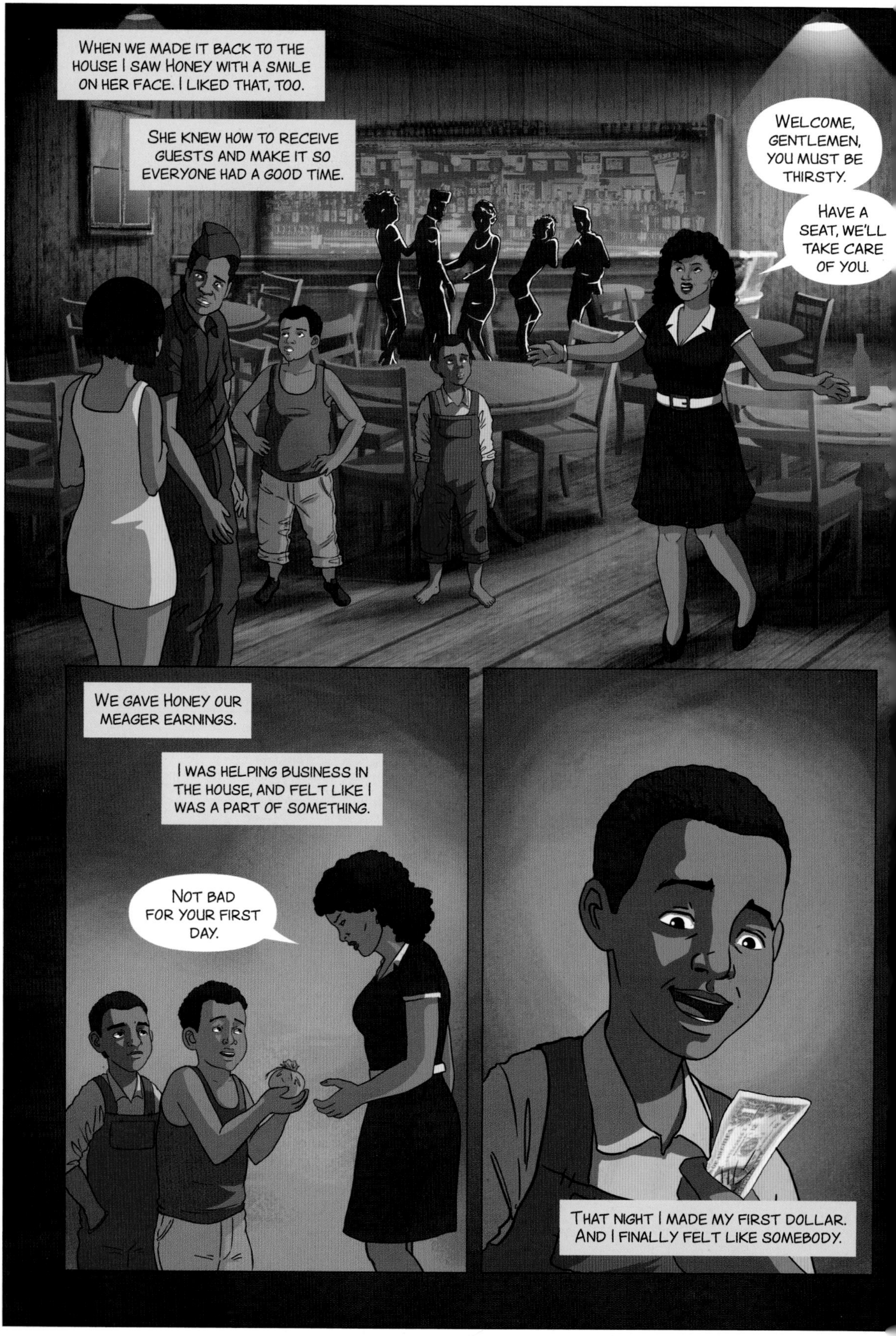
WHEN WE MADE IT BACK TO THE HOUSE I SAW HONEY WITH A SMILE ON HER FACE. I LIKED THAT, TOO.
SHE KNEW HOW TO RECEIVE GUESTS AND MAKE IT SO EVERYONE HAD A GOOD TIME.
WELCOME, GENTLEMEN, YOU MUST BE THIRSTY.
HAVE A SEAT, WE'LL TAKE CARE OF YOU.
WE GAVE HONEY OUR MEAGER EARNINGS.
I WAS HELPING BUSINESS IN THE HOUSE, AND FELT LIKE I WAS A PART OF SOMETHING.
NOT BAD FOR YOUR FIRST DAY.
THAT NIGHT I MADE MY FIRST DOLLAR. AND I FINALLY FELT LIKE SOMEBODY.

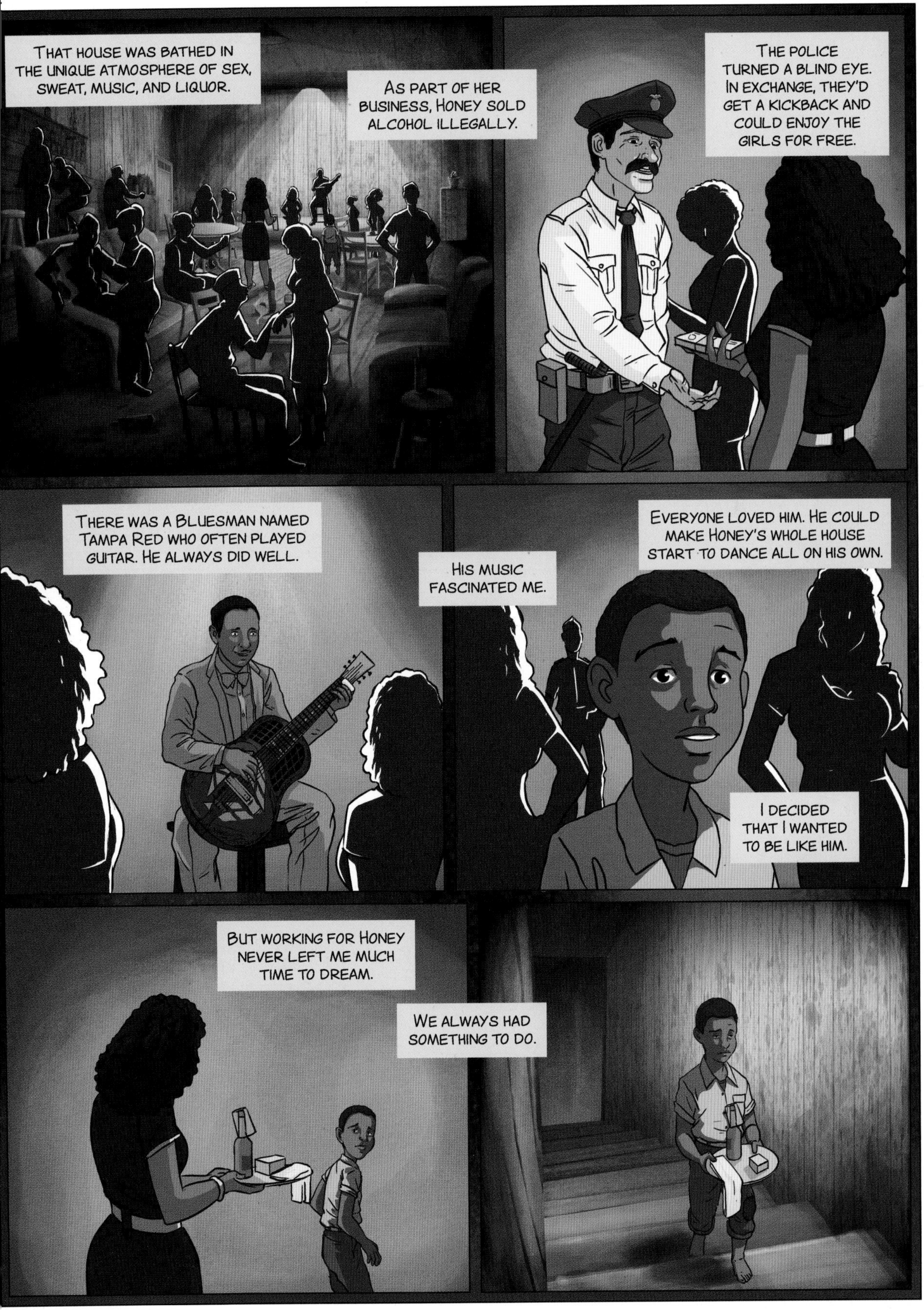

THAT HOUSE WAS BATHED IN THE UNIQUE ATMOSPHERE OF SEX, SWEAT, MUSIC, AND LIQUOR.
AS PART OF HER BUSINESS, HONEY SOLD ALCOHOL ILLEGALLY.
THE POLICE TURNED A BLIND EYE. IN EXCHANGE, THEY'D GET A KICKBACK AND COULD ENJOY THE GIRLS FOR FREE.
THERE WAS A BLUESMAN NAMED TAMPA RED WHO OFTEN PLAYED GUITAR. HE ALWAYS DID WELL.
HIS MUSIC FASCINATED ME.
EVERYONE LOVED HIM. HE COULD MAKE HONEY'S WHOLE HOUSE START TO DANCE ALL ON HIS OWN.
I DECIDED THAT I WANTED TO BE LIKE HIM.
BUT WORKING FOR HONEY NEVER LEFT ME MUCH TIME TO DREAM.
WE ALWAYS HAD SOMETHING TO DO.

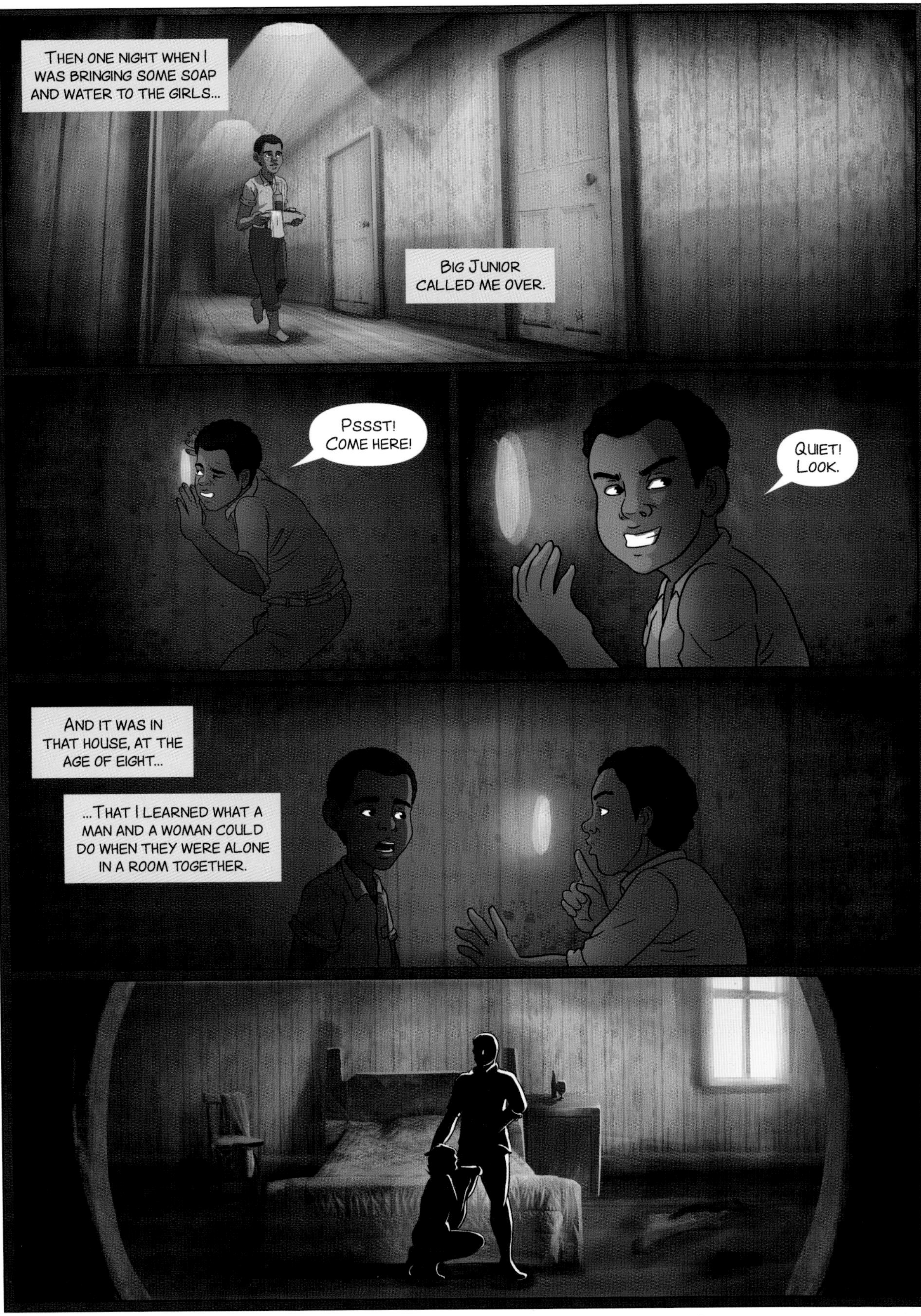
THEN ONE NIGHT WHEN I WAS BRINGING SOME SOAP AND WATER TO THE GIRLS...
BIG JUNIOR CALLED ME OVER.
PSSST! COME HERE!
QUIET! LOOK.
AND IT WAS IN THAT HOUSE, AT THE AGE OF EIGHT...
...THAT I LEARNED WHAT A MAN AND A WOMAN COULD DO WHEN THEY WERE ALONE IN A ROOM TOGETHER.

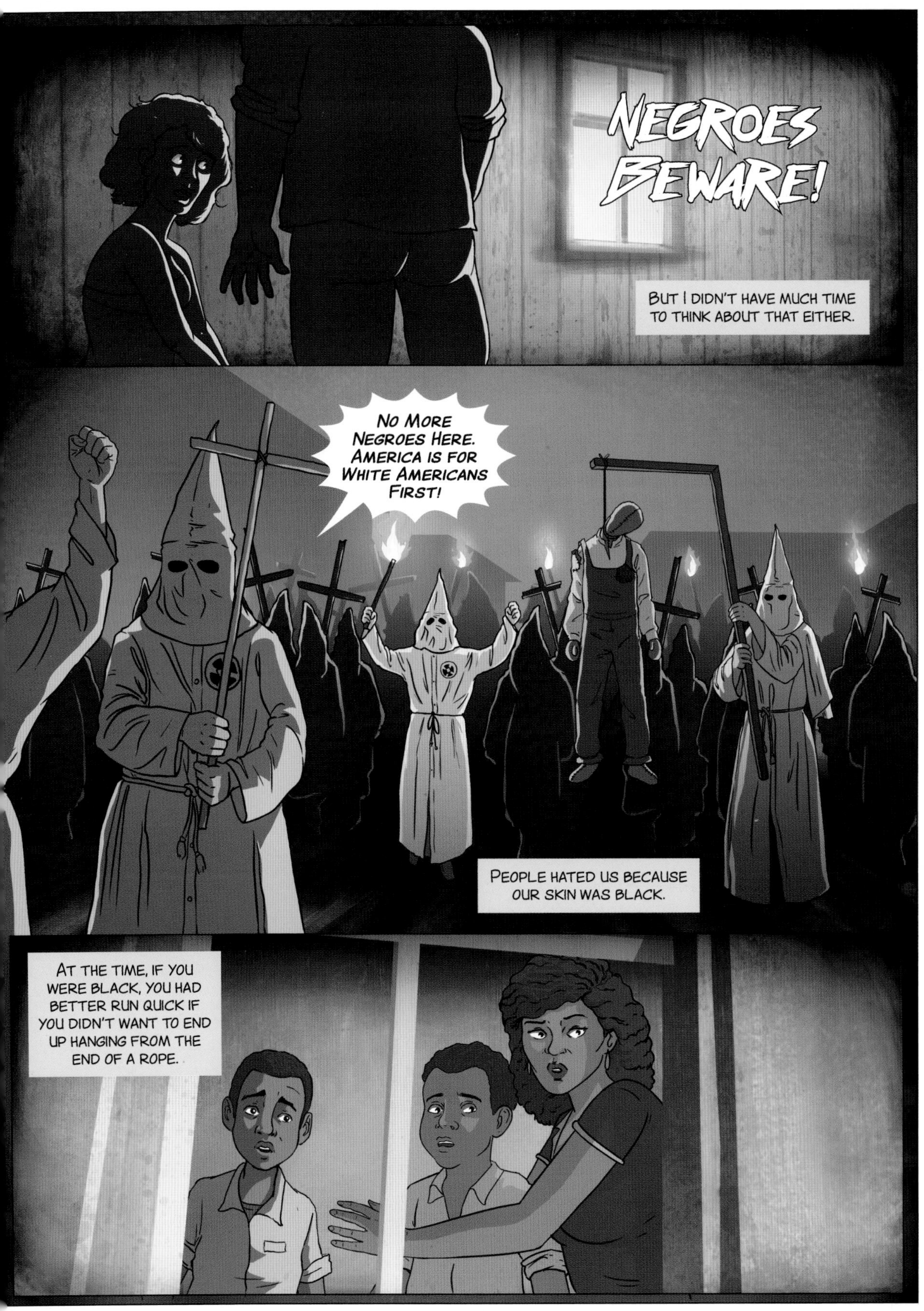
NEGROES BEWARE!
BUT I DIDN'T HAVE MUCH TIME TO THINK ABOUT THAT EITHER.
NO MORE NEGROES HERE. AMERICA IS FOR WHITE AMERICANS FIRST!
PEOPLE HATED US BECAUSE OUR SKIN WAS BLACK.
AT THE TIME, IF YOU WERE BLACK, YOU HAD BETTER RUN QUICK IF YOU DIDN'T WANT TO END UP HANGING FROM THE END OF A ROPE.

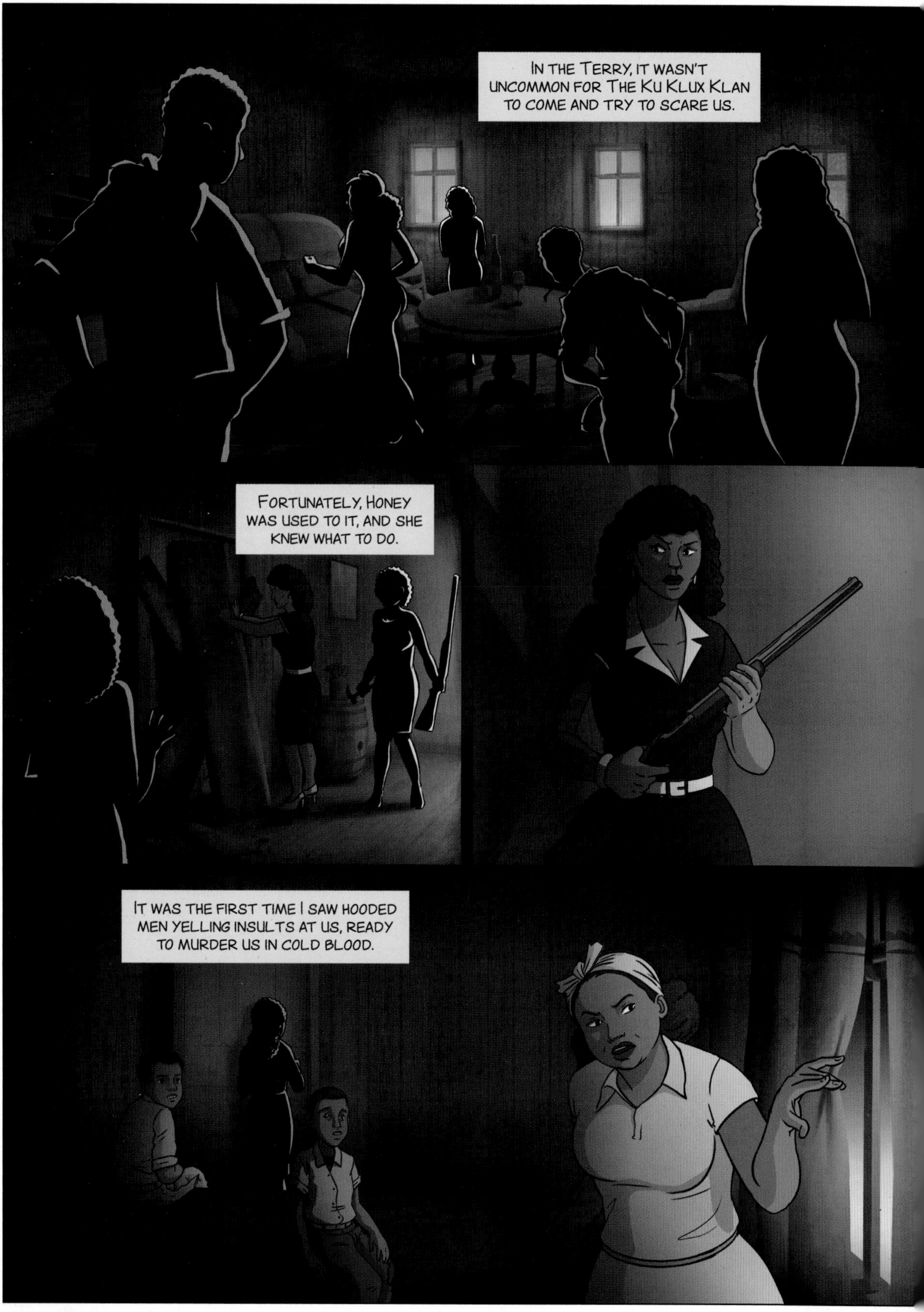
In the Terry, it wasn't uncommon for The Ku Klux Klan to come and try to scare us.
Fortunately, Honey was used to it, and she knew what to do.
It was the first time I saw hooded men yelling insults at us, ready to murder us in cold blood.

06.22 1938

Joe Louis, nicknamed the Brown Bomber, became the world heavyweight champion in Chicago in 1937, and held the title until 1949. He only lost three times in his career. The first time was on June 6th in 1936, against the pro-Aryan German, Max Schmeling.

On June 22nd, 1938, Louis and Schmeling had their rematch in Yankee Stadium in front of 80,000 spectators. Joe Louis laid out the colossal Schmeling during the 1st round in just two minutes.

The idol of the Nazi Regime was KOed.

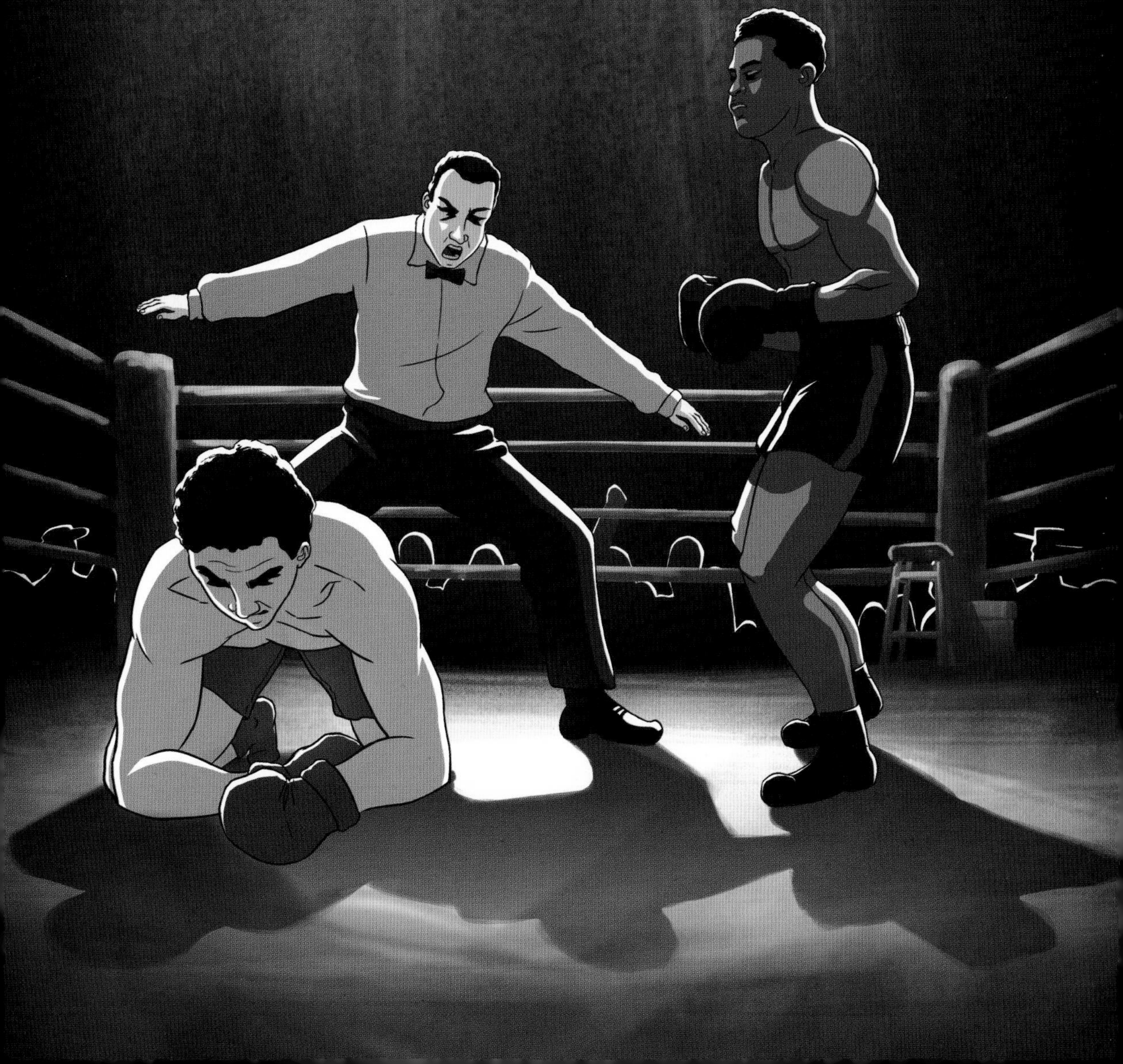

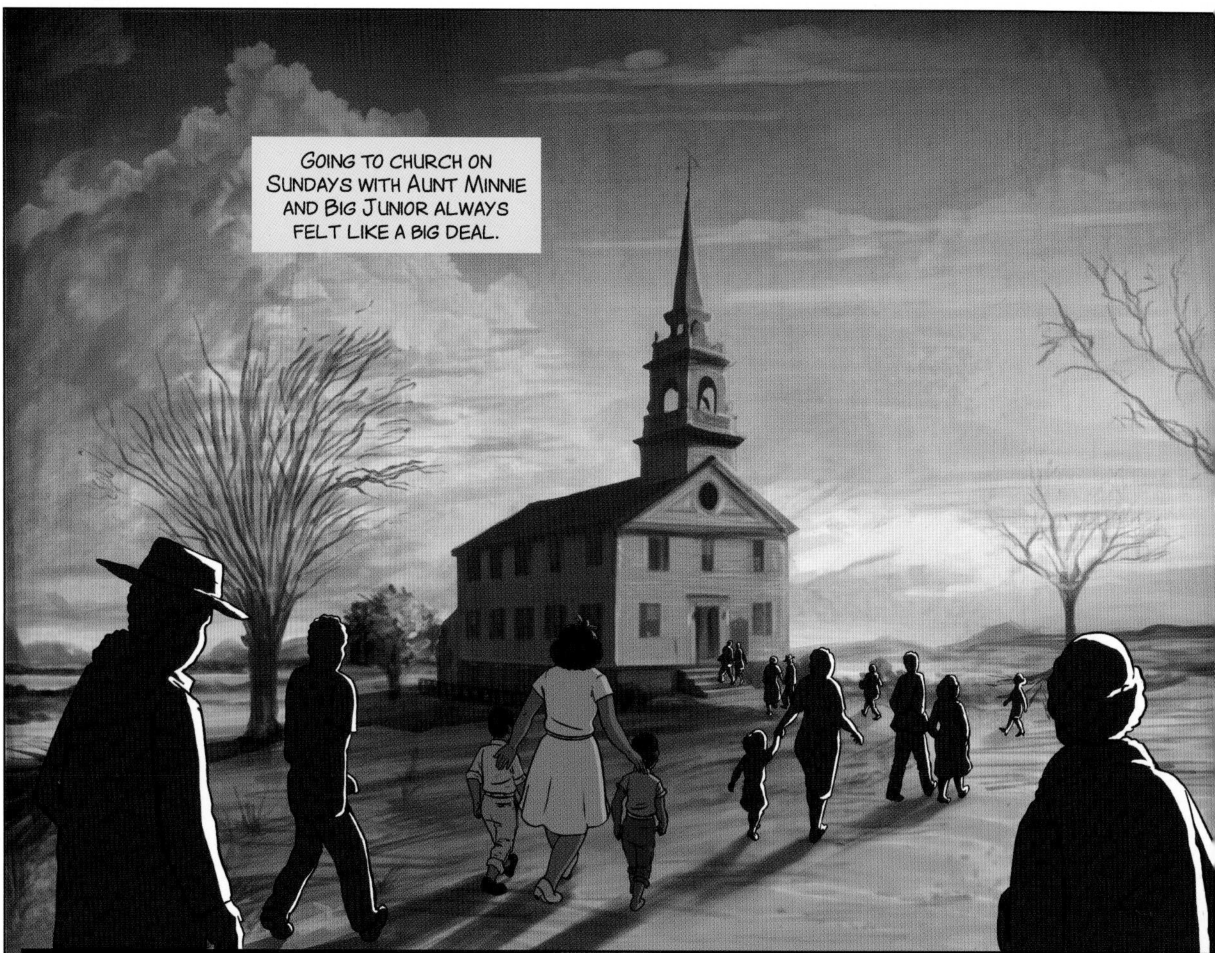
GOING TO CHURCH ON SUNDAYS WITH AUNT MINNIE AND BIG JUNIOR ALWAYS FELT LIKE A BIG DEAL.

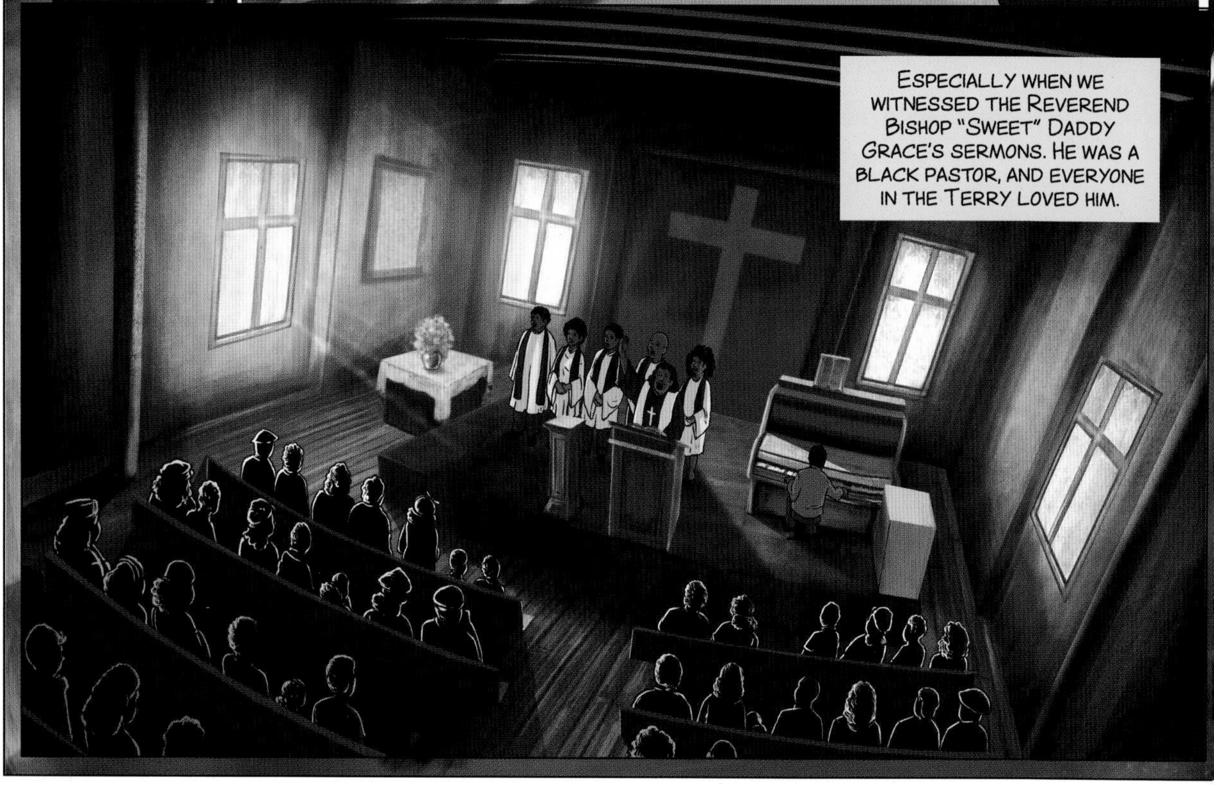
ESPECIALLY WHEN WE WITNESSED THE REVEREND BISHOP "SWEET" DADDY GRACE'S SERMONS. HE WAS A BLACK PASTOR, AND EVERYONE IN THE TERRY LOVED HIM.

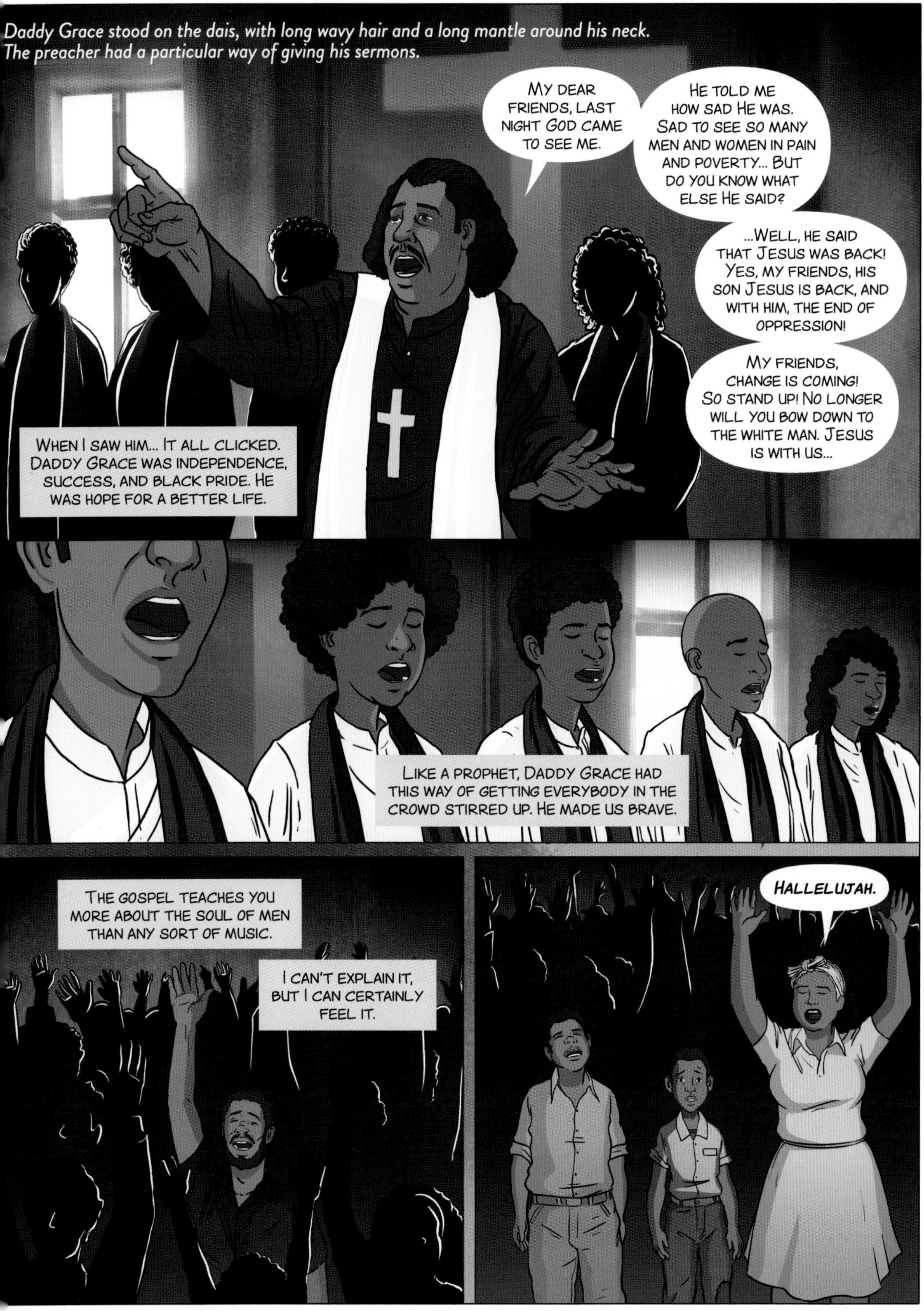
Daddy Grace stood on the dais, with long wavy hair and a long mantle around his neck. The preacher had a particular way of giving his sermons.
MY DEAR FRIENDS, LAST NIGHT GOD CAME TO SEE ME.
HE TOLD ME HOW SAD HE WAS. SAD TO SEE SO MANY MEN AND WOMEN IN PAIN AND POVERTY... BUT DO YOU KNOW WHAT ELSE HE SAID?
...WELL, HE SAID THAT JESUS WAS BACK! YES, MY FRIENDS, HIS SON JESUS IS BACK, AND WITH HIM, THE END OF OPPRESSION!
MY FRIENDS, CHANGE IS COMING! SO STAND UP! NO LONGER WILL YOU BOW DOWN TO THE WHITE MAN. JESUS IS WITH US...
WHEN I SAW HIM... IT ALL CLICKED. DADDY GRACE WAS INDEPENDENCE, SUCCESS, AND BLACK PRIDE. HE WAS HOPE FOR A BETTER LIFE.
LIKE A PROPHET, DADDY GRACE HAD THIS WAY OF GETTING EVERYBODY IN THE CROWD STIRRED UP. HE MADE US BRAVE.
THE GOSPEL TEACHES YOU MORE ABOUT THE SOUL OF MEN THAN ANY SORT OF MUSIC.
I CAN'T EXPLAIN IT, BUT I CAN CERTAINLY FEEL IT.
HALLELUJAH.

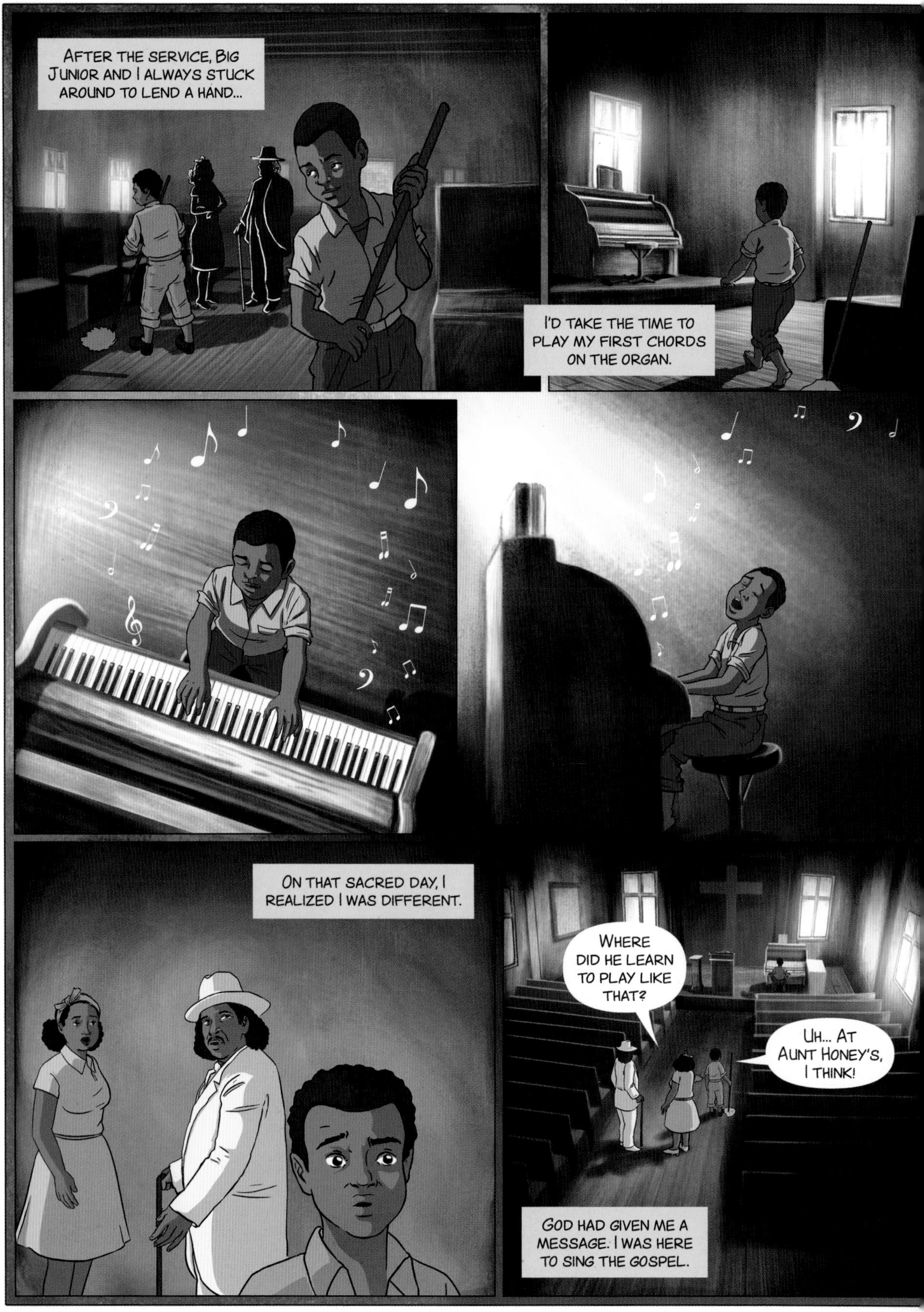

AFTER THE SERVICE, BIG JUNIOR AND I ALWAYS STUCK AROUND TO LEND A HAND...
I'D TAKE THE TIME TO PLAY MY FIRST CHORDS ON THE ORGAN.
ON THAT SACRED DAY, I REALIZED I WAS DIFFERENT.
WHERE DID HE LEARN TO PLAY LIKE THAT?
UH... AT AUNT HONEY'S, I THINK!
GOD HAD GIVEN ME A MESSAGE. I WAS HERE TO SING THE GOSPEL.

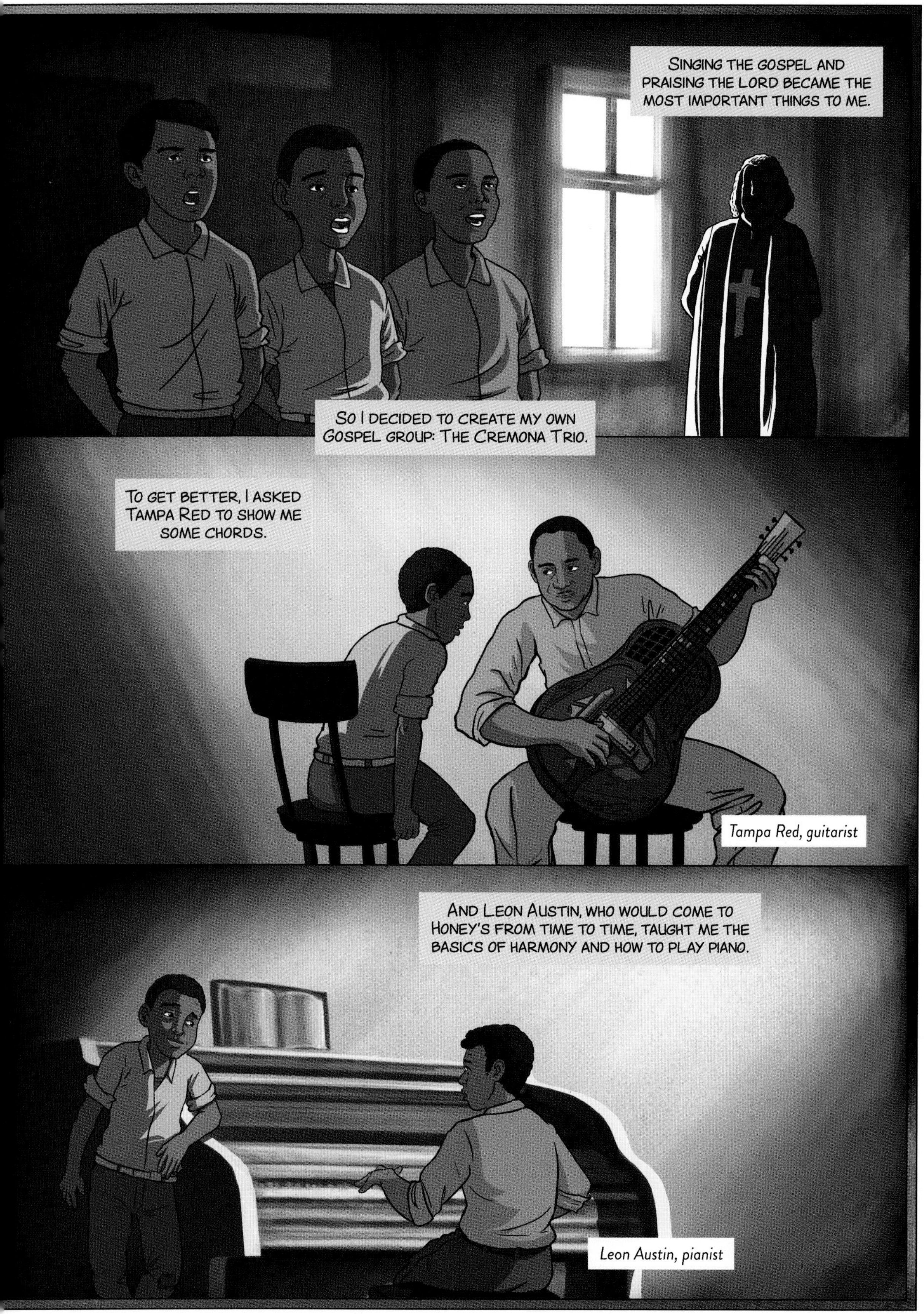
Singing the gospel and praising the Lord became the most important things to me.
So I decided to create my own Gospel group: The Cremona Trio.
To get better, I asked Tampa Red to show me some chords.
Tampa Red, guitarist
And Leon Austin, who would come to Honey's from time to time, taught me the basics of harmony and how to play piano.
Leon Austin, pianist

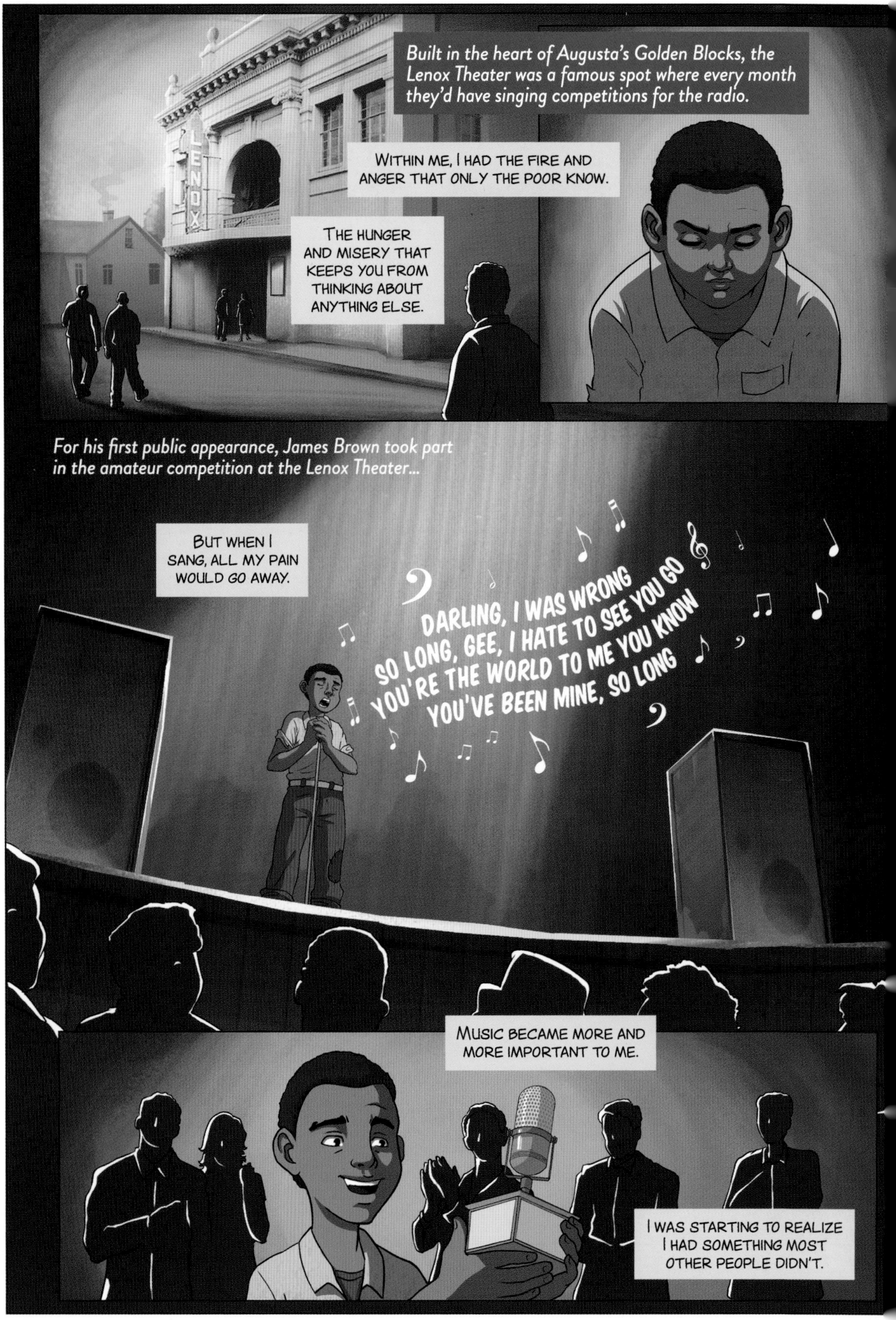

Built in the heart of Augusta's Golden Blocks, the Lenox Theater was a famous spot where every month they'd have singing competitions for the radio.
LENOX
WITHIN ME, I HAD THE FIRE AND ANGER THAT ONLY THE POOR KNOW.
THE HUNGER AND MISERY THAT KEEPS YOU FROM THINKING ABOUT ANYTHING ELSE.
For his first public appearance, James Brown took part in the amateur competition at the Lenox Theater...
BUT WHEN I SANG, ALL MY PAIN WOULD GO AWAY.
DARLING, I WAS WRONG
SO LONG, GEE, I HATE TO SEE YOU GO
YOU'RE THE WORLD TO ME YOU KNOW
YOU'VE BEEN MINE, SO LONG
MUSIC BECAME MORE AND MORE IMPORTANT TO ME.
I WAS STARTING TO REALIZE I HAD SOMETHING MOST OTHER PEOPLE DIDN'T.

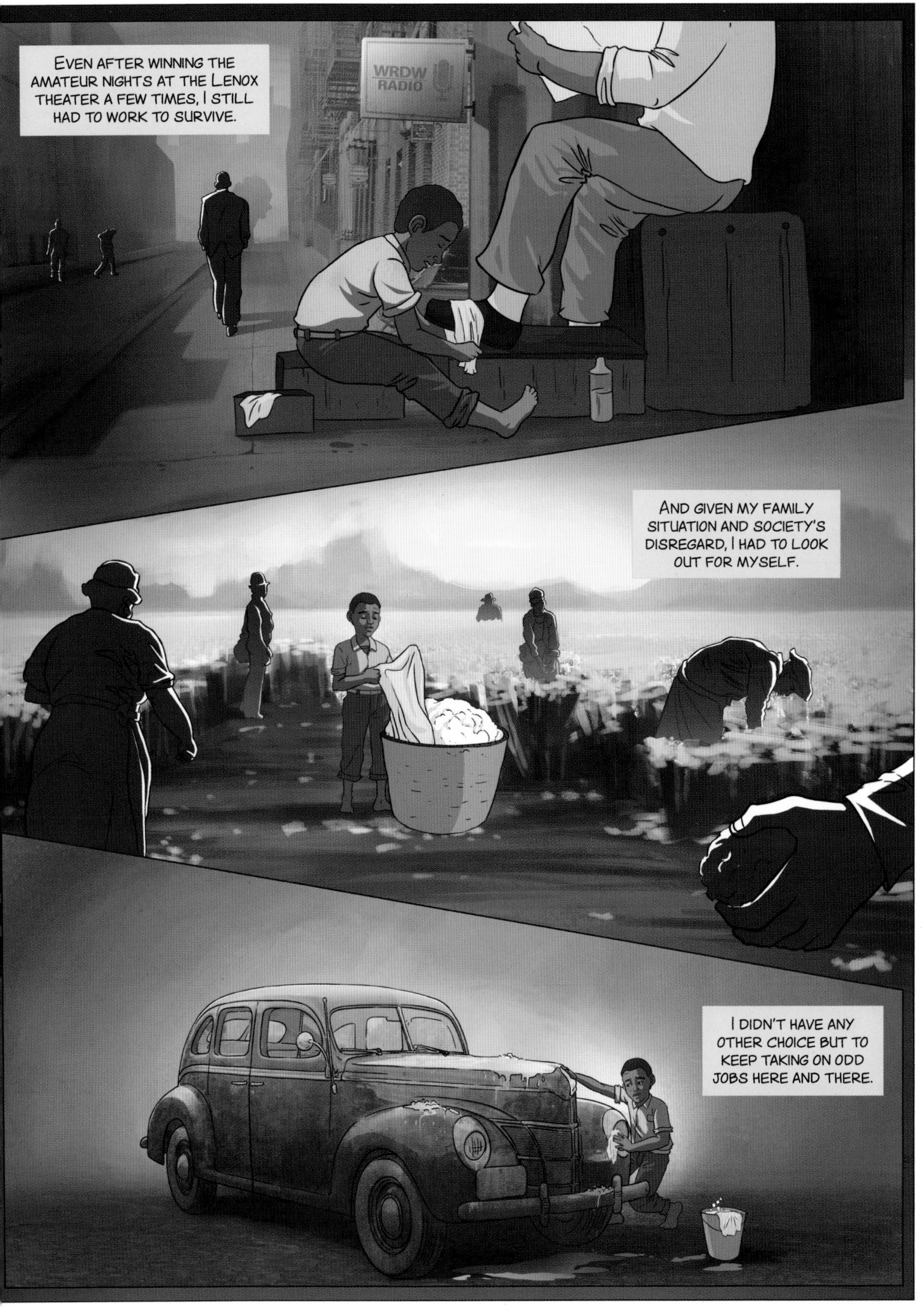
Even after winning the amateur nights at the Lenox theater a few times, I still had to work to survive.
WRDW RADIO
And given my family situation and society's disregard, I had to look out for myself.
I didn't have any other choice but to keep taking on odd jobs here and there.

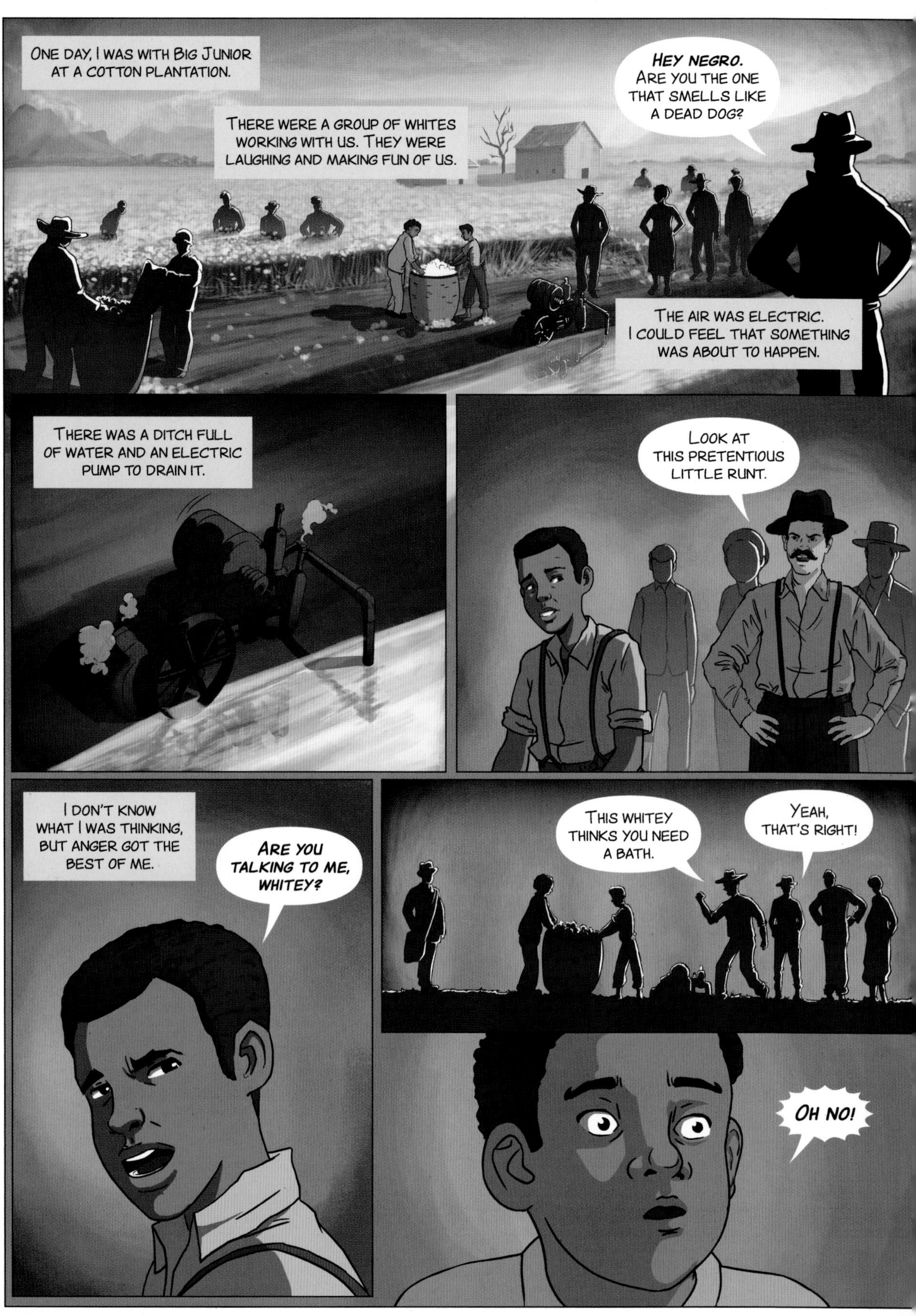
ONE DAY, I WAS WITH BIG JUNIOR AT A COTTON PLANTATION.
THERE WERE A GROUP OF WHITES WORKING WITH US. THEY WERE LAUGHING AND MAKING FUN OF US.
HEY NEGRO. ARE YOU THE ONE THAT SMELLS LIKE A DEAD DOG?
THE AIR WAS ELECTRIC. I COULD FEEL THAT SOMETHING WAS ABOUT TO HAPPEN.
THERE WAS A DITCH FULL OF WATER AND AN ELECTRIC PUMP TO DRAIN IT.
LOOK AT THIS PRETENTIOUS LITTLE RUNT.
I DON'T KNOW WHAT I WAS THINKING, BUT ANGER GOT THE BEST OF ME.
ARE YOU TALKING TO ME, WHITEY?
THIS WHITEY THINKS YOU NEED A BATH.
YEAH, THAT'S RIGHT!
OH NO!

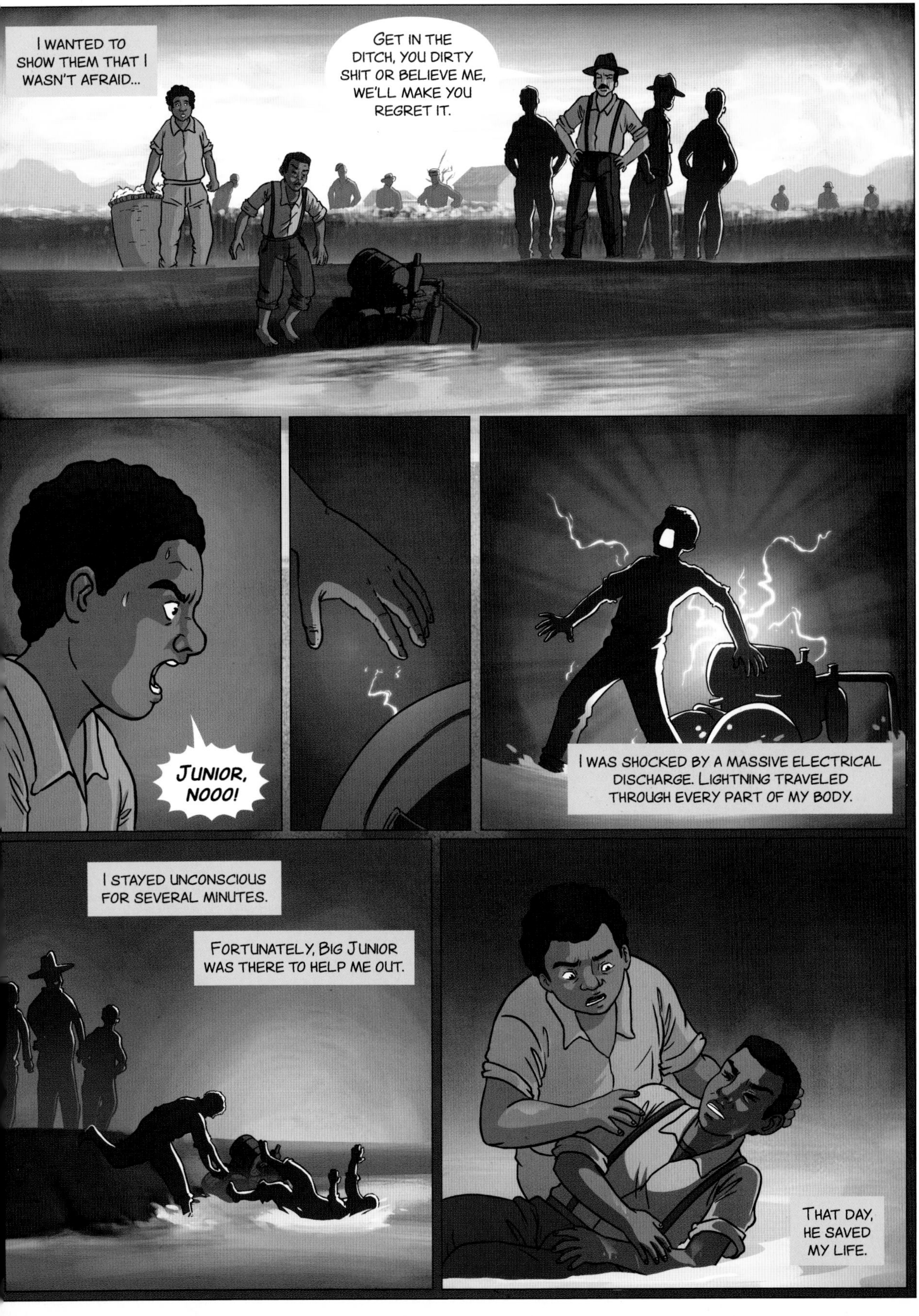
I WANTED TO SHOW THEM THAT I WASN'T AFRAID...
GET IN THE DITCH, YOU DIRTY SHIT OR BELIEVE ME, WE'LL MAKE YOU REGRET IT.
JUNIOR, NOOO!
I WAS SHOCKED BY A MASSIVE ELECTRICAL DISCHARGE. LIGHTNING TRAVELED THROUGH EVERY PART OF MY BODY.
I STAYED UNCONSCIOUS FOR SEVERAL MINUTES.
FORTUNATELY, BIG JUNIOR WAS THERE TO HELP ME OUT.
THAT DAY, HE SAVED MY LIFE.

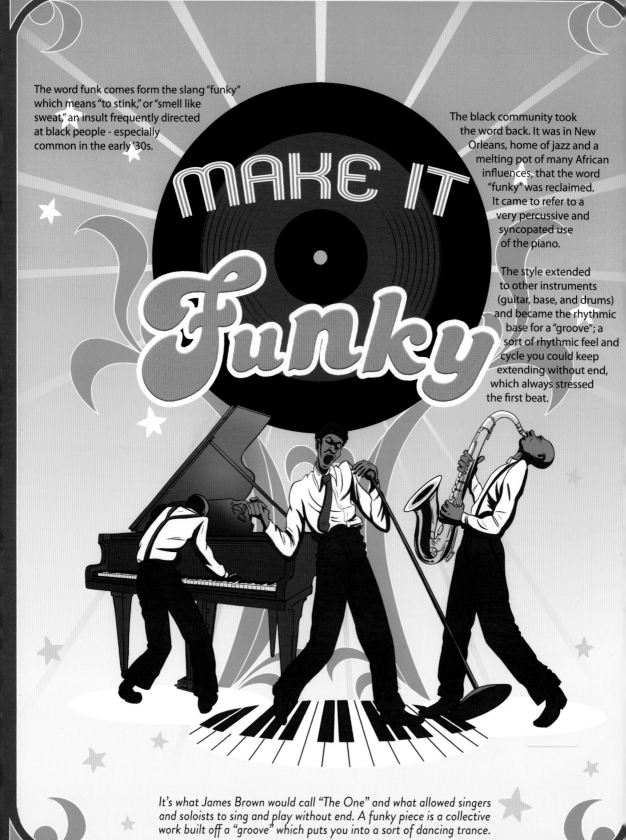

The word funk comes form the slang "funky" which means "to stink," or "smell like sweat," an insult frequently directed at black people - especially common in the early '30s.

The black community took the word back. It was in New Orleans, home of jazz and a melting pot of many African influences, that the word "funky" was reclaimed. It came to refer to a very percussive and syncopated use of the piano.

The style extended to other instruments (guitar, base, and drums) and became the rhythmic base for a "groove"; a sort of rhythmic feel and cycle you could keep extending without end, which always stressed the first beat.

MAKE IT Funky

It's what James Brown would call "The One" and what allowed singers and soloists to sing and play without end. A funky piece is a collective work built off a "groove" which puts you into a sort of dancing trance.

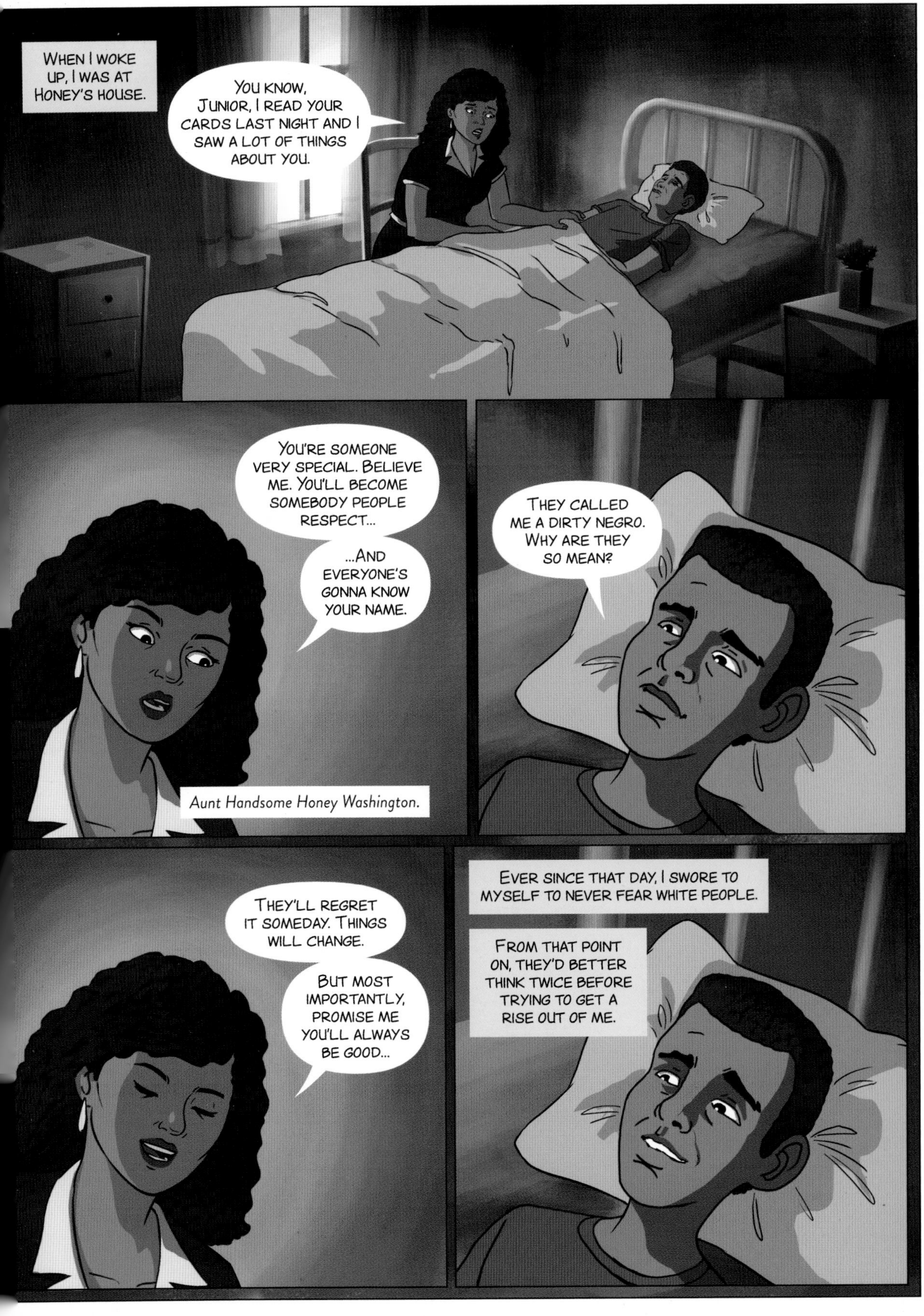
WHEN I WOKE UP, I WAS AT HONEY'S HOUSE.
YOU KNOW, JUNIOR, I READ YOUR CARDS LAST NIGHT AND I SAW A LOT OF THINGS ABOUT YOU.
YOU'RE SOMEONE VERY SPECIAL. BELIEVE ME. YOU'LL BECOME SOMEBODY PEOPLE RESPECT...
...AND EVERYONE'S GONNA KNOW YOUR NAME.
Aunt Handsome Honey Washington.
THEY CALLED ME A DIRTY NEGRO. WHY ARE THEY SO MEAN?
THEY'LL REGRET IT SOMEDAY. THINGS WILL CHANGE.
BUT MOST IMPORTANTLY, PROMISE ME YOU'LL ALWAYS BE GOOD...
EVER SINCE THAT DAY, I SWORE TO MYSELF TO NEVER FEAR WHITE PEOPLE.
FROM THAT POINT ON, THEY'D BETTER THINK TWICE BEFORE TRYING TO GET A RISE OUT OF ME.

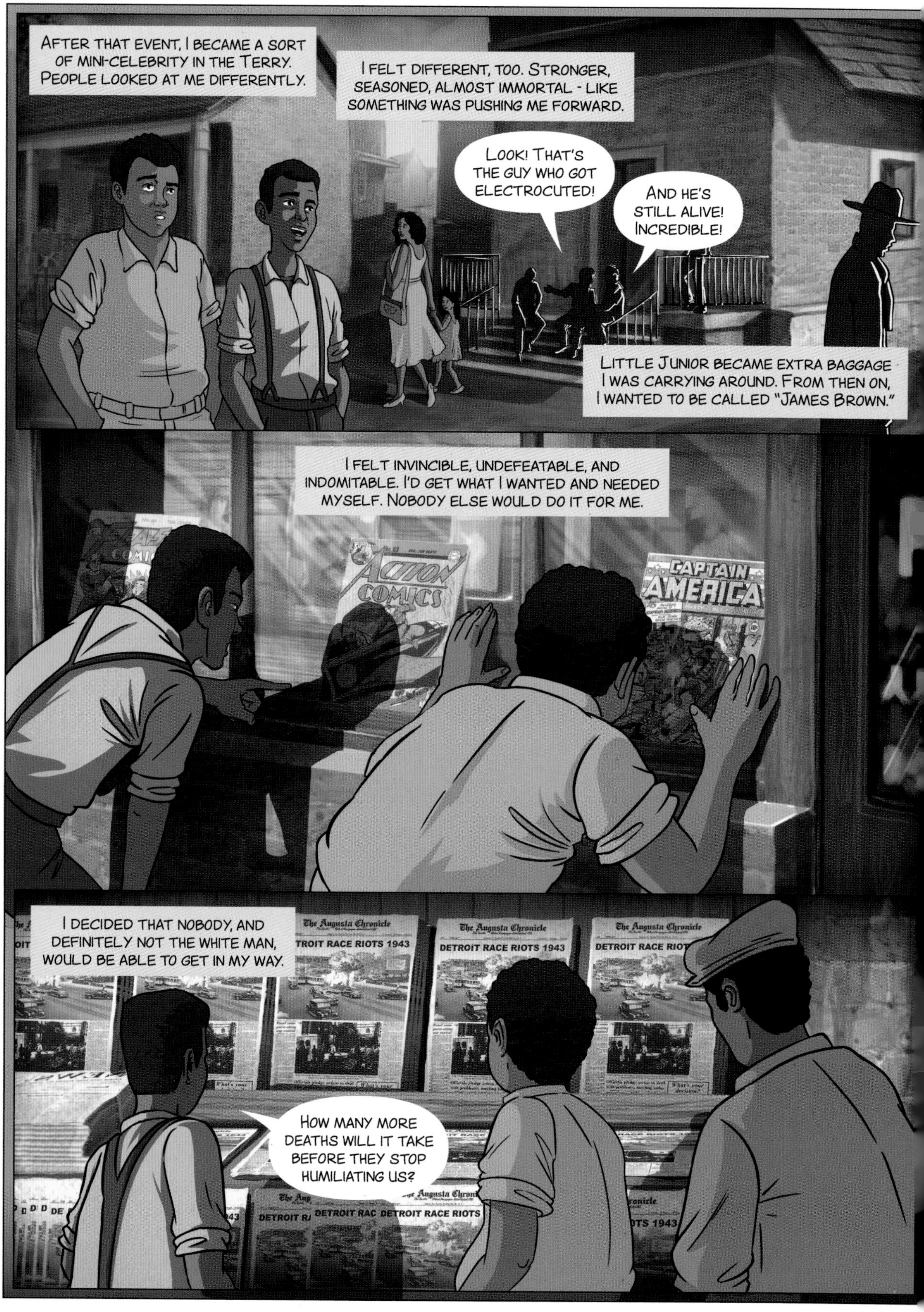
AFTER THAT EVENT, I BECAME A SORT OF MINI-CELEBRITY IN THE TERRY. PEOPLE LOOKED AT ME DIFFERENTLY.
I FELT DIFFERENT, TOO. STRONGER, SEASONED, ALMOST IMMORTAL - LIKE SOMETHING WAS PUSHING ME FORWARD.
LOOK! THAT'S THE GUY WHO GOT ELECTROCUTED!
AND HE'S STILL ALIVE! INCREDIBLE!
LITTLE JUNIOR BECAME EXTRA BAGGAGE I WAS CARRYING AROUND. FROM THEN ON, I WANTED TO BE CALLED "JAMES BROWN."
I FELT INVINCIBLE, UNDEFEATABLE, AND INDOMITABLE. I'D GET WHAT I WANTED AND NEEDED MYSELF. NOBODY ELSE WOULD DO IT FOR ME.
ACTION COMICS
CAPTAIN AMERICA
I DECIDED THAT NOBODY, AND DEFINITELY NOT THE WHITE MAN, WOULD BE ABLE TO GET IN MY WAY.
The Augusta Chronicle
DETROIT RACE RIOTS 1943
HOW MANY MORE DEATHS WILL IT TAKE BEFORE THEY STOP HUMILIATING US?

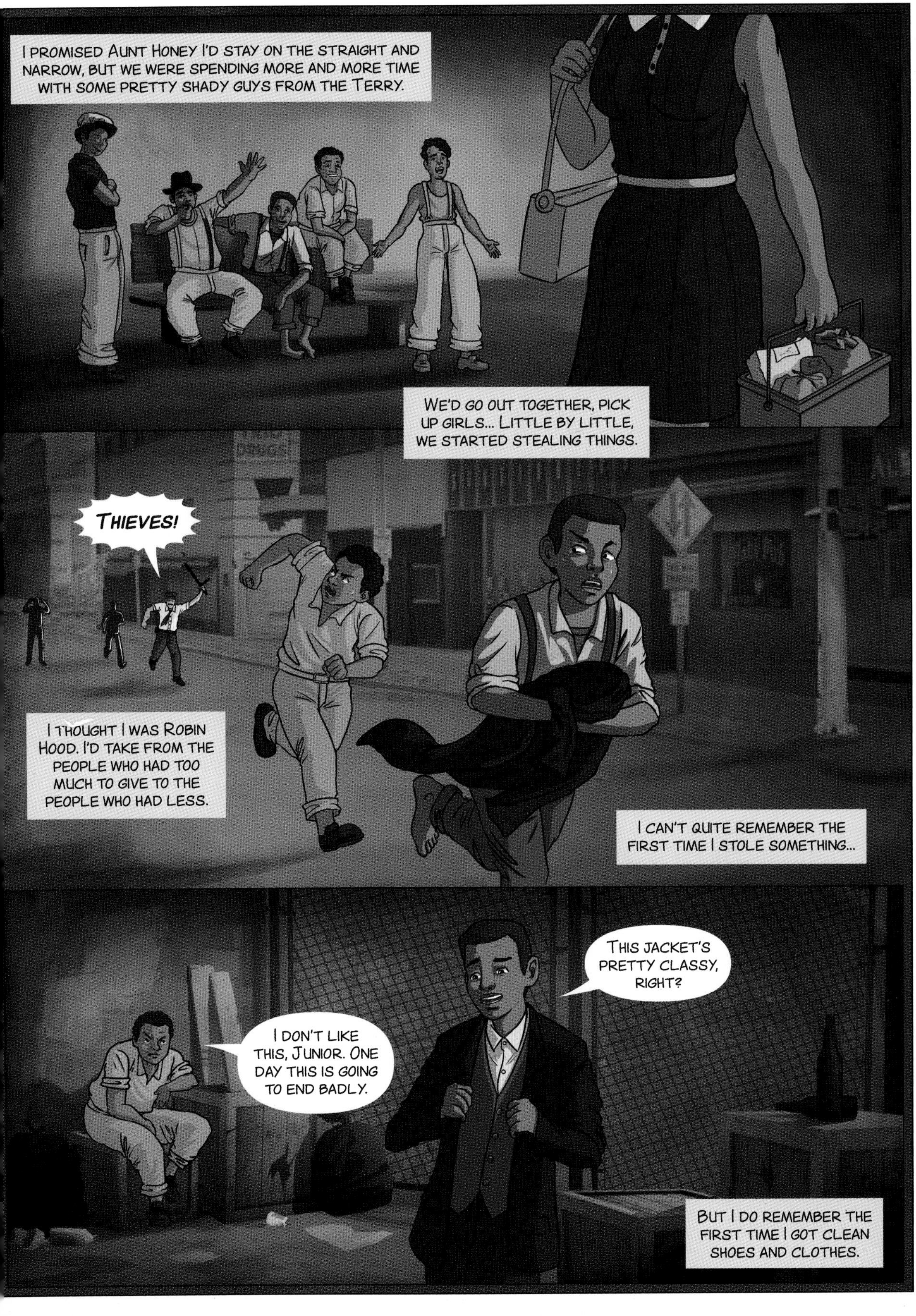
I PROMISED AUNT HONEY I'D STAY ON THE STRAIGHT AND NARROW, BUT WE WERE SPENDING MORE AND MORE TIME WITH SOME PRETTY SHADY GUYS FROM THE TERRY.
WE'D GO OUT TOGETHER, PICK UP GIRLS... LITTLE BY LITTLE, WE STARTED STEALING THINGS.
DRUGS
THIEVES!
I THOUGHT I WAS ROBIN HOOD. I'D TAKE FROM THE PEOPLE WHO HAD TOO MUCH TO GIVE TO THE PEOPLE WHO HAD LESS.
I CAN'T QUITE REMEMBER THE FIRST TIME I STOLE SOMETHING...
THIS JACKET'S PRETTY CLASSY, RIGHT?
I DON'T LIKE THIS, JUNIOR. ONE DAY THIS IS GOING TO END BADLY.
BUT I DO REMEMBER THE FIRST TIME I GOT CLEAN SHOES AND CLOTHES.

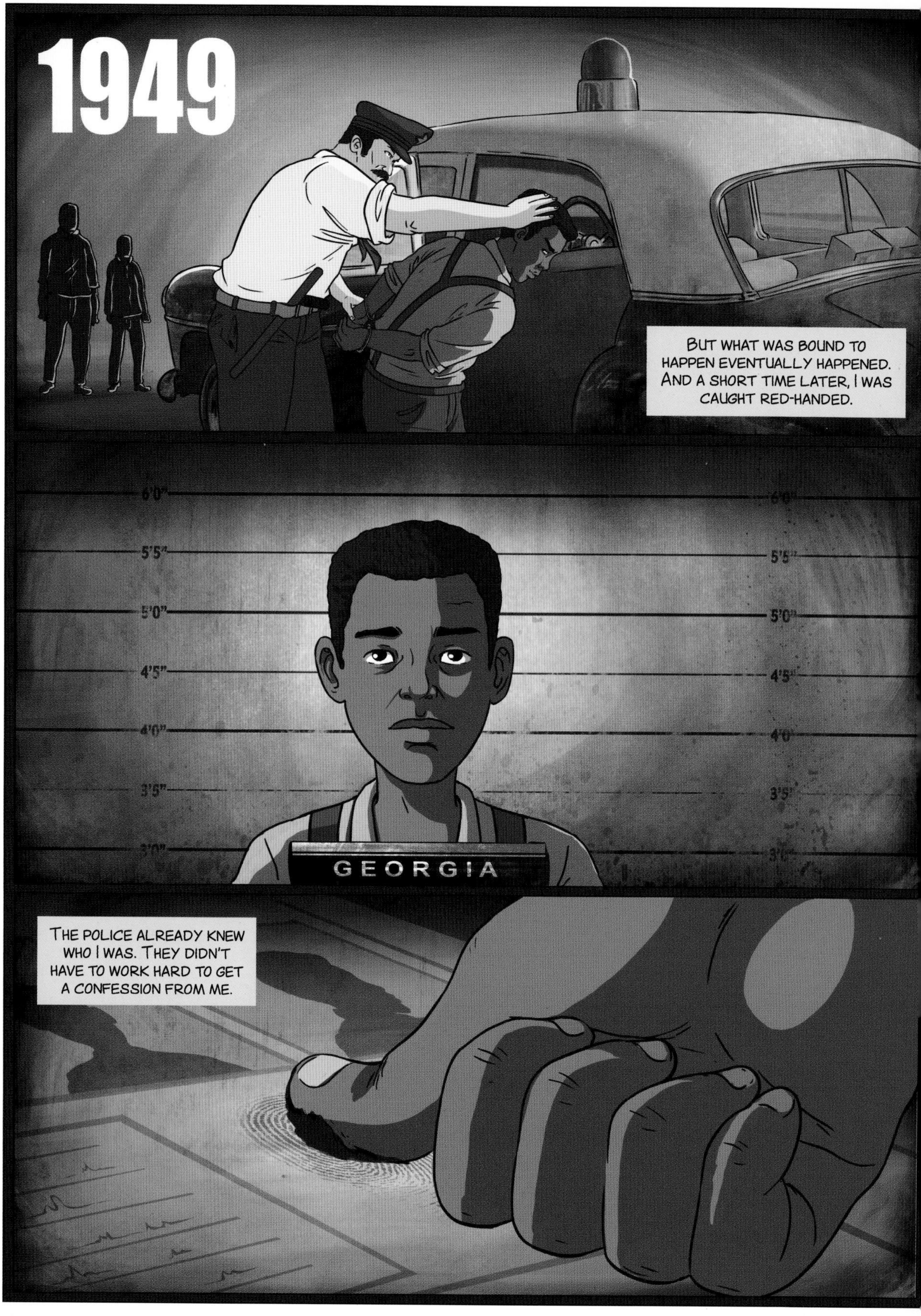
1949
BUT WHAT WAS BOUND TO HAPPEN EVENTUALLY HAPPENED. AND A SHORT TIME LATER, I WAS CAUGHT RED-HANDED.
6'0"
5'5"
5'0"
4'5"
4'0"
3'5"
3'0"
GEORGIA
THE POLICE ALREADY KNEW WHO I WAS. THEY DIDN'T HAVE TO WORK HARD TO GET A CONFESSION FROM ME.

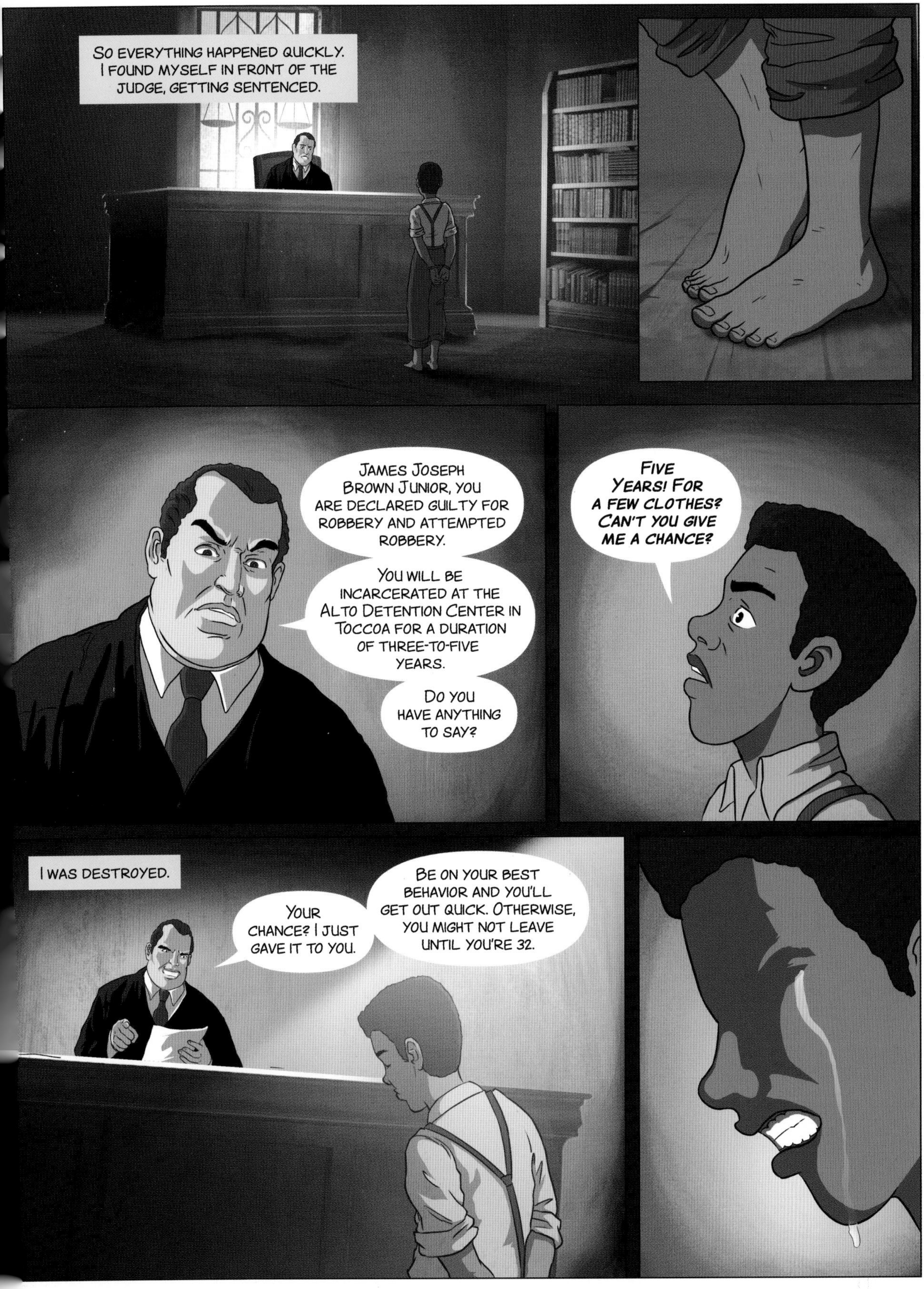
SO EVERYTHING HAPPENED QUICKLY. I FOUND MYSELF IN FRONT OF THE JUDGE, GETTING SENTENCED.
JAMES JOSEPH BROWN JUNIOR, YOU ARE DECLARED GUILTY FOR ROBBERY AND ATTEMPTED ROBBERY.
YOU WILL BE INCARCERATED AT THE ALTO DETENTION CENTER IN TOCCOA FOR A DURATION OF THREE-TO-FIVE YEARS.
DO YOU HAVE ANYTHING TO SAY?
FIVE YEARS! FOR A FEW CLOTHES? CAN'T YOU GIVE ME A CHANCE?
I WAS DESTROYED.
YOUR CHANCE? I JUST GAVE IT TO YOU.
BE ON YOUR BEST BEHAVIOR AND YOU'LL GET OUT QUICK. OTHERWISE, YOU MIGHT NOT LEAVE UNTIL YOU'RE 32.

THIS TIME, IT ALL CAUGHT UP TO ME. FIVE YEARS IN THE SLAMMER. IT WAS THE USUAL AMOUNT FOR A YOUNG NEGRO LIKE ME.

THE THING THAT HURT THE MOST WAS THAT I WOULDN'T SEE BIG JUNIOR OR AUNT MINNIE FOR SOME TIME...

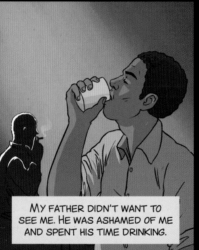

MY FATHER DIDN'T WANT TO SEE ME. HE WAS ASHAMED OF ME AND SPENT HIS TIME DRINKING.

HONEY'S HOUSE WAS CLOSED. THE WAR WAS OVER, AND THERE WASN'T ANY NEED FOR A BROTHEL FOR SOLDIERS.

I WAS 16 YEARS OLD, AND I WAS IN PRISON. AND ONCE MORE, I WAS ALONE.

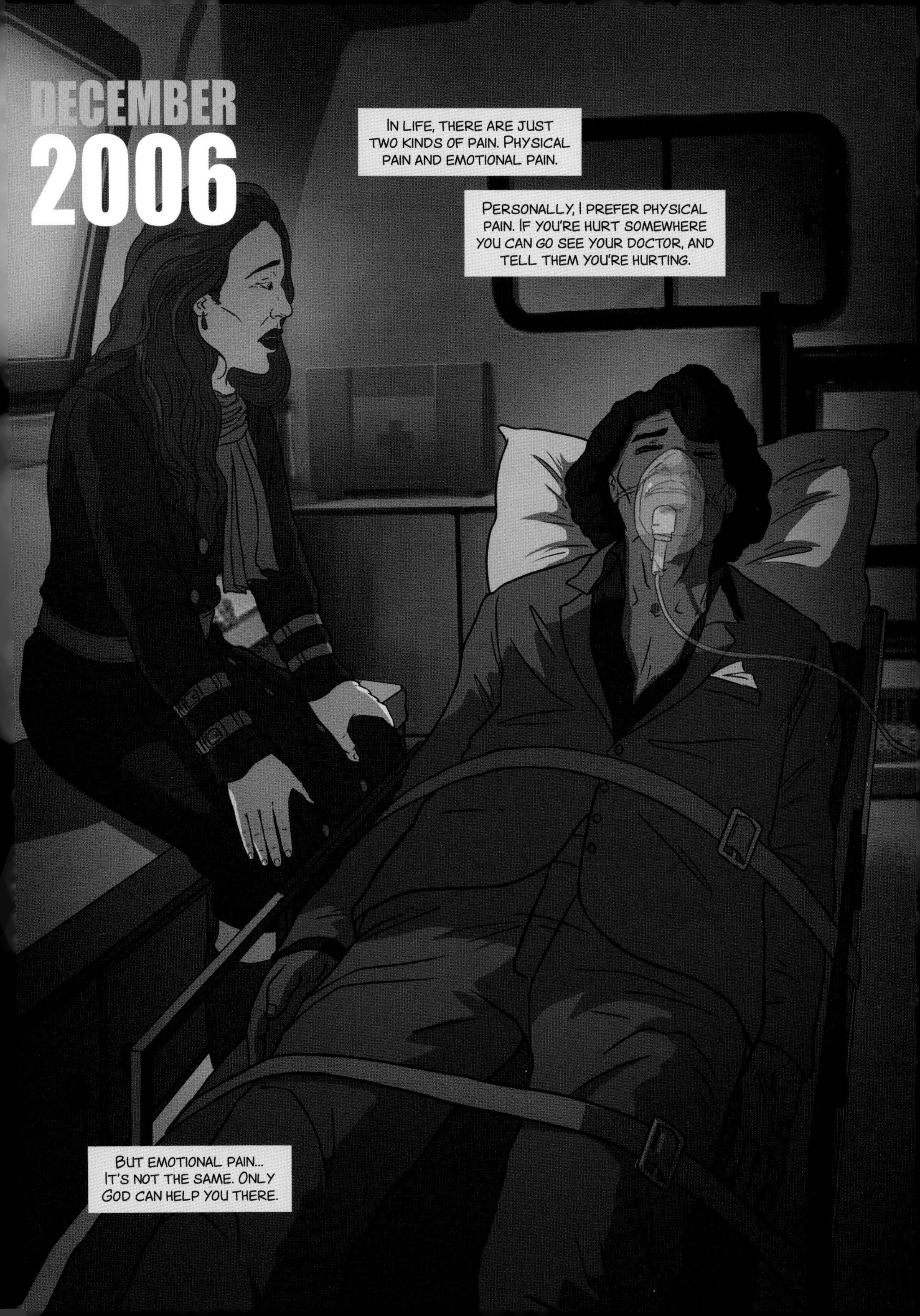
DECEMBER 2006
IN LIFE, THERE ARE JUST TWO KINDS OF PAIN. PHYSICAL PAIN AND EMOTIONAL PAIN.
PERSONALLY, I PREFER PHYSICAL PAIN. IF YOU'RE HURT SOMEWHERE YOU CAN GO SEE YOUR DOCTOR, AND TELL THEM YOU'RE HURTING.
BUT EMOTIONAL PAIN... IT'S NOT THE SAME. ONLY GOD CAN HELP YOU THERE.

So, I created
James Brown
from scratch...

It was the
only way.

-2-
MUSiC iS THE KEY

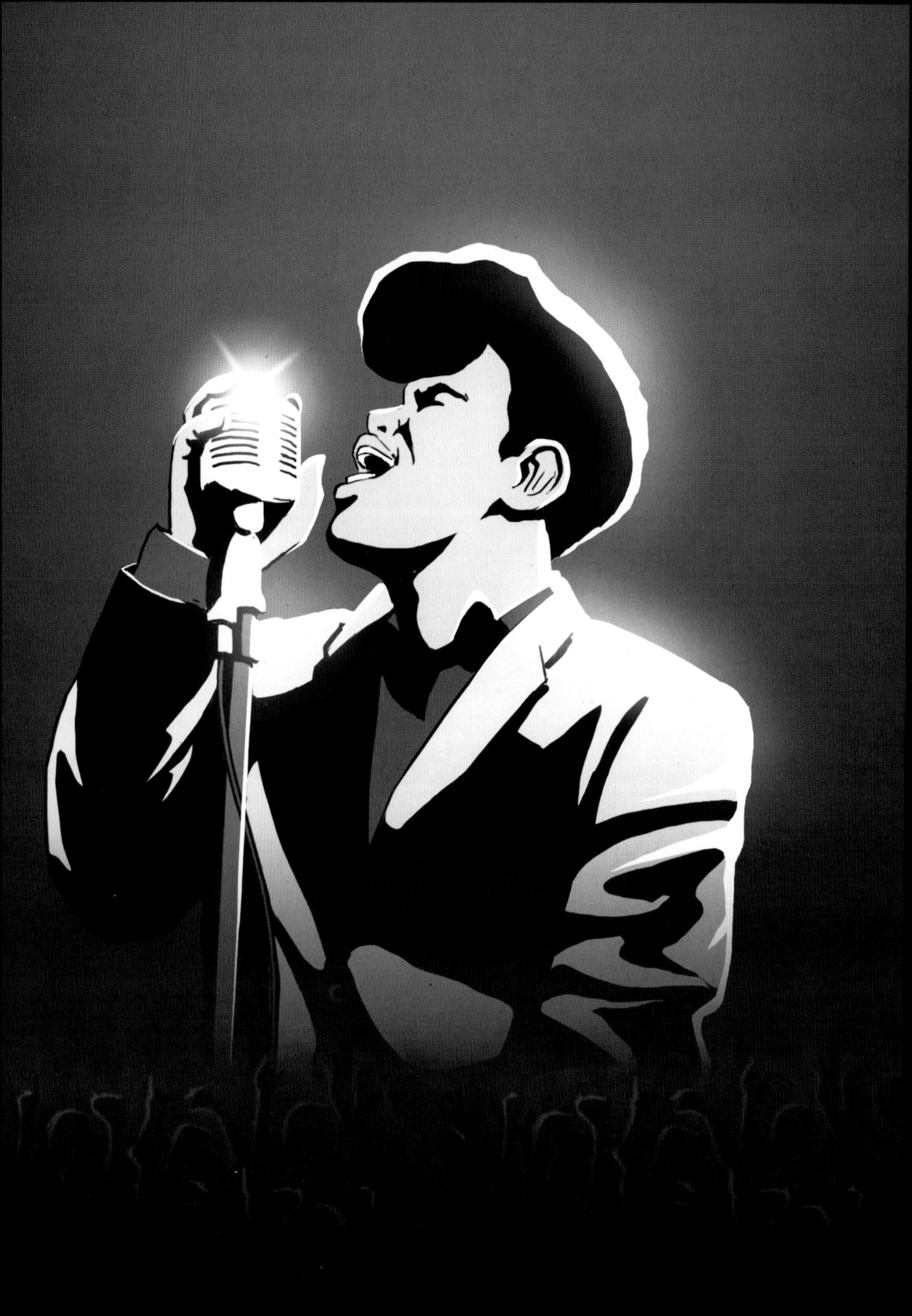

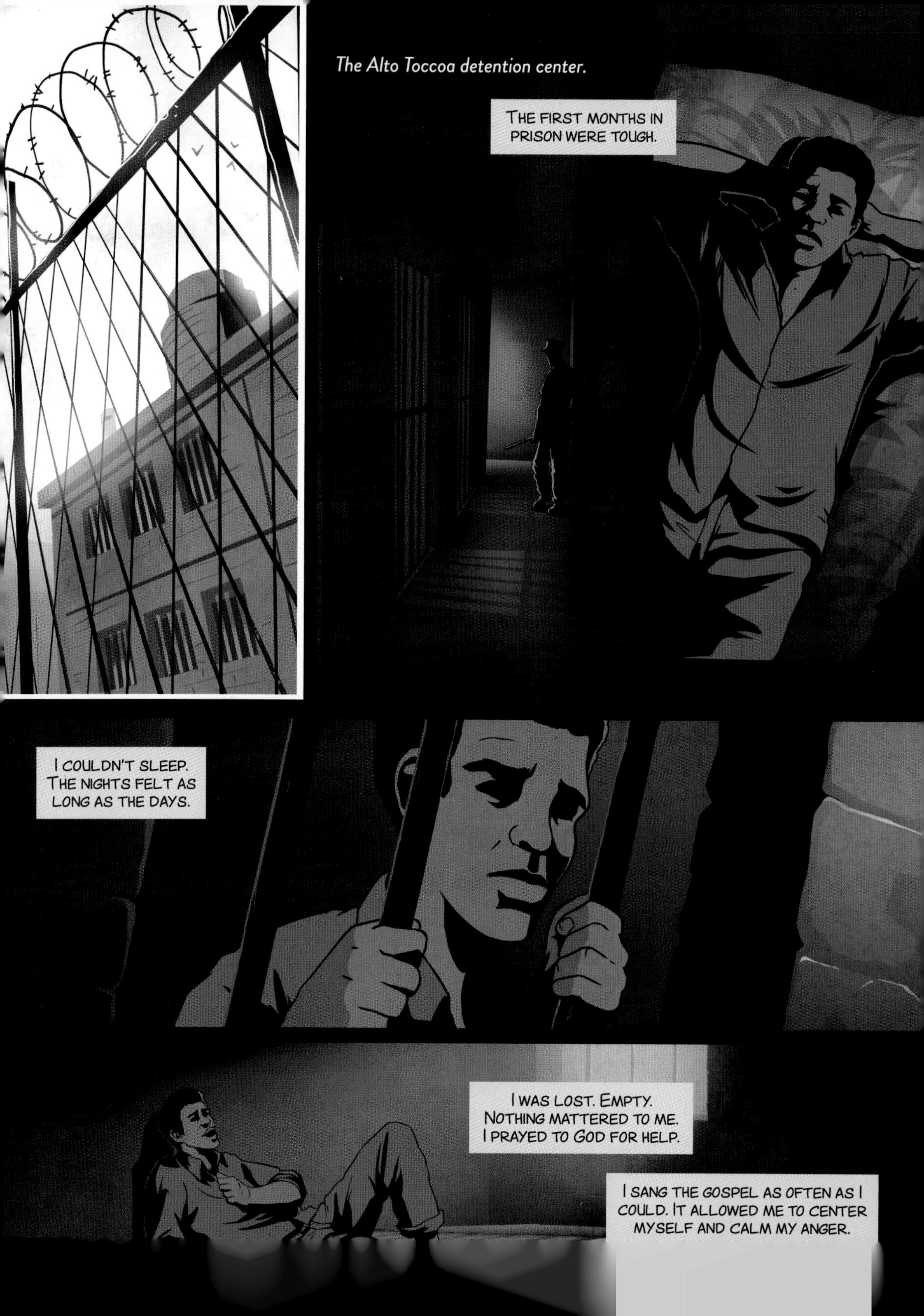
The Alto Toccoa detention center.
THE FIRST MONTHS IN PRISON WERE TOUGH.
I COULDN'T SLEEP. THE NIGHTS FELT AS LONG AS THE DAYS.
I WAS LOST. EMPTY. NOTHING MATTERED TO ME. I PRAYED TO GOD FOR HELP.
I SANG THE GOSPEL AS OFTEN AS I COULD. IT ALLOWED ME TO CENTER MYSELF AND CALM MY ANGER.

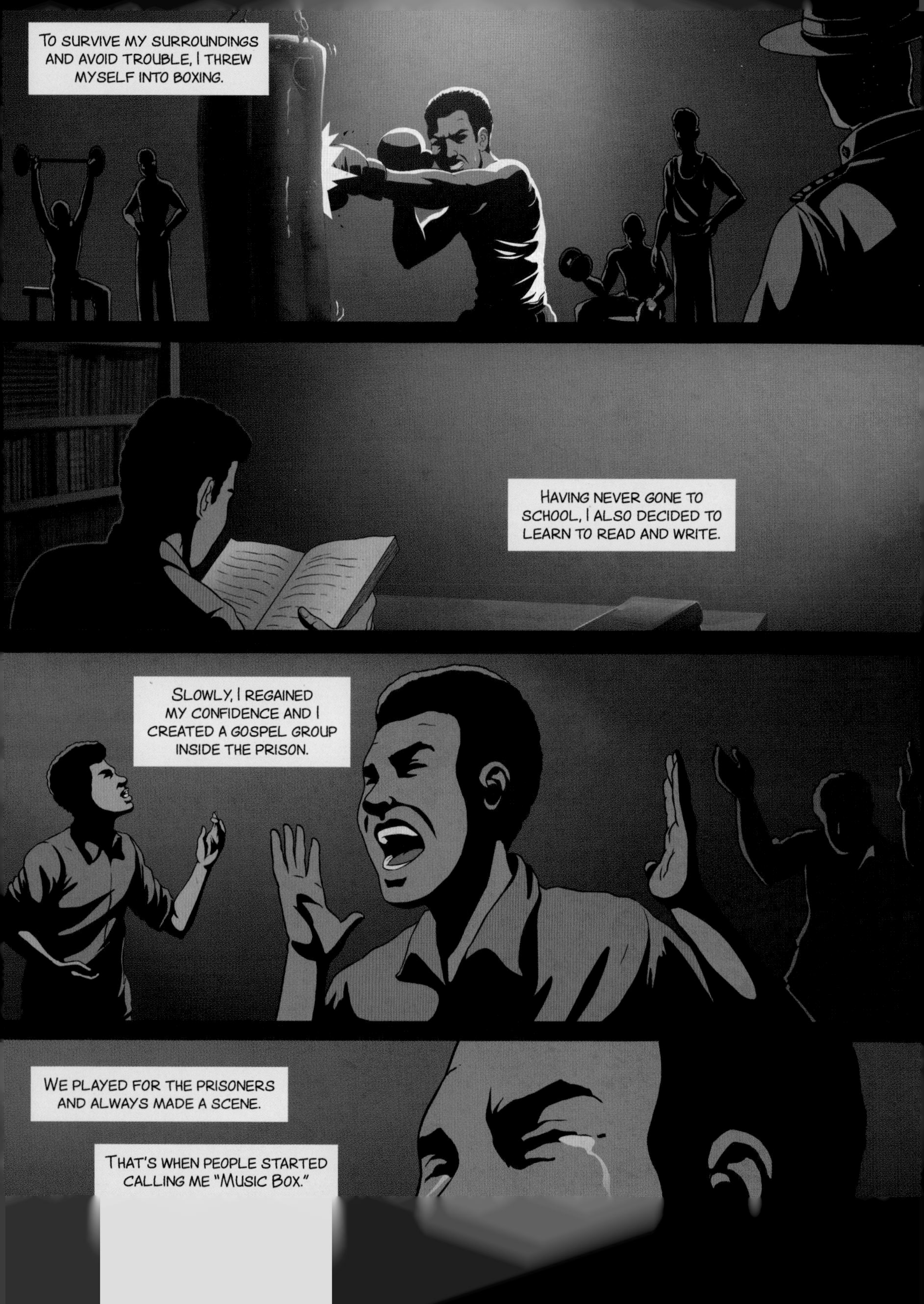
To survive my surroundings and avoid trouble, I threw myself into boxing.
Having never gone to school, I also decided to learn to read and write.
Slowly, I regained my confidence and I created a gospel group inside the prison.
We played for the prisoners and always made a scene.
That's when people started calling me "Music Box."

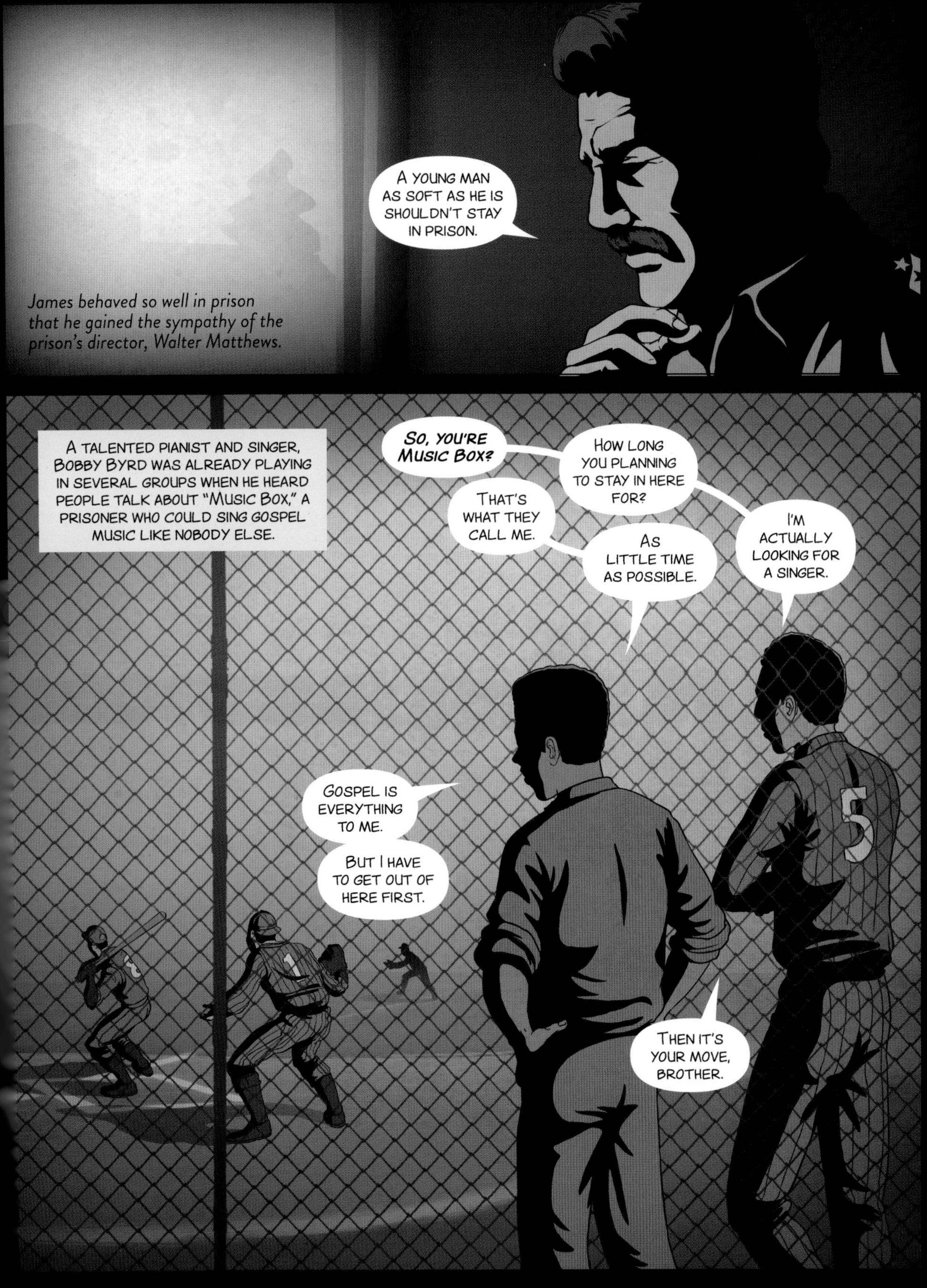
James behaved so well in prison that he gained the sympathy of the prison's director, Walter Matthews.
A YOUNG MAN AS SOFT AS HE IS SHOULDN'T STAY IN PRISON.
A TALENTED PIANIST AND SINGER, BOBBY BYRD WAS ALREADY PLAYING IN SEVERAL GROUPS WHEN HE HEARD PEOPLE TALK ABOUT "MUSIC BOX," A PRISONER WHO COULD SING GOSPEL MUSIC LIKE NOBODY ELSE.
SO, YOU'RE MUSIC BOX?
THAT'S WHAT THEY CALL ME.
HOW LONG YOU PLANNING TO STAY IN HERE FOR?
AS LITTLE TIME AS POSSIBLE.
I'M ACTUALLY LOOKING FOR A SINGER.
GOSPEL IS EVERYTHING TO ME.
BUT I HAVE TO GET OUT OF HERE FIRST.
THEN IT'S YOUR MOVE, BROTHER.

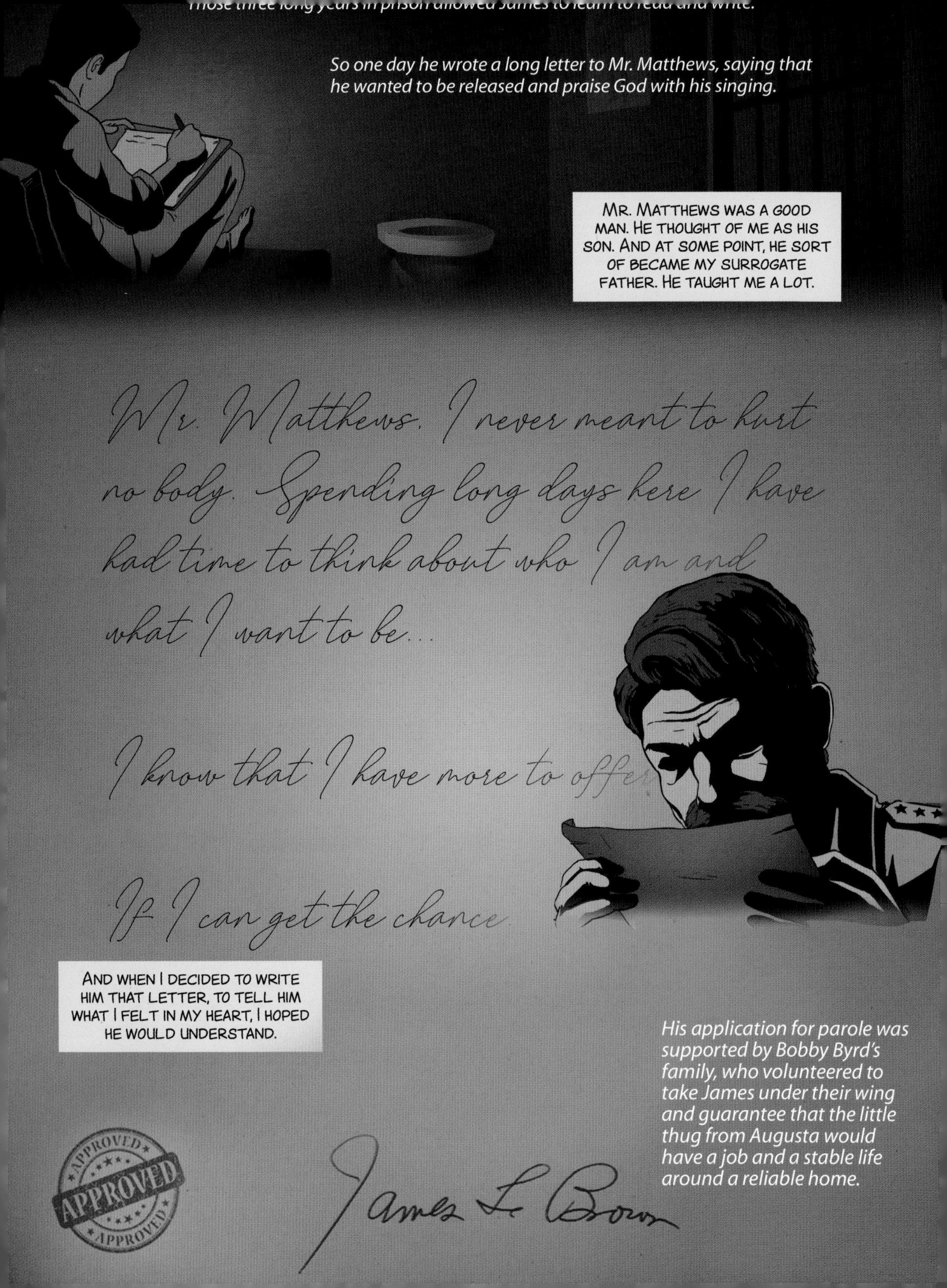

Those three long years in prison allowed James to learn to read and write.

So one day he wrote a long letter to Mr. Matthews, saying that he wanted to be released and praise God with his singing.

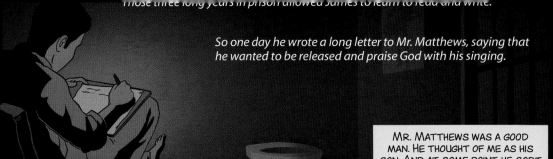

MR. MATTHEWS WAS A GOOD MAN. HE THOUGHT OF ME AS HIS SON. AND AT SOME POINT, HE SORT OF BECAME MY SURROGATE FATHER. HE TAUGHT ME A LOT.

Mr. Matthews. I never meant to hurt no body. Spending long days here I have had time to think about who I am and what I want to be...

I know that I have more to offer

If I can get the chance

AND WHEN I DECIDED TO WRITE HIM THAT LETTER, TO TELL HIM WHAT I FELT IN MY HEART, I HOPED HE WOULD UNDERSTAND.

His application for parole was supported by Bobby Byrd's family, who volunteered to take James under their wing and guarantee that the little thug from Augusta would have a job and a stable life around a reliable home.

James L. Brown

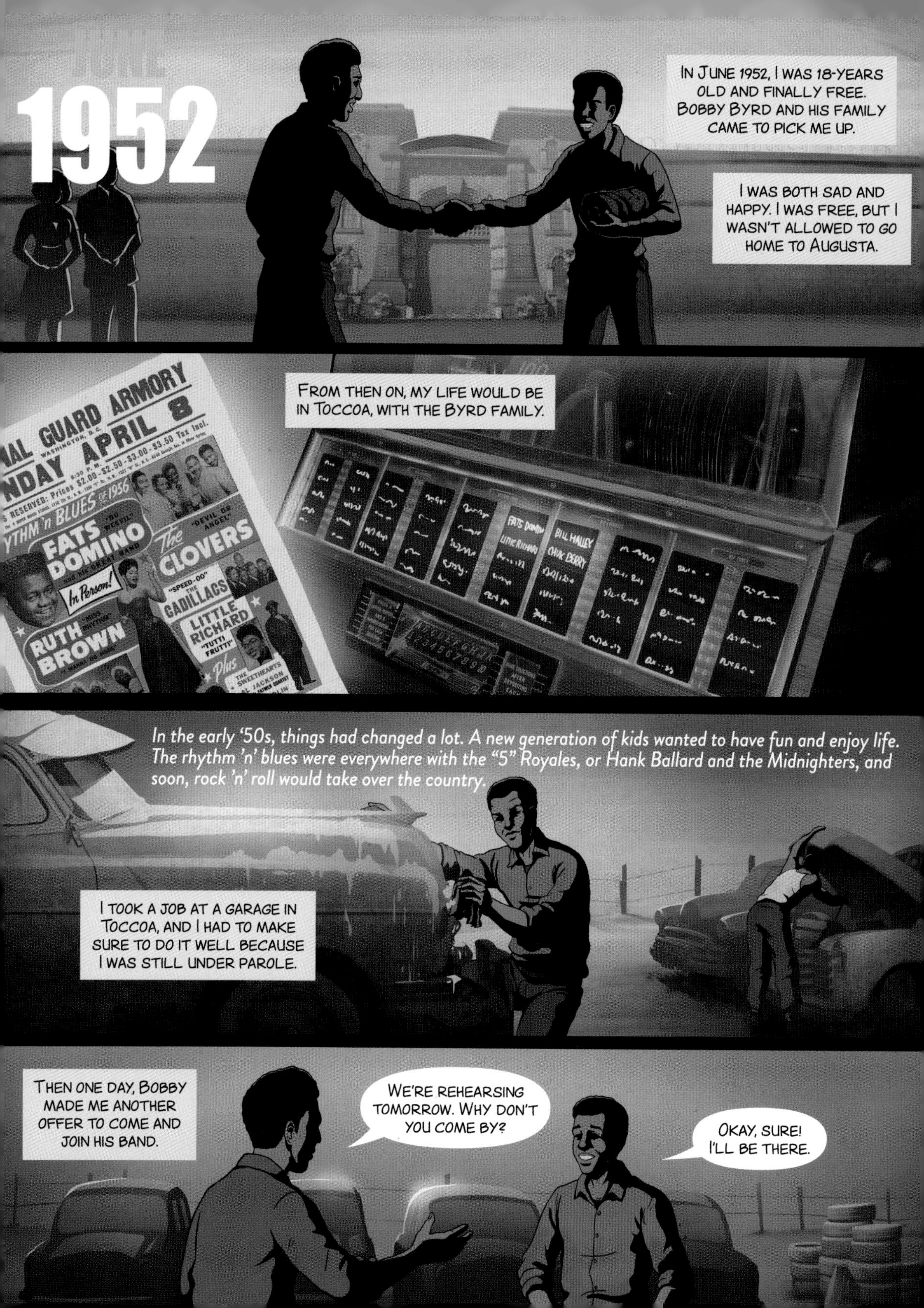
1952
IN JUNE 1952, I WAS 18-YEARS OLD AND FINALLY FREE. BOBBY BYRD AND HIS FAMILY CAME TO PICK ME UP.
I WAS BOTH SAD AND HAPPY. I WAS FREE, BUT I WASN'T ALLOWED TO GO HOME TO AUGUSTA.
FROM THEN ON, MY LIFE WOULD BE IN TOCCOA, WITH THE BYRD FAMILY.
GUARD ARMORY
APRIL 8
FATS DOMINO
THE CLOVERS
THE CADILLACS
LITTLE RICHARD
RUTH BROWN
In the early '50s, things had changed a lot. A new generation of kids wanted to have fun and enjoy life. The rhythm 'n' blues were everywhere with the "5" Royales, or Hank Ballard and the Midnighters, and soon, rock 'n' roll would take over the country.
I TOOK A JOB AT A GARAGE IN TOCCOA, AND I HAD TO MAKE SURE TO DO IT WELL BECAUSE I WAS STILL UNDER PAROLE.
THEN ONE DAY, BOBBY MADE ME ANOTHER OFFER TO COME AND JOIN HIS BAND.
WE'RE REHEARSING TOMORROW. WHY DON'T YOU COME BY?
OKAY, SURE! I'LL BE THERE.

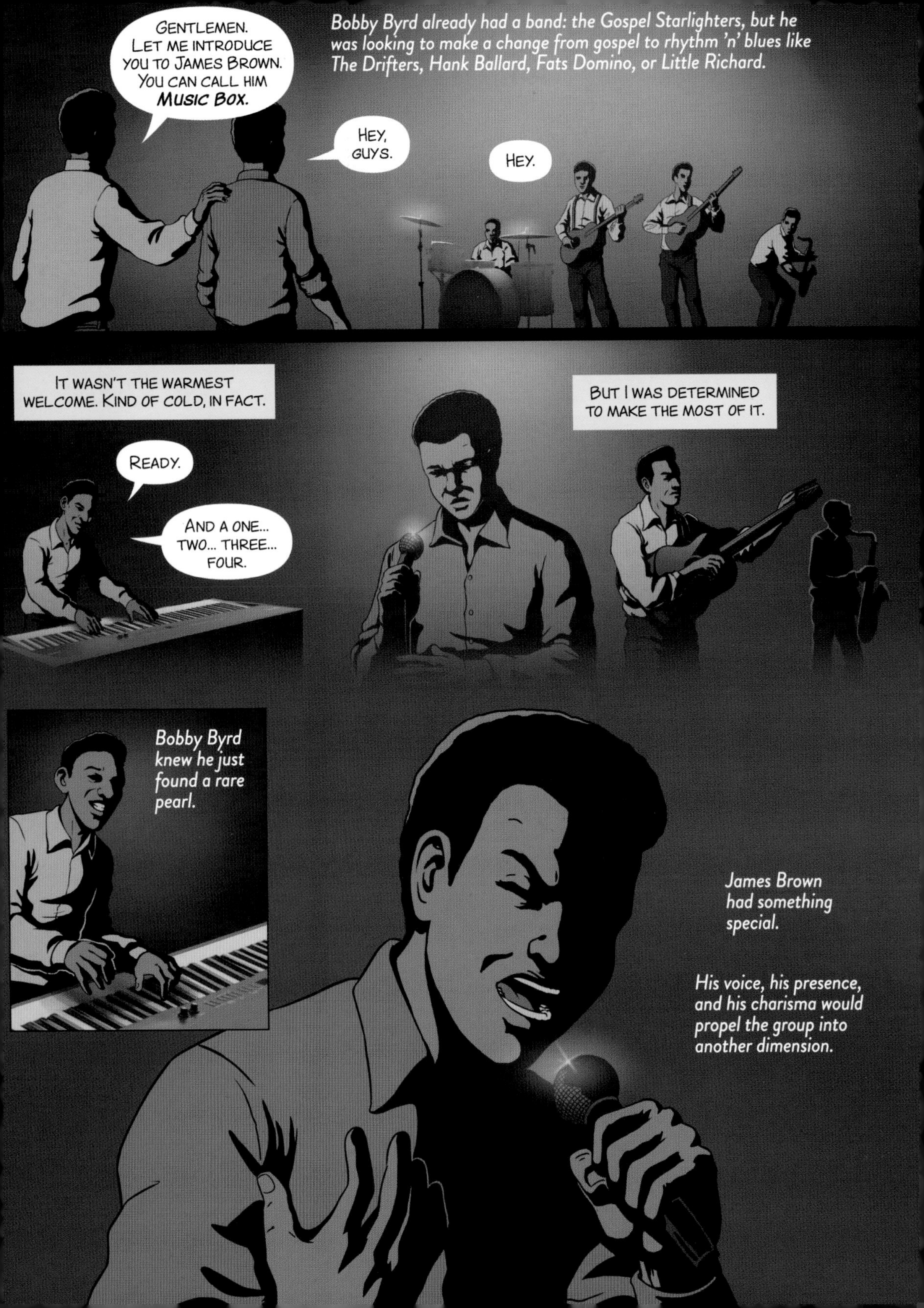
Gentlemen. Let me introduce you to James Brown. You can call him Music Box.
Bobby Byrd already had a band: the Gospel Starlighters, but he was looking to make a change from gospel to rhythm 'n' blues like The Drifters, Hank Ballard, Fats Domino, or Little Richard.
Hey, guys.
Hey.
It wasn't the warmest welcome. Kind of cold, in fact.
Ready.
And a one... two... three... four.
But I was determined to make the most of it.
Bobby Byrd knew he just found a rare pearl.
James Brown had something special.
His voice, his presence, and his charisma would propel the group into another dimension.

Since 1870 and the end of the Civil War, the Jim Crow laws had been the core rules governing segregation in the USA. "Separate but equal" was one of the founding principles that made people think that colored men had the same rights as whites. In reality, it was another story entirely, especially in the South.

In the early '50s, rhythm 'n' blues and rock 'n' roll brought young white and black people together, while the racists fought to keep them apart.

"THEY WANT TO MIX WHITE AND BLACK CHILDREN IN THE MELTING POT OF INTEGRATION, FOR THEM TO INTERBREED?"

"...A WHOLE SET OF MULATTO BASTARDS!"

"LET YOUR DAUGHTERS LISTEN TO NEGRO MUSIC, AND TOMORROW THEY'LL BE GIVING BIRTH TO BLACK BABIES!"

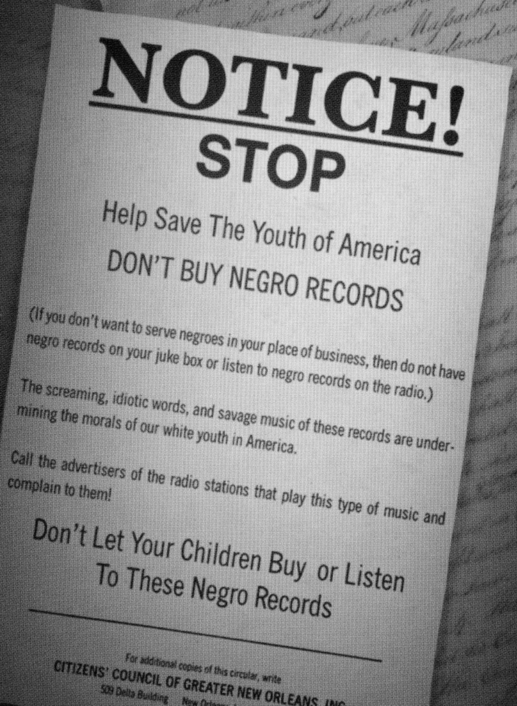

NOTICE!

STOP

Help Save The Youth of America

DON'T BUY NEGRO RECORDS

(If you don't want to serve negroes in your place of business, then do not have negro records on your juke box or listen to negro records on the radio.)

The screaming, idiotic words, and savage music of these records are undermining the morals of our white youth in America.

Call the advertisers of the radio stations that play this type of music and complain to them!

Don't Let Your Children Buy or Listen To These Negro Records

For additional copies of this circular, write

CITIZENS' COUNCIL OF GREATER NEW ORLEANS, INC.

509 Delta Building New Orleans, Louisiana 70112

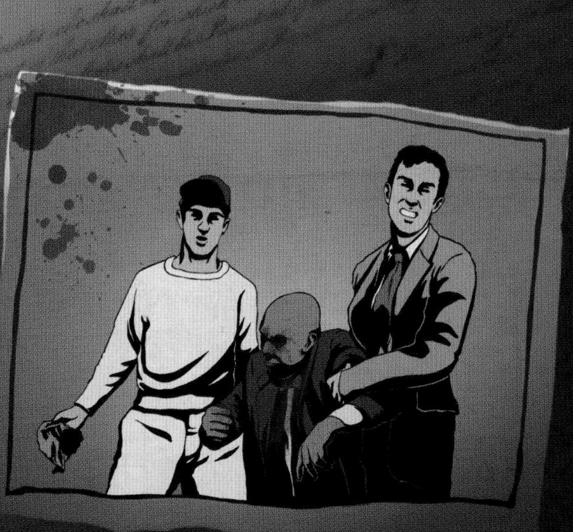

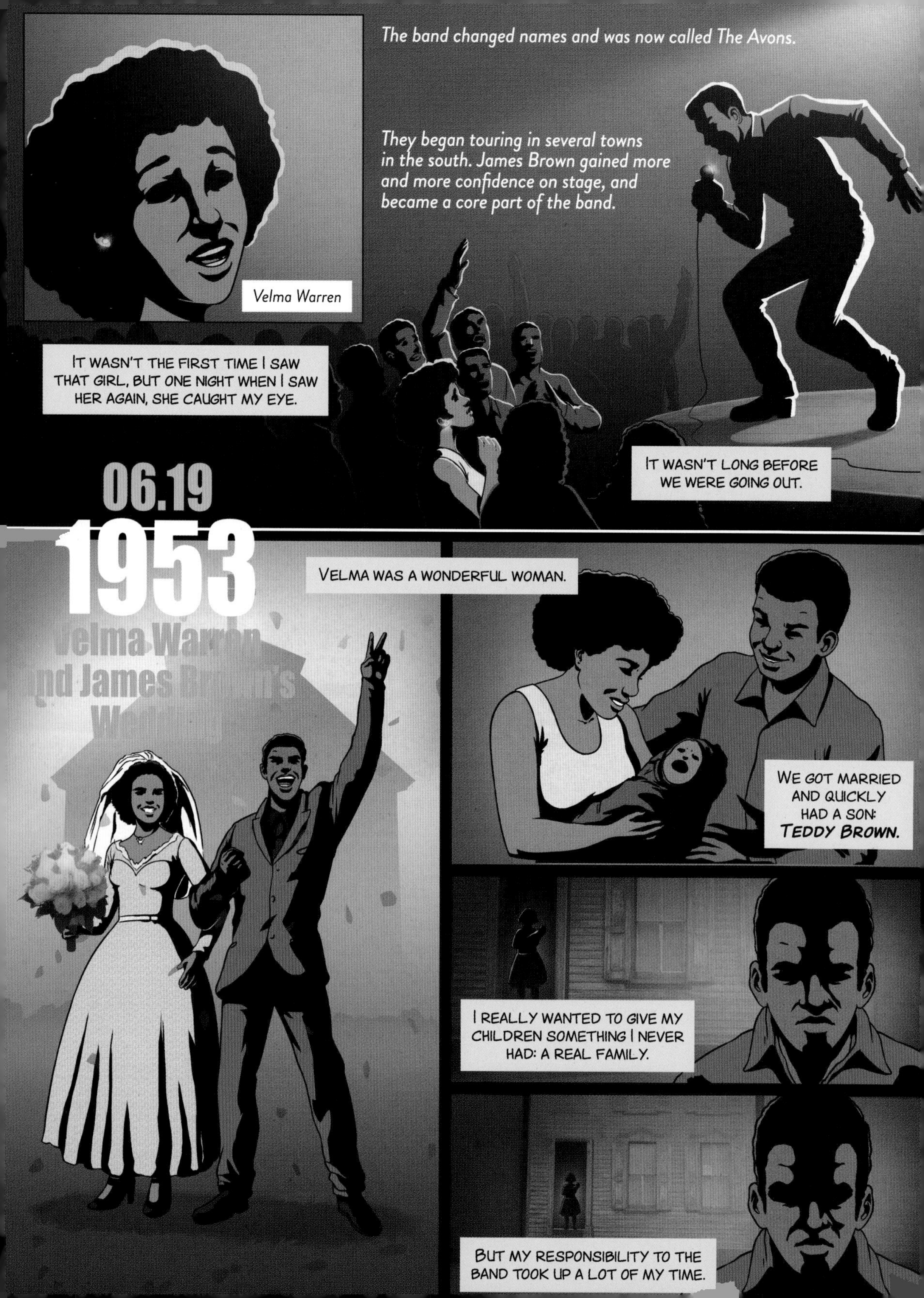

The band changed names and was now called The Avons.
Velma Warren
They began touring in several towns in the south. James Brown gained more and more confidence on stage, and became a core part of the band.
IT WASN'T THE FIRST TIME I SAW THAT GIRL, BUT ONE NIGHT WHEN I SAW HER AGAIN, SHE CAUGHT MY EYE.
IT WASN'T LONG BEFORE WE WERE GOING OUT.
06.19
1953
VELMA WAS A WONDERFUL WOMAN.
WE GOT MARRIED AND QUICKLY HAD A SON: TEDDY BROWN.
I REALLY WANTED TO GIVE MY CHILDREN SOMETHING I NEVER HAD: A REAL FAMILY.
BUT MY RESPONSIBILITY TO THE BAND TOOK UP A LOT OF MY TIME.

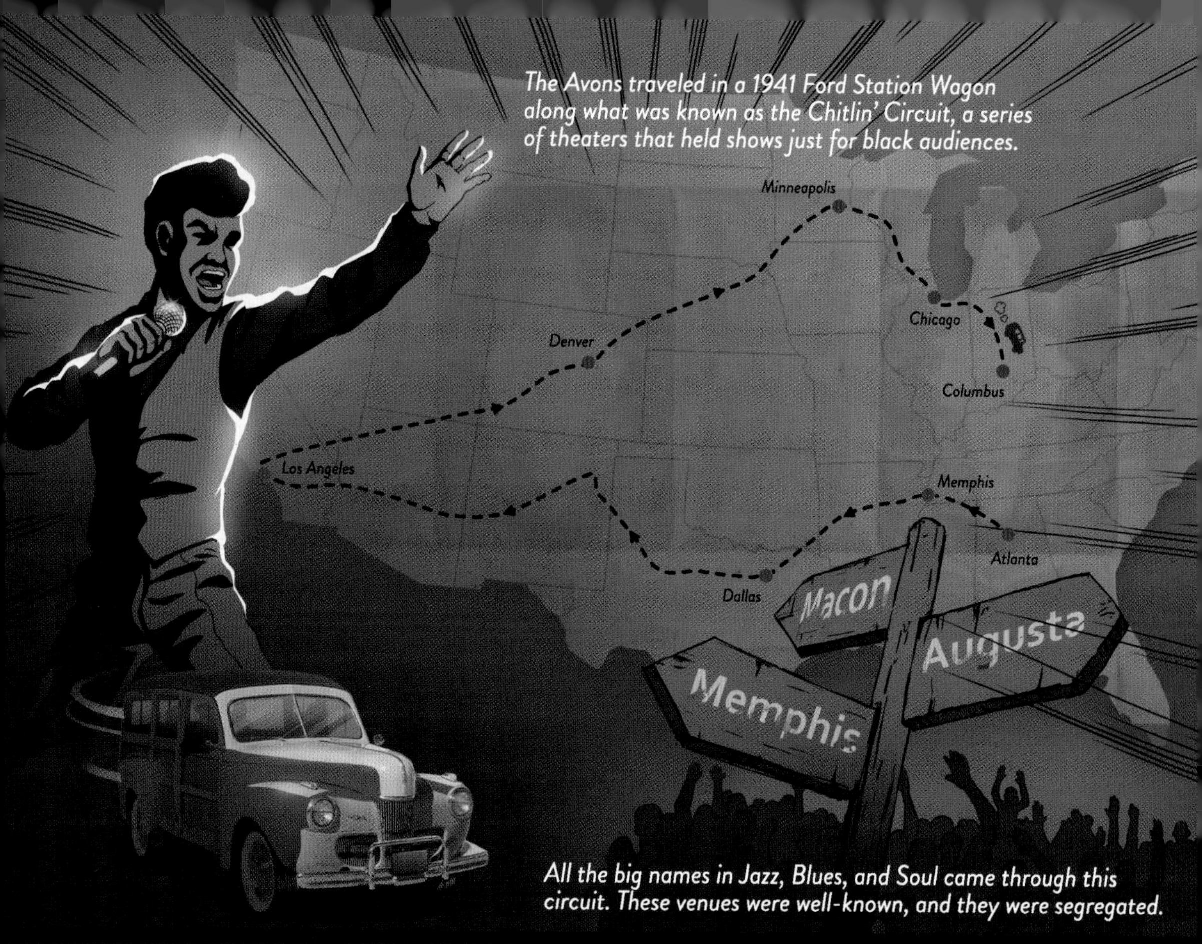
The Avons traveled in a 1941 Ford Station Wagon along what was known as the Chitlin' Circuit, a series of theaters that held shows just for black audiences.
Minneapolis
Chicago
Denver
Columbus
Los Angeles
Memphis
Atlanta
Dallas
Macon
Augusta
Memphis
All the big names in Jazz, Blues, and Soul came through this circuit. These venues were well-known, and they were segregated.

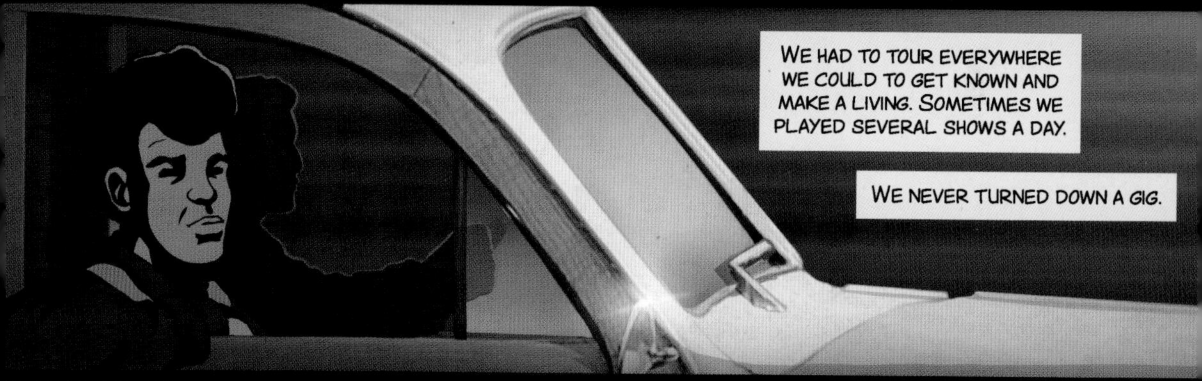
WE HAD TO TOUR EVERYWHERE WE COULD TO GET KNOWN AND MAKE A LIVING. SOMETIMES WE PLAYED SEVERAL SHOWS A DAY.
WE NEVER TURNED DOWN A GIG.

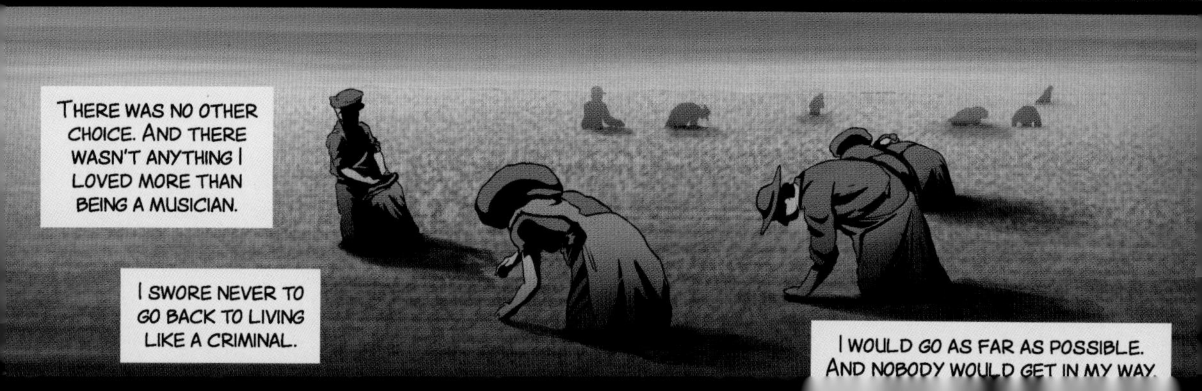
THERE WAS NO OTHER CHOICE. AND THERE WASN'T ANYTHING I LOVED MORE THAN BEING A MUSICIAN.
I SWORE NEVER TO GO BACK TO LIVING LIKE A CRIMINAL.
I WOULD GO AS FAR AS POSSIBLE. AND NOBODY WOULD GET IN MY WAY.

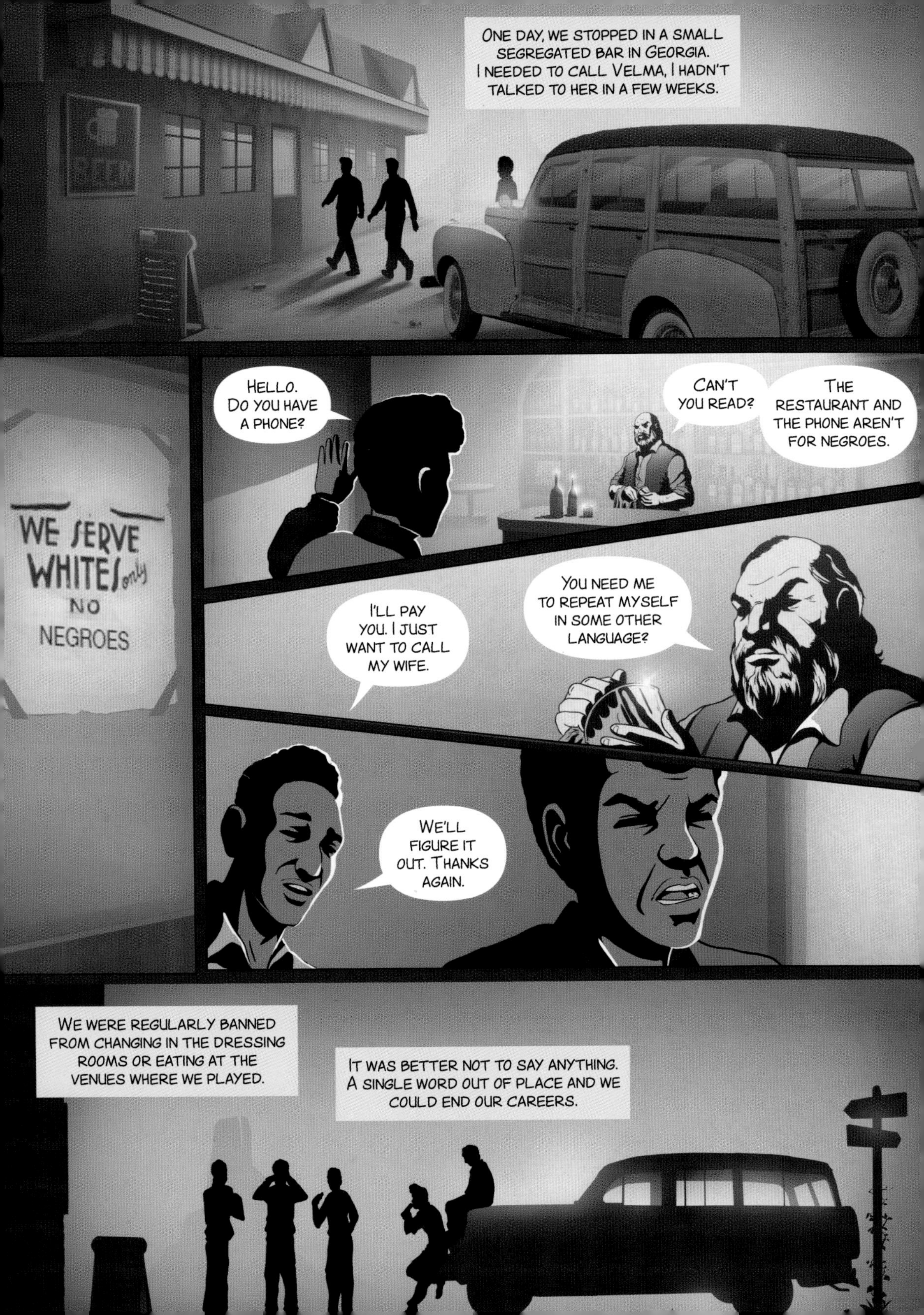
ONE DAY, WE STOPPED IN A SMALL SEGREGATED BAR IN GEORGIA. I NEEDED TO CALL VELMA, I HADN'T TALKED TO HER IN A FEW WEEKS.
BEER
WE SERVE WHITES only NO NEGROES
HELLO. DO YOU HAVE A PHONE?
CAN'T YOU READ?
THE RESTAURANT AND THE PHONE AREN'T FOR NEGROES.
I'LL PAY YOU. I JUST WANT TO CALL MY WIFE.
YOU NEED ME TO REPEAT MYSELF IN SOME OTHER LANGUAGE?
WE'LL FIGURE IT OUT. THANKS AGAIN.
WE WERE REGULARLY BANNED FROM CHANGING IN THE DRESSING ROOMS OR EATING AT THE VENUES WHERE WE PLAYED.
IT WAS BETTER NOT TO SAY ANYTHING. A SINGLE WORD OUT OF PLACE AND WE COULD END OUR CAREERS.

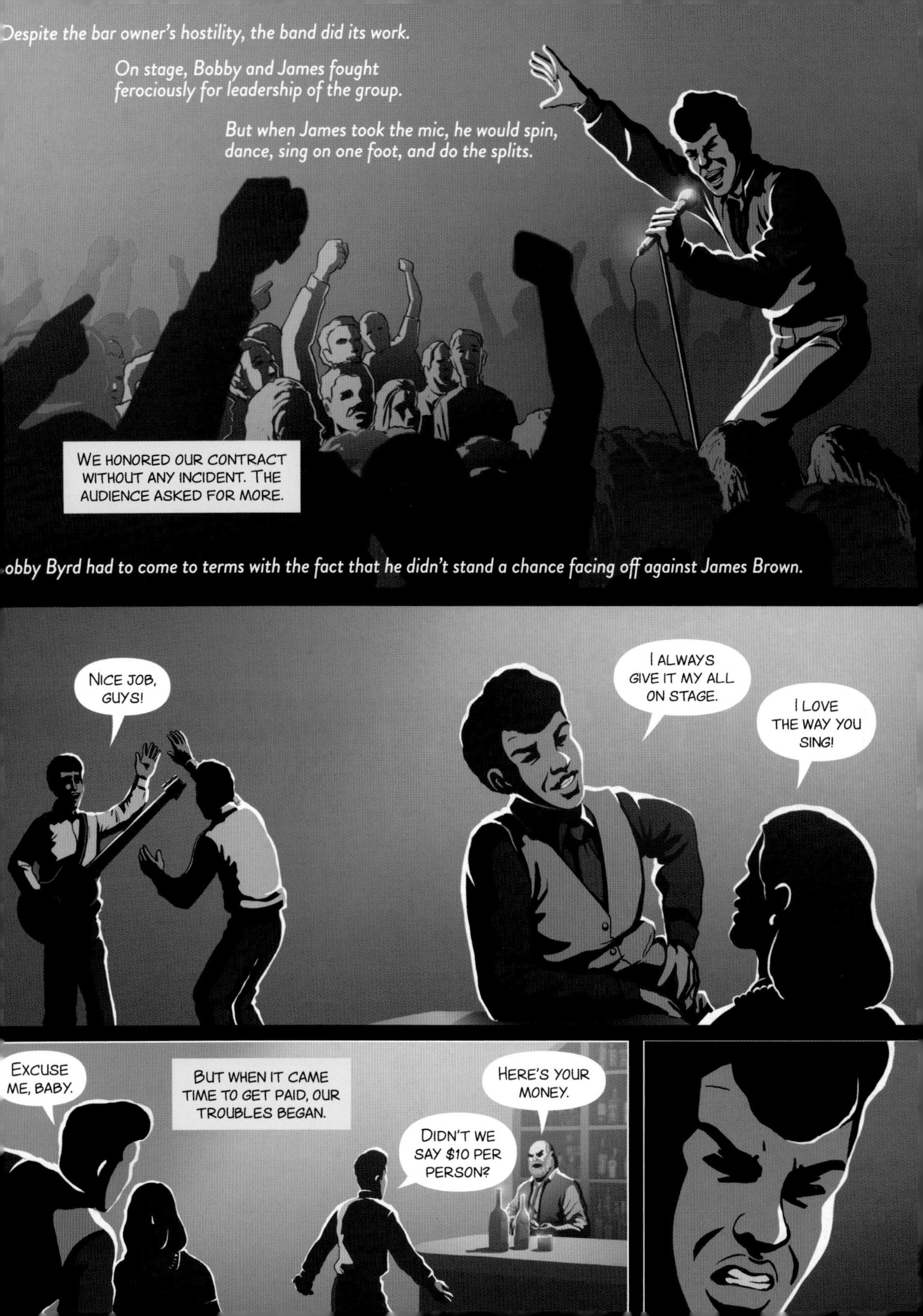
Despite the bar owner's hostility, the band did its work.
On stage, Bobby and James fought ferociously for leadership of the group.
But when James took the mic, he would spin, dance, sing on one foot, and do the splits.
WE HONORED OUR CONTRACT WITHOUT ANY INCIDENT. THE AUDIENCE ASKED FOR MORE.
obby Byrd had to come to terms with the fact that he didn't stand a chance facing off against James Brown.
NICE JOB, GUYS!
I ALWAYS GIVE IT MY ALL ON STAGE.
I LOVE THE WAY YOU SING!
EXCUSE ME, BABY.
BUT WHEN IT CAME TIME TO GET PAID, OUR TROUBLES BEGAN.
HERE'S YOUR MONEY.
DIDN'T WE SAY $10 PER PERSON?

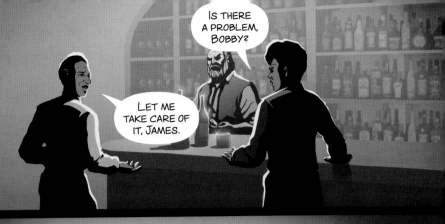

BECAUSE THE BAR OWNER DIDN'T WANT TO PAY US WHAT WE WERE DUE.

IS THERE A PROBLEM, BOBBY?

LET ME TAKE CARE OF IT, JAMES.

NO WAY AROUND IT. THIS GUY'S A THIEF!

WHO YOU CALLING A THIEF? DIRTY NIGGER!

GET OUT OF HERE BEFORE I PUT YOU DOWN LIKE THE DOG YOU ARE.

FINE. I GOT IT.

DO YOU REALIZE WHAT ALMOST HAPPENED THERE?

THAT GUY DOESN'T RESPECT US.

IT'S NONE OF OUR BUSINESS.

YES, IT IS.

BUT FACED WITH THE THREAT OF ENDING UP BURIED IN A HOLE, OR GETTING THE GROUP SHOT UP, I DECIDED TO BACK DOWN.

AND I LEFT ANGRY...

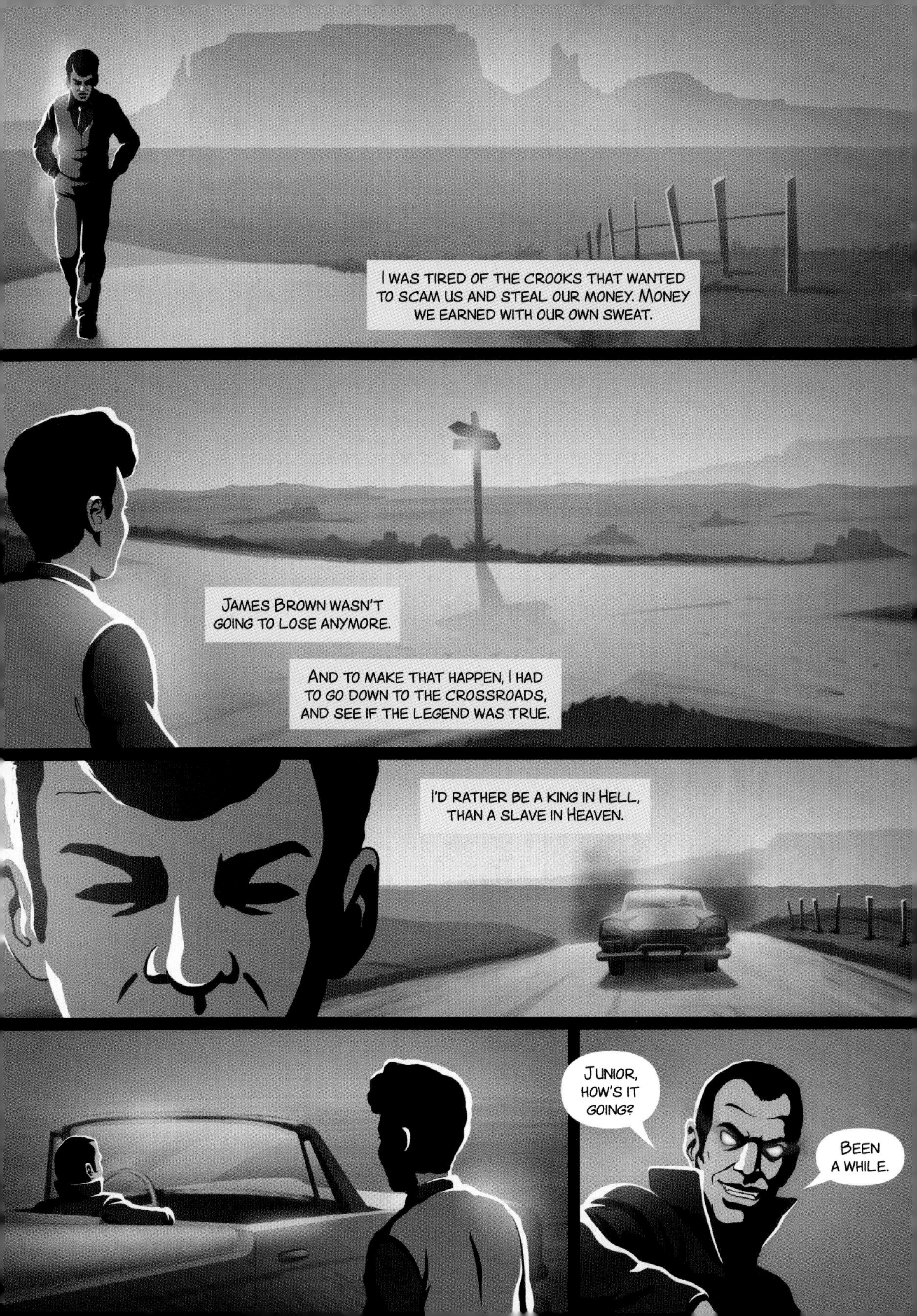
I WAS TIRED OF THE CROOKS THAT WANTED TO SCAM US AND STEAL OUR MONEY. MONEY WE EARNED WITH OUR OWN SWEAT.
JAMES BROWN WASN'T GOING TO LOSE ANYMORE.
AND TO MAKE THAT HAPPEN, I HAD TO GO DOWN TO THE CROSSROADS, AND SEE IF THE LEGEND WAS TRUE.
I'D RATHER BE A KING IN HELL, THAN A SLAVE IN HEAVEN.
JUNIOR, HOW'S IT GOING?
BEEN A WHILE.

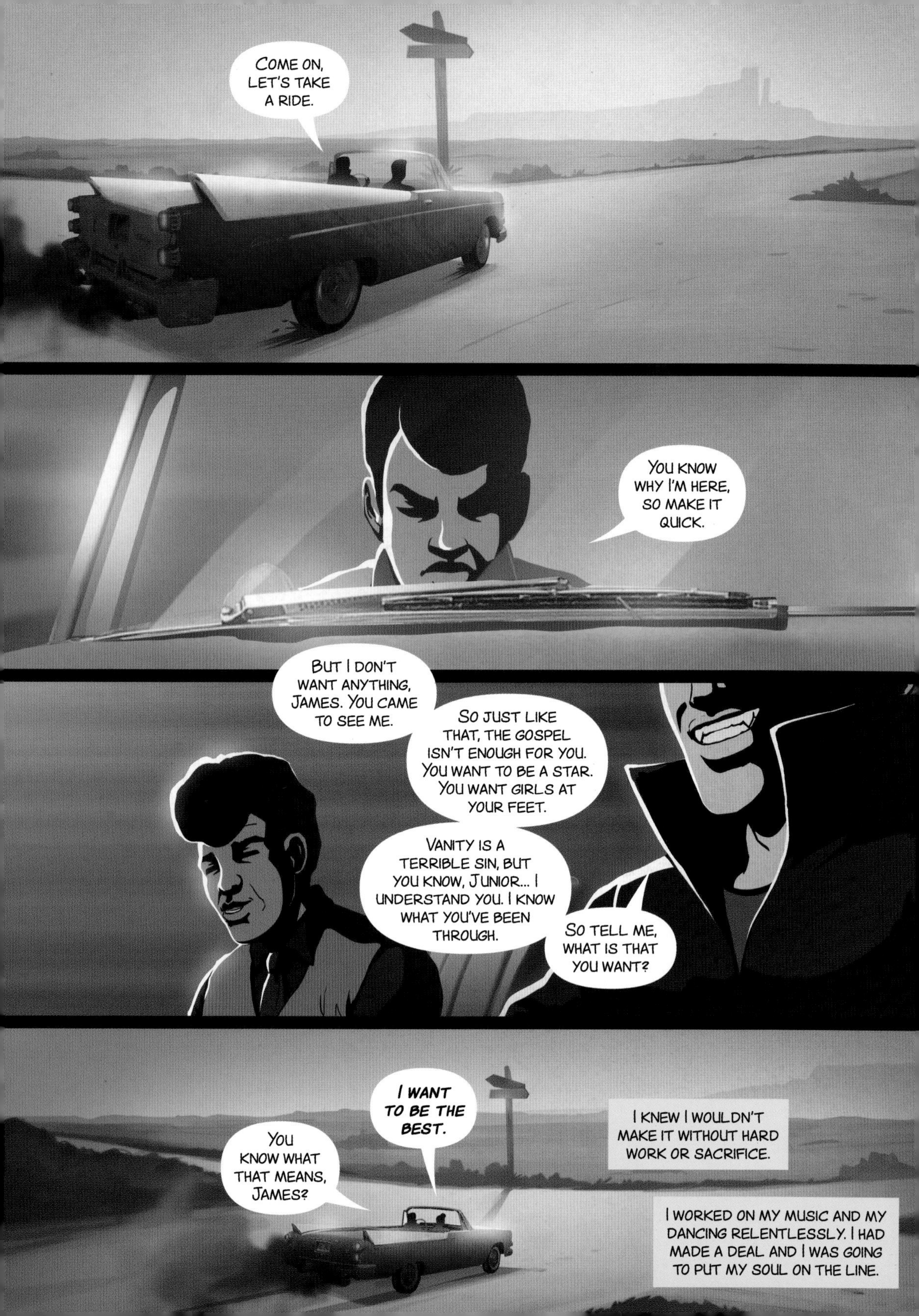
COME ON, LET'S TAKE A RIDE.
YOU KNOW WHY I'M HERE, SO MAKE IT QUICK.
BUT I DON'T WANT ANYTHING, JAMES. YOU CAME TO SEE ME.
SO JUST LIKE THAT, THE GOSPEL ISN'T ENOUGH FOR YOU. YOU WANT TO BE A STAR. YOU WANT GIRLS AT YOUR FEET.
VANITY IS A TERRIBLE SIN, BUT YOU KNOW, JUNIOR... I UNDERSTAND YOU. I KNOW WHAT YOU'VE BEEN THROUGH.
SO TELL ME, WHAT IS THAT YOU WANT?
I WANT TO BE THE BEST.
YOU KNOW WHAT THAT MEANS, JAMES?
I KNEW I WOULDN'T MAKE IT WITHOUT HARD WORK OR SACRIFICE.
I WORKED ON MY MUSIC AND MY DANCING RELENTLESSLY. I HAD MADE A DEAL AND I WAS GOING TO PUT MY SOUL ON THE LINE.

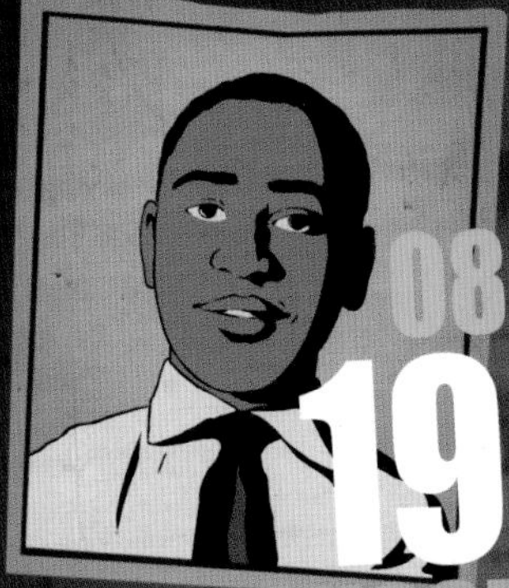

08.28 1955 MISSISSIPPI

Emmett Till, a young 14-year old boy originally from Chicago, who was on vacation visiting his uncle in Mississippi, was found in the Tallahatchie river, violently murdered. A few days later, during the funeral, his mother opened his casket, revealing the mutilated body of her son in order to show the entire world the horror of the crime committed. Pictures of Emmett Till's deformed face spread across the world. His death shook the whole of America, and the year 1955 marked the beginning of a long fight for African-Americans.

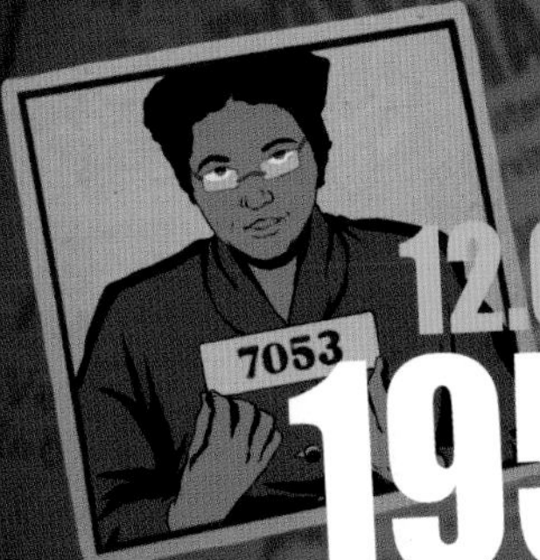
7053

12.01 1955 MONTGOMERY

A woman by the name of Rosa Parks refused to give up her seat to a white person in a crowded bus. Even though she was seated in a section designated for black people, the driver had her arrested for breaking one of the South's tacit laws, which stated that a black must give up their place to a white if the bus was full. Rosa Park's arrest provoked intense reactions, and she received support from the N.A.A.C.P. (National Association for the Advancement of Colored People). This movement gained momentum and led to the boycott of the Montgomery bus system, led by a young black pastor named Martin Luther King, Jr.

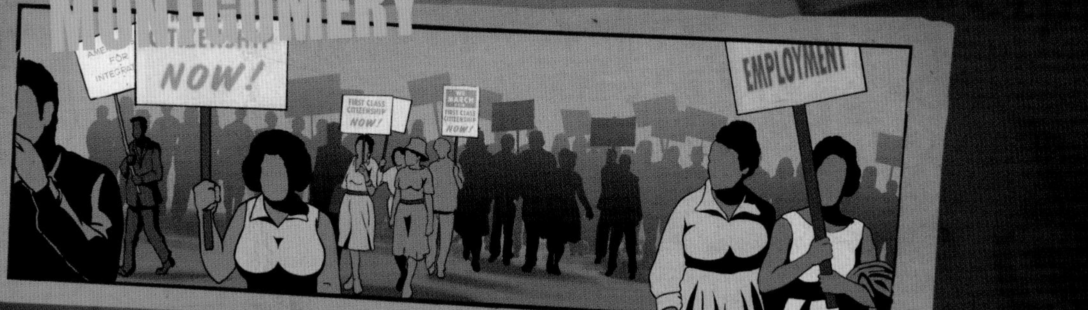
NOW!
FIRST CLASS CITIZENSHIP NOW!
FIRST CLASS CITIZENSHIP NOW!
EMPLOYMENT

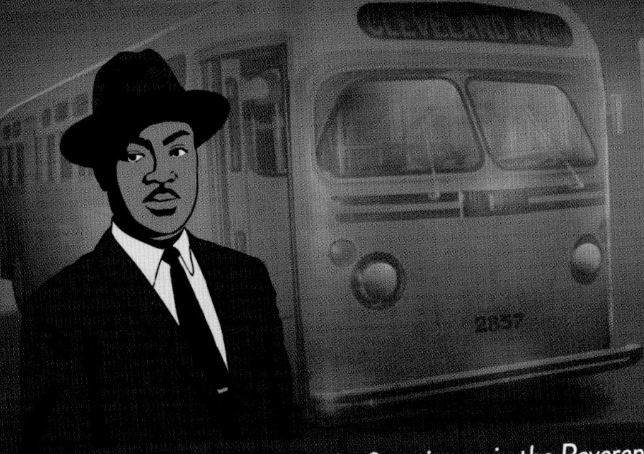
2857

The boycott of the Montgomery buses was the first campaign led by Reverend Martin Luther King, Jr. and would result in the Supreme Court of the United States ruling that the laws of the State of Alabama imposing racial segregation in buses were unconstitutional.

This amounted to the first victory in the Reverend's fight for civil rights for black Americans.

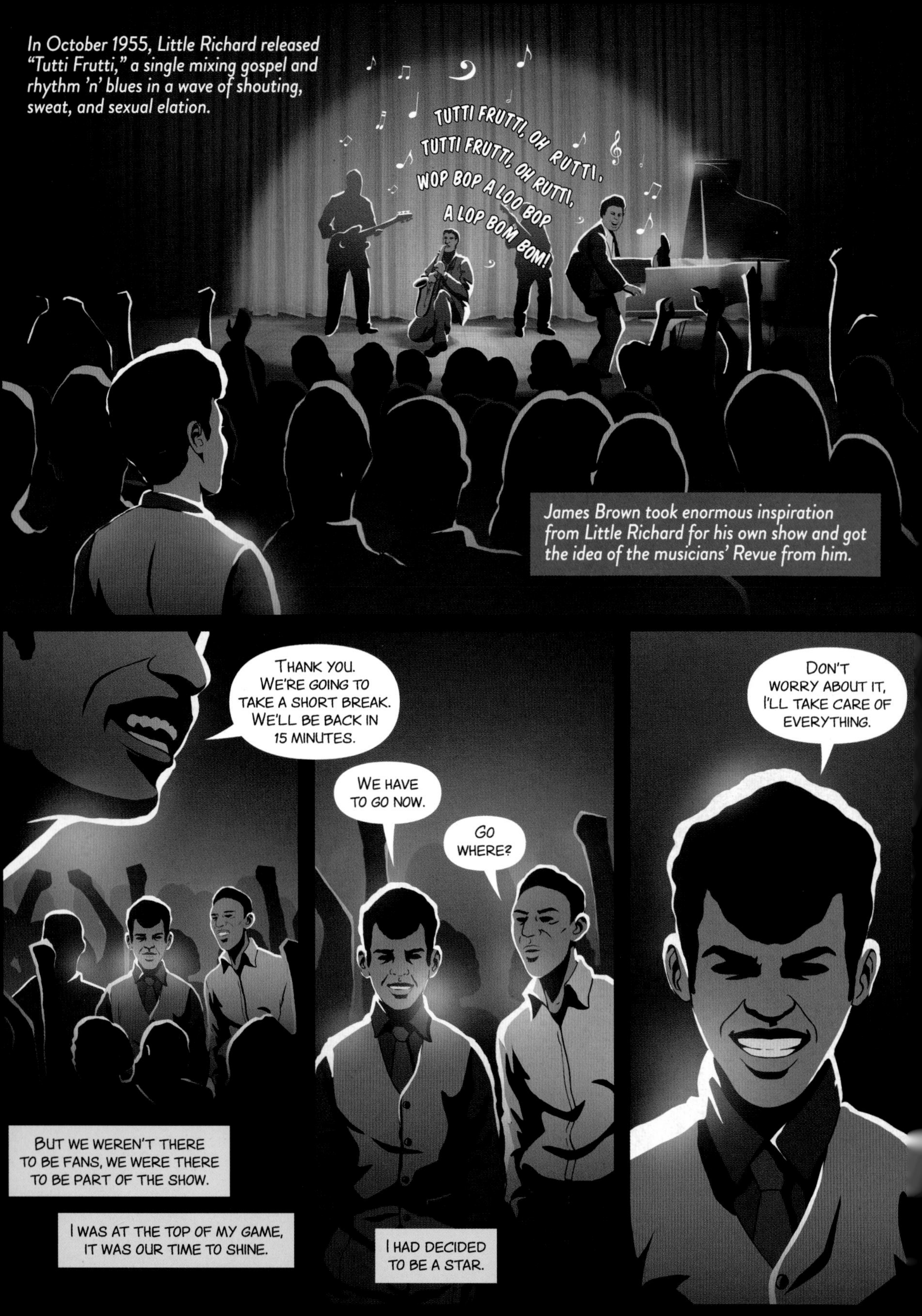
In October 1955, Little Richard released "Tutti Frutti," a single mixing gospel and rhythm 'n' blues in a wave of shouting, sweat, and sexual elation.
TUTTI FRUTTI, OH RUTTI, TUTTI FRUTTI, OH RUTTI, WOP BOP A LOO BOP A LOP BOM BOM!
James Brown took enormous inspiration from Little Richard for his own show and got the idea of the musicians' Revue from him.
THANK YOU. WE'RE GOING TO TAKE A SHORT BREAK. WE'LL BE BACK IN 15 MINUTES.
BUT WE WEREN'T THERE TO BE FANS, WE WERE THERE TO BE PART OF THE SHOW.
I WAS AT THE TOP OF MY GAME, IT WAS OUR TIME TO SHINE.
WE HAVE TO GO NOW.
GO WHERE?
I HAD DECIDED TO BE A STAR.
DON'T WORRY ABOUT IT, I'LL TAKE CARE OF EVERYTHING.

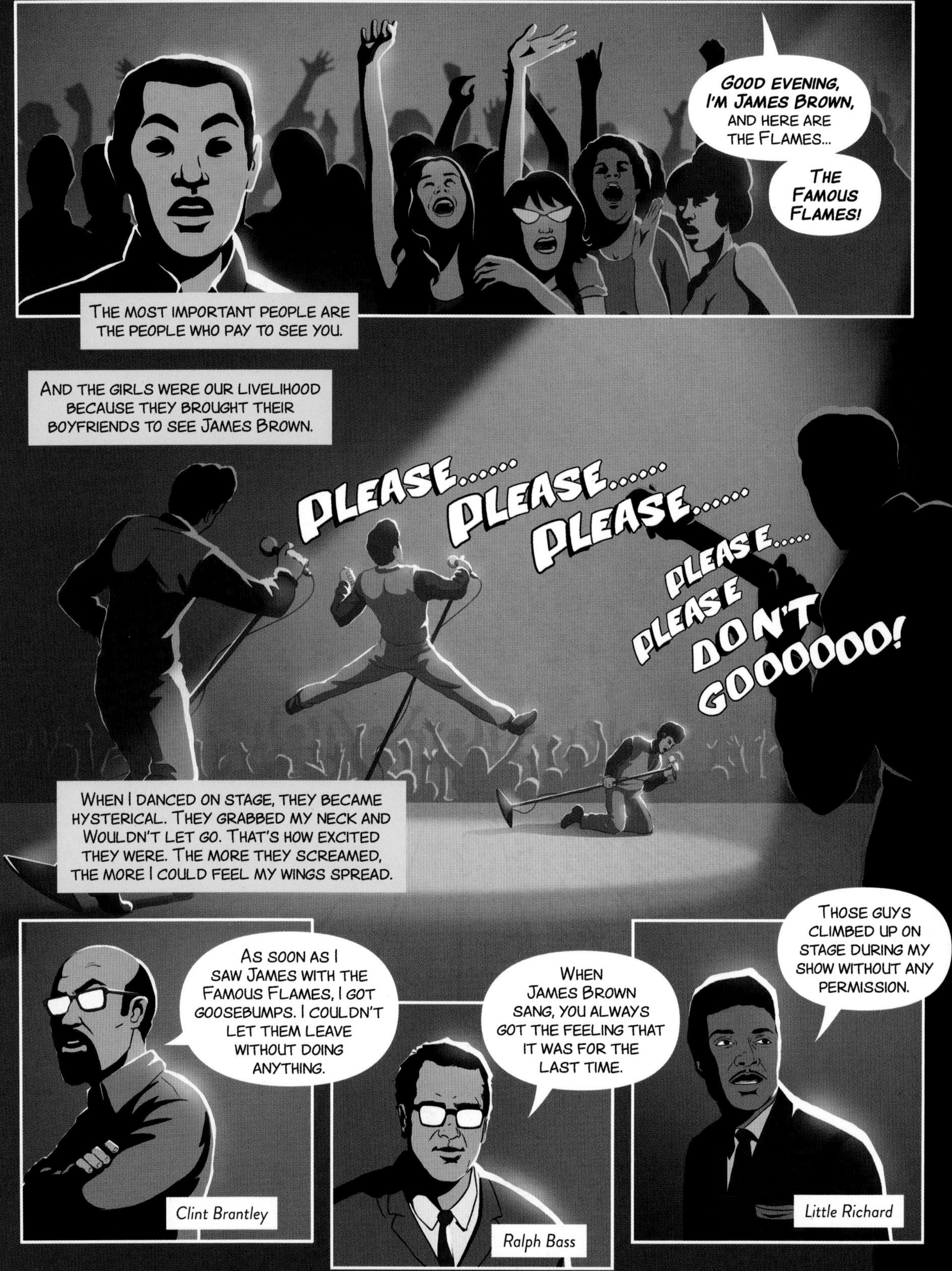
GOOD EVENING, I'M JAMES BROWN, AND HERE ARE THE FLAMES...
THE FAMOUS FLAMES!
THE MOST IMPORTANT PEOPLE ARE THE PEOPLE WHO PAY TO SEE YOU.
AND THE GIRLS WERE OUR LIVELIHOOD BECAUSE THEY BROUGHT THEIR BOYFRIENDS TO SEE JAMES BROWN.
PLEASE...... PLEASE...... PLEASE...... PLEASE..... PLEASE DON'T GOOOOOO!
WHEN I DANCED ON STAGE, THEY BECAME HYSTERICAL. THEY GRABBED MY NECK AND WOULDN'T LET GO. THAT'S HOW EXCITED THEY WERE. THE MORE THEY SCREAMED, THE MORE I COULD FEEL MY WINGS SPREAD.
AS SOON AS I SAW JAMES WITH THE FAMOUS FLAMES, I GOT GOOSEBUMPS. I COULDN'T LET THEM LEAVE WITHOUT DOING ANYTHING.
Clint Brantley
WHEN JAMES BROWN SANG, YOU ALWAYS GOT THE FEELING THAT IT WAS FOR THE LAST TIME.
Ralph Bass
THOSE GUYS CLIMBED UP ON STAGE DURING MY SHOW WITHOUT ANY PERMISSION.
Little Richard

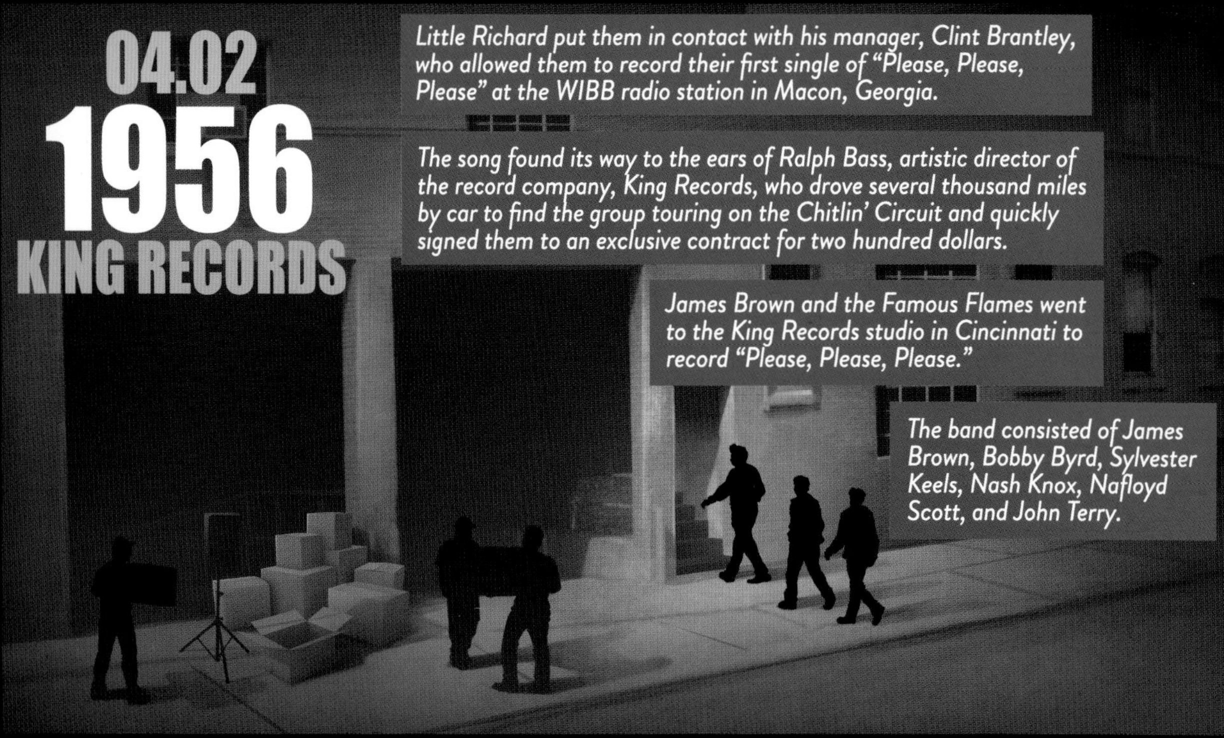
04.02
1956
KING RECORDS
Little Richard put them in contact with his manager, Clint Brantley, who allowed them to record their first single of "Please, Please, Please" at the WIBB radio station in Macon, Georgia.
The song found its way to the ears of Ralph Bass, artistic director of the record company, King Records, who drove several thousand miles by car to find the group touring on the Chitlin' Circuit and quickly signed them to an exclusive contract for two hundred dollars.
James Brown and the Famous Flames went to the King Records studio in Cincinnati to record "Please, Please, Please."
The band consisted of James Brown, Bobby Byrd, Sylvester Keels, Nash Knox, Nafloyd Scott, and John Terry.

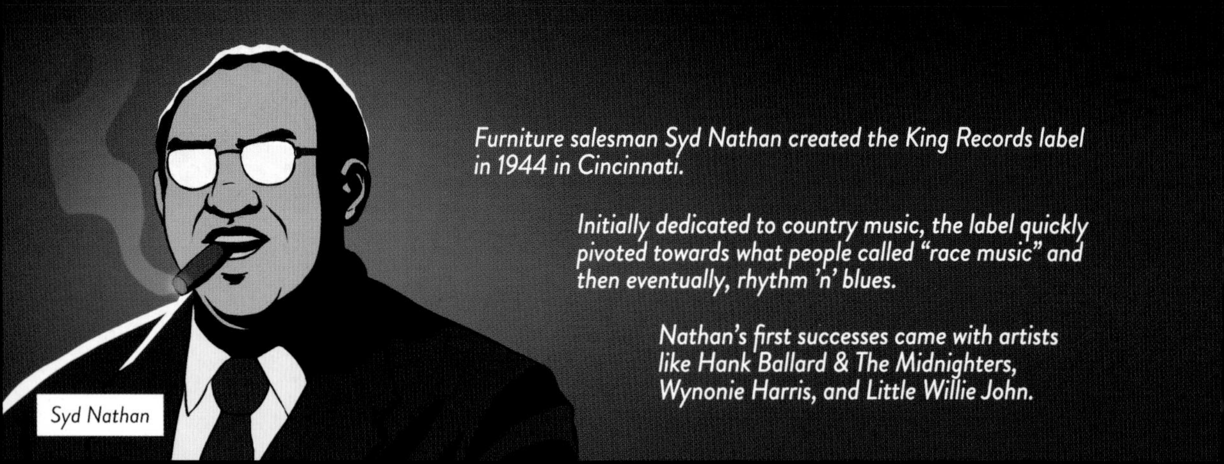
Syd Nathan
Furniture salesman Syd Nathan created the King Records label in 1944 in Cincinnati.
Initially dedicated to country music, the label quickly pivoted towards what people called "race music" and then eventually, rhythm 'n' blues.
Nathan's first successes came with artists like Hank Ballard & The Midnighters, Wynonie Harris, and Little Willie John.

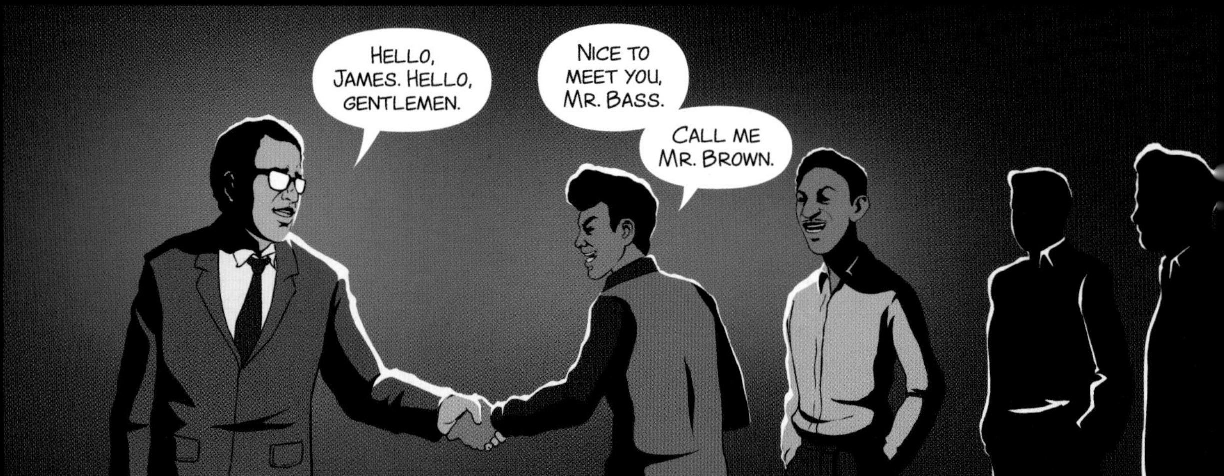
HELLO, JAMES. HELLO, GENTLEMEN.
NICE TO MEET YOU, MR. BASS.
CALL ME MR. BROWN.

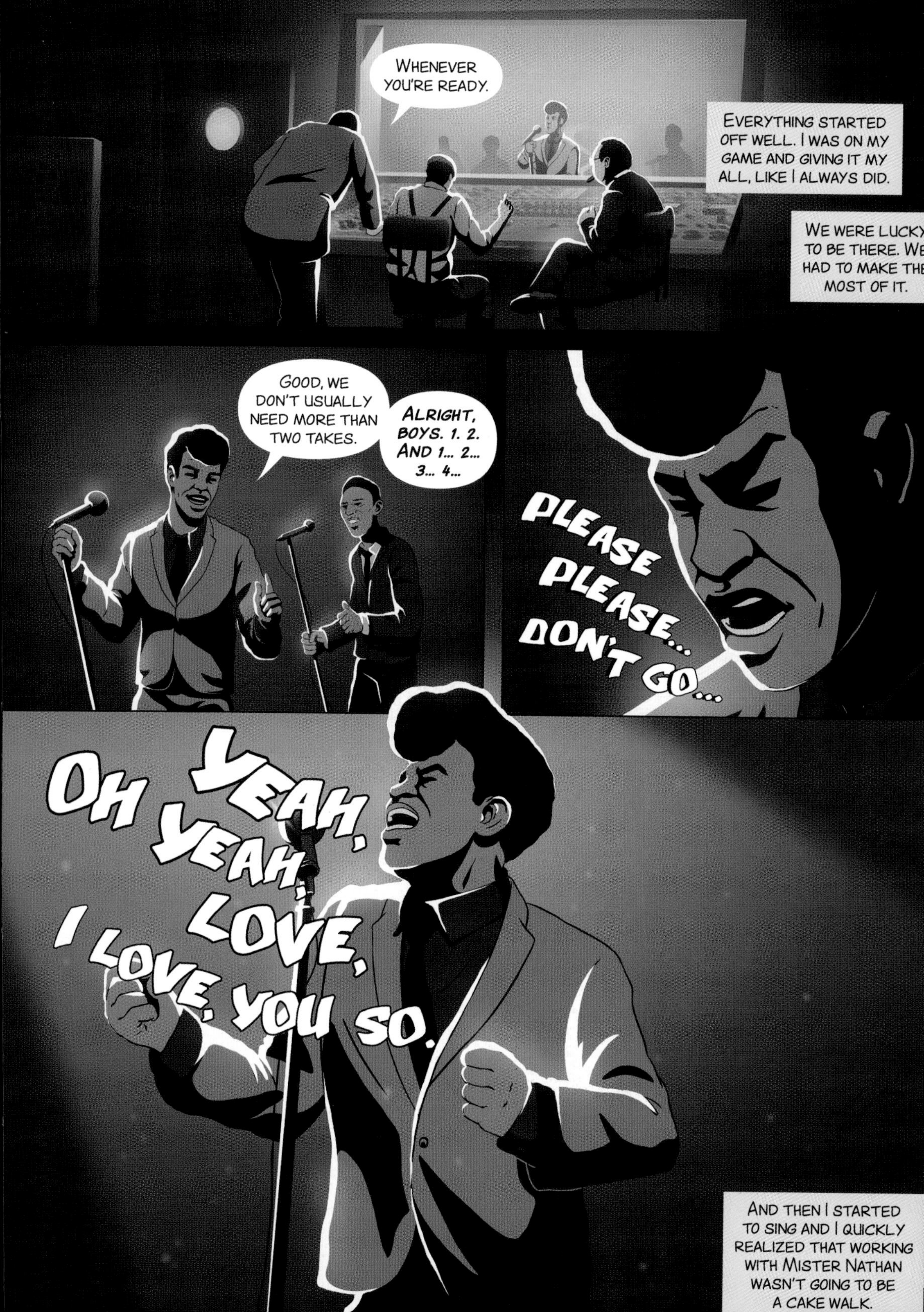
WHENEVER YOU'RE READY.
EVERYTHING STARTED OFF WELL. I WAS ON MY GAME AND GIVING IT MY ALL, LIKE I ALWAYS DID.
WE WERE LUCKY TO BE THERE. WE HAD TO MAKE THE MOST OF IT.
GOOD, WE DON'T USUALLY NEED MORE THAN TWO TAKES.
ALRIGHT, BOYS. 1. 2. AND 1... 2... 3... 4...
PLEASE PLEASE... DON'T GO...
OH YEAH, YEAH, LOVE, I LOVE, YOU SO.
AND THEN I STARTED TO SING AND I QUICKLY REALIZED THAT WORKING WITH MISTER NATHAN WASN'T GOING TO BE A CAKE WALK.

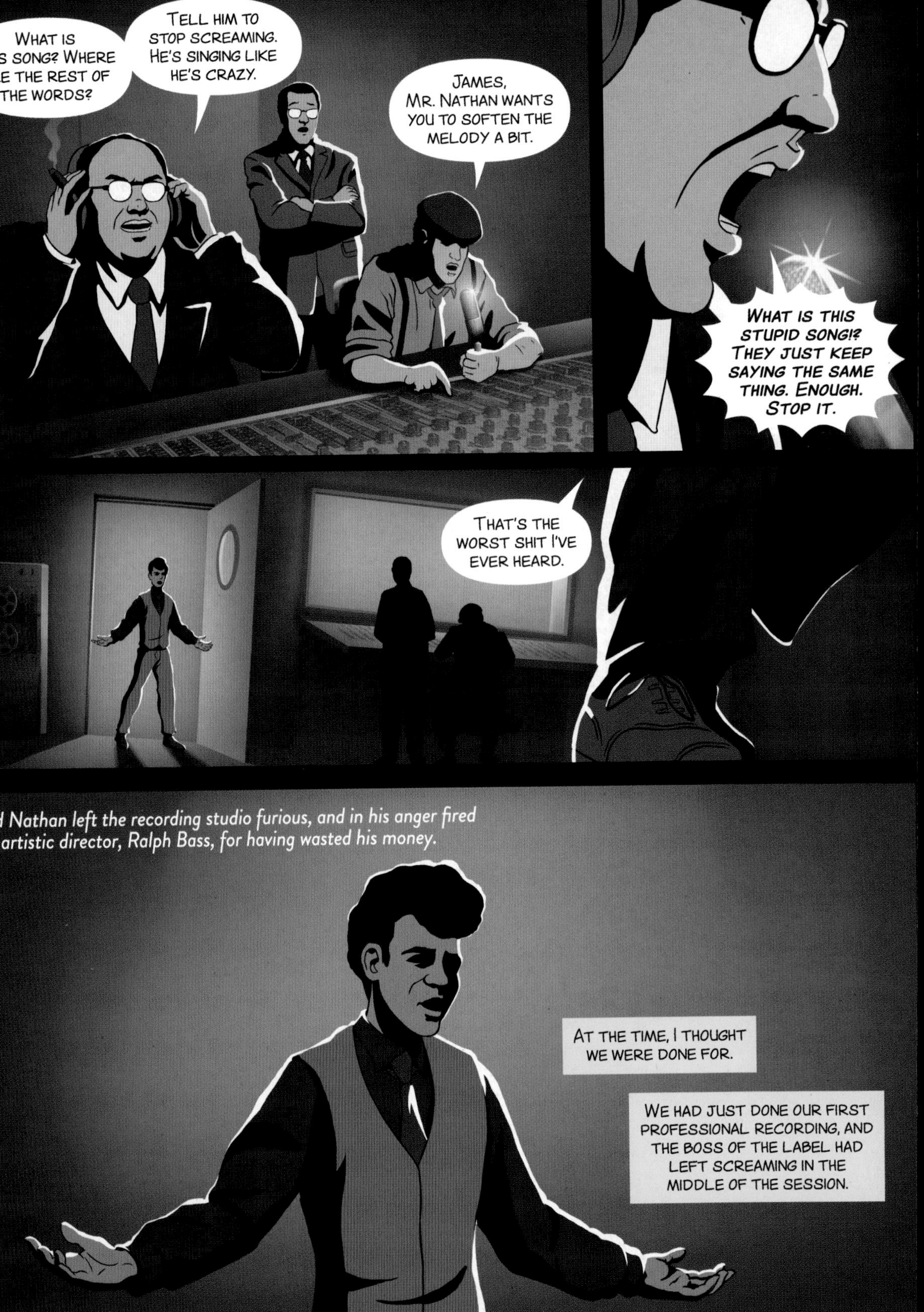
WHAT IS
S SONG? WHERE
E THE REST OF
THE WORDS?
TELL HIM TO STOP SCREAMING. HE'S SINGING LIKE HE'S CRAZY.
JAMES, MR. NATHAN WANTS YOU TO SOFTEN THE MELODY A BIT.
WHAT IS THIS STUPID SONG!? THEY JUST KEEP SAYING THE SAME THING. ENOUGH. STOP IT.
THAT'S THE WORST SHIT I'VE EVER HEARD.
d Nathan left the recording studio furious, and in his anger fired
artistic director, Ralph Bass, for having wasted his money.
AT THE TIME, I THOUGHT WE WERE DONE FOR.
WE HAD JUST DONE OUR FIRST PROFESSIONAL RECORDING, AND THE BOSS OF THE LABEL HAD LEFT SCREAMING IN THE MIDDLE OF THE SESSION.

MARCH 3, 1956
PLEASE PLEASE PLEASE
HELLO EVERYBODY, TODAY WE HAVE A WHOLE NEW SONG BY JAMES BROWN AND HIS FAMOUS FLAMES.
NOW LISTEN TO THIS. IT'S TOO COOL, BABY!
Reluctantly, Syd Nathan eventually decided to release "Please, Please, Please" as a single under Federal Records, a sub-label of King Records.
The single entered the Top 5 best selling rhythm 'n' blues records and sold more than a million copies. It played on all the radio stations in the South. Alan Freed, one of the first white disc-jockeys to support rhythm 'n' blues, would play the single on a loop.
HEY, VELMA.
HEY, BOBBY.
JAMES BROWN AND HIS FAMOUS FLAMES.
But when the group discovered that the band was listed on the sleeve as James Brown and HIS Famous Flames, their relationship deteriorated.
JAMES, WE CAN'T ACCEPT THESE CONDITIONS.
YOU HAVE TO MAKE A DECISION, BOBBY. EITHER YOU'RE WITH ME, OR YOU'RE NOT.
OF COURSE I AM, BUT WHAT ABOUT THE REST OF THE GROUP?
WHO CARES? THERE CAN ONLY BE ONE JAMES BROWN.
DON'T GET IN MY WAY.
YOU THINK I WANT TO TAKE YOUR PLACE?
Despite years of working together, James Brown and the group broke up.
DOES THE NAME BOBBY BYRD SELL RECORDS?
I'M DOING 95% OF THE WORK. THE GIRLS ARE CRAZY FOR JAMES BROWN.
THAT'S WHAT SELLS RECORDS, BOBBY. AND YOU KNOW IT AS WELL AS I DO.
THAT'S IT. I'VE HEARD ENOUGH!

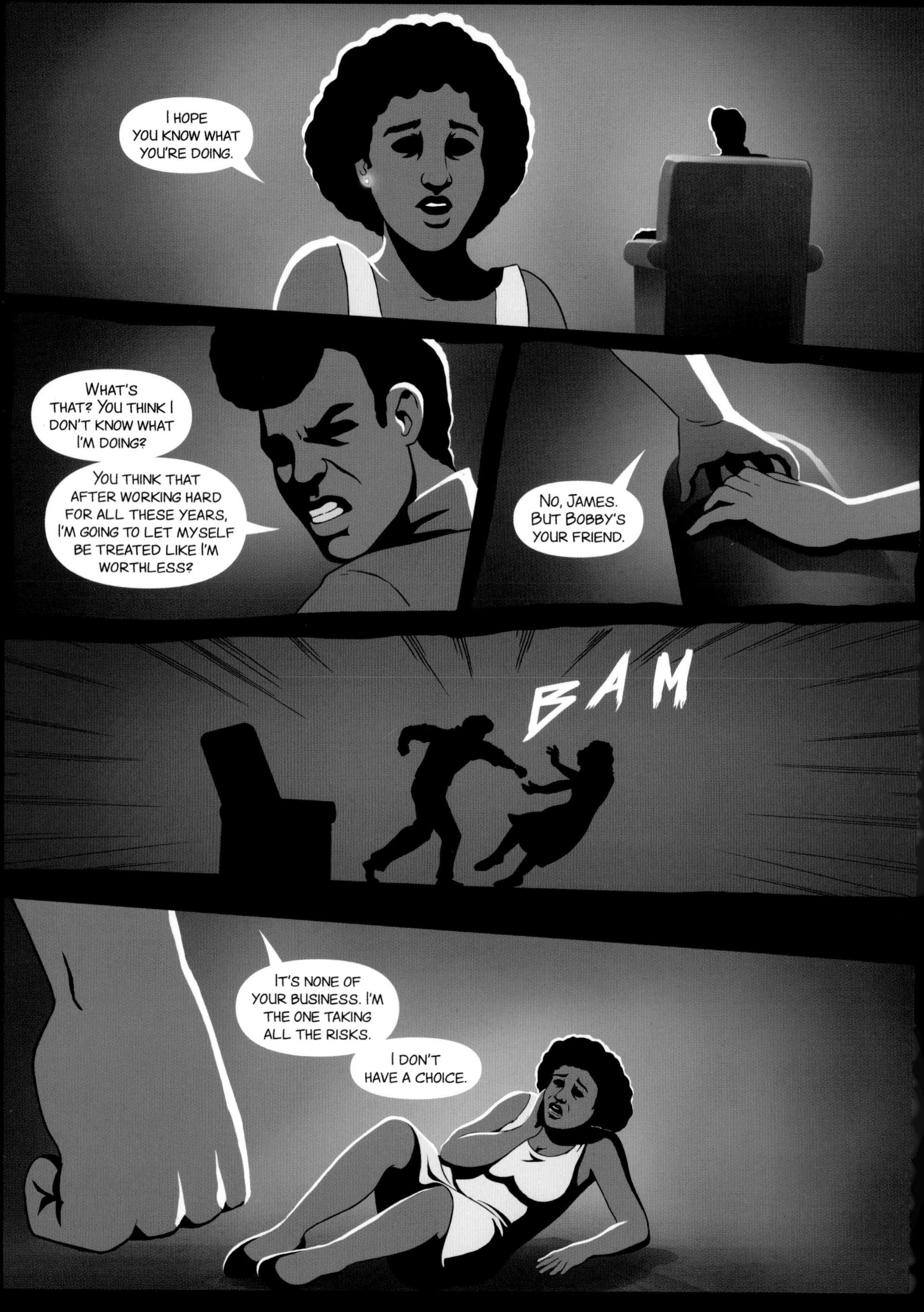
I HOPE YOU KNOW WHAT YOU'RE DOING.
WHAT'S THAT? YOU THINK I DON'T KNOW WHAT I'M DOING?
YOU THINK THAT AFTER WORKING HARD FOR ALL THESE YEARS, I'M GOING TO LET MYSELF BE TREATED LIKE I'M WORTHLESS?
NO, JAMES. BUT BOBBY'S YOUR FRIEND.
BAM
IT'S NONE OF YOUR BUSINESS. I'M THE ONE TAKING ALL THE RISKS.
I DON'T HAVE A CHOICE.

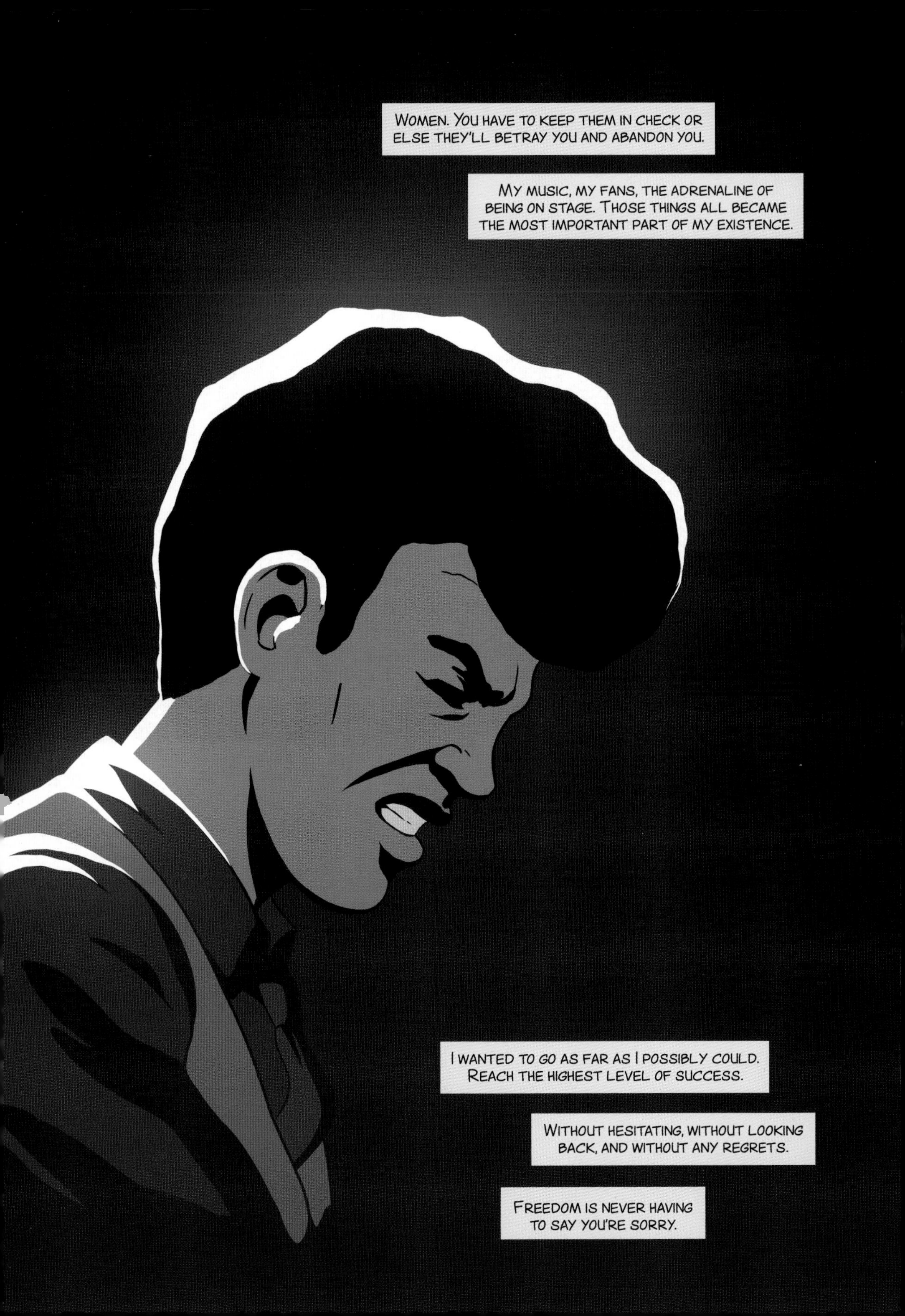
WOMEN. YOU HAVE TO KEEP THEM IN CHECK OR ELSE THEY'LL BETRAY YOU AND ABANDON YOU.
MY MUSIC, MY FANS, THE ADRENALINE OF BEING ON STAGE. THOSE THINGS ALL BECAME THE MOST IMPORTANT PART OF MY EXISTENCE.
I WANTED TO GO AS FAR AS I POSSIBLY COULD. REACH THE HIGHEST LEVEL OF SUCCESS.
WITHOUT HESITATING, WITHOUT LOOKING BACK, AND WITHOUT ANY REGRETS.
FREEDOM IS NEVER HAVING TO SAY YOU'RE SORRY.

SOUL IS
BORN FROM THE
SUFFERING OF A
COMMUNITY THAT
COULD NO LONGER
STAND THEIR
HUMILIATION.

-3-
SOUL BROTHER Nº 1

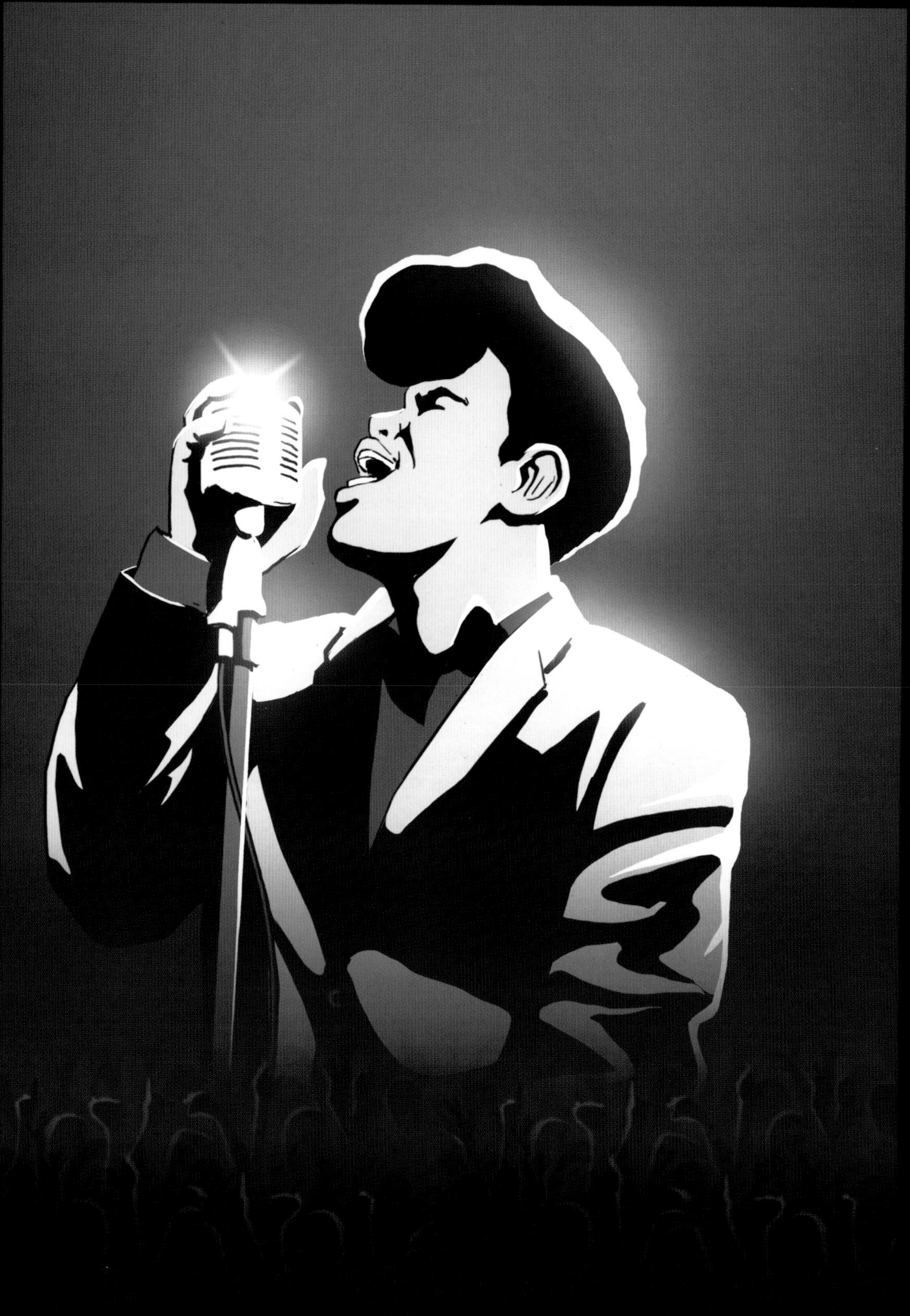

Despite the enormous success of the single "Please, Please, Please," James Brown found himself alone and without a band.

Still under contract at King Records, and under the artistic supervision of Syd Nathan, James Brown changed paths. He adopted a "crooner" style, which didn't suit him, and for almost two years, he chased one disappointment and failure after another.

James Brown and Syd Nathan's relationship worsened day by day. Nathan no longer believed in him and didn't want to spend another cent.

Nathan even billed James Brown for all his expenses: nights in hotels, recording time in the studio, soundtracks, phone calls, and meals.

STUDIO BILL

OCTOBER
1958
TRY ME

But James persevered until he found success. In 1958, with the help of Clint Brantley and Little Richard's band The Dominoes, whom he had toured with, James recorded a ballad called "Try Me."

It was James Brown's last chance. Against all expectations, the song reached number 1 on the R&B charts. At the last possible moment, this success relaunched his career.

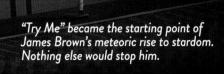

"Try Me" became the starting point of James Brown's meteoric rise to stardom. Nothing else would stop him.

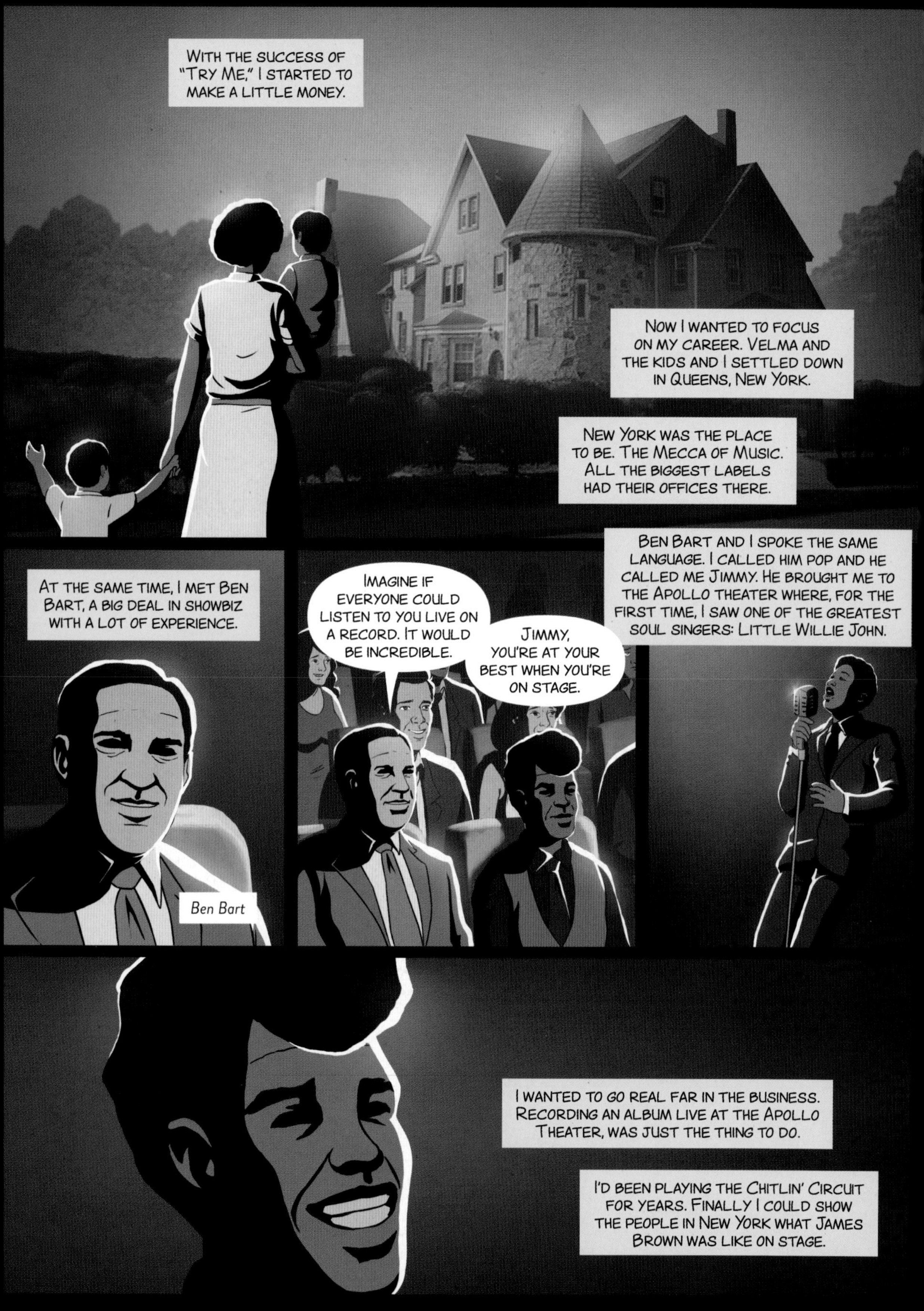

WITH THE SUCCESS OF "TRY ME," I STARTED TO MAKE A LITTLE MONEY.
NOW I WANTED TO FOCUS ON MY CAREER. VELMA AND THE KIDS AND I SETTLED DOWN IN QUEENS, NEW YORK.
NEW YORK WAS THE PLACE TO BE. THE MECCA OF MUSIC. ALL THE BIGGEST LABELS HAD THEIR OFFICES THERE.
AT THE SAME TIME, I MET BEN BART, A BIG DEAL IN SHOWBIZ WITH A LOT OF EXPERIENCE.
Ben Bart
IMAGINE IF EVERYONE COULD LISTEN TO YOU LIVE ON A RECORD. IT WOULD BE INCREDIBLE.
JIMMY, YOU'RE AT YOUR BEST WHEN YOU'RE ON STAGE.
BEN BART AND I SPOKE THE SAME LANGUAGE. I CALLED HIM POP AND HE CALLED ME JIMMY. HE BROUGHT ME TO THE APOLLO THEATER WHERE, FOR THE FIRST TIME, I SAW ONE OF THE GREATEST SOUL SINGERS: LITTLE WILLIE JOHN.
I WANTED TO GO REAL FAR IN THE BUSINESS. RECORDING AN ALBUM LIVE AT THE APOLLO THEATER, WAS JUST THE THING TO DO.
I'D BEEN PLAYING THE CHITLIN' CIRCUIT FOR YEARS. FINALLY I COULD SHOW THE PEOPLE IN NEW YORK WHAT JAMES BROWN WAS LIKE ON STAGE.

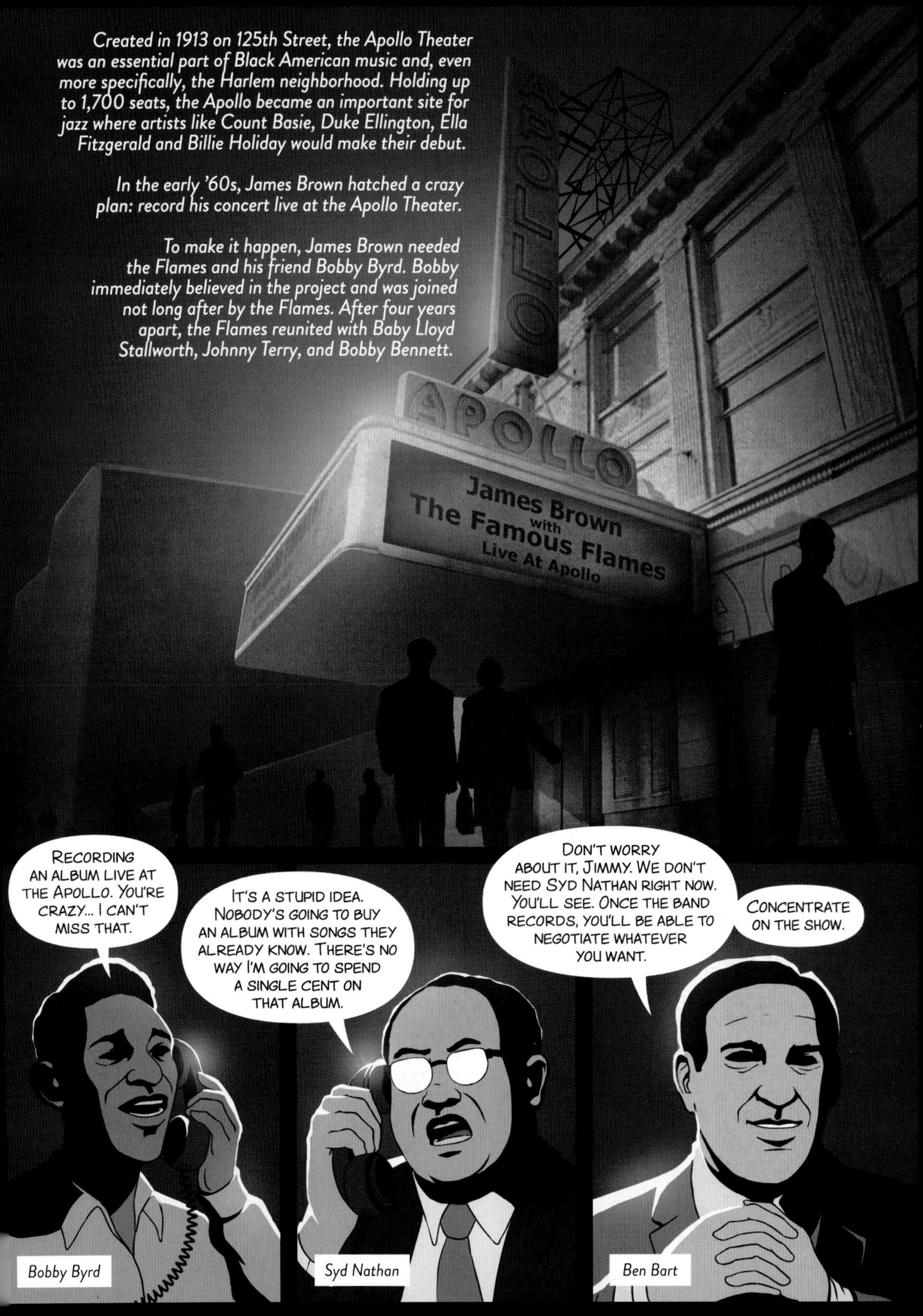
Created in 1913 on 125th Street, the Apollo Theater was an essential part of Black American music and, even more specifically, the Harlem neighborhood. Holding up to 1,700 seats, the Apollo became an important site for jazz where artists like Count Basie, Duke Ellington, Ella Fitzgerald and Billie Holiday would make their debut.
In the early '60s, James Brown hatched a crazy plan: record his concert live at the Apollo Theater.
To make it happen, James Brown needed the Flames and his friend Bobby Byrd. Bobby immediately believed in the project and was joined not long after by the Flames. After four years apart, the Flames reunited with Baby Lloyd Stallworth, Johnny Terry, and Bobby Bennett.
APOLLO
James Brown with The Famous Flames Live At Apollo
RECORDING AN ALBUM LIVE AT THE APOLLO. YOU'RE CRAZY... I CAN'T MISS THAT.
Bobby Byrd
IT'S A STUPID IDEA. NOBODY'S GOING TO BUY AN ALBUM WITH SONGS THEY ALREADY KNOW. THERE'S NO WAY I'M GOING TO SPEND A SINGLE CENT ON THAT ALBUM.
Syd Nathan
DON'T WORRY ABOUT IT, JIMMY. WE DON'T NEED SYD NATHAN RIGHT NOW. YOU'LL SEE. ONCE THE BAND RECORDS, YOU'LL BE ABLE TO NEGOTIATE WHATEVER YOU WANT.
CONCENTRATE ON THE SHOW.
Ben Bart

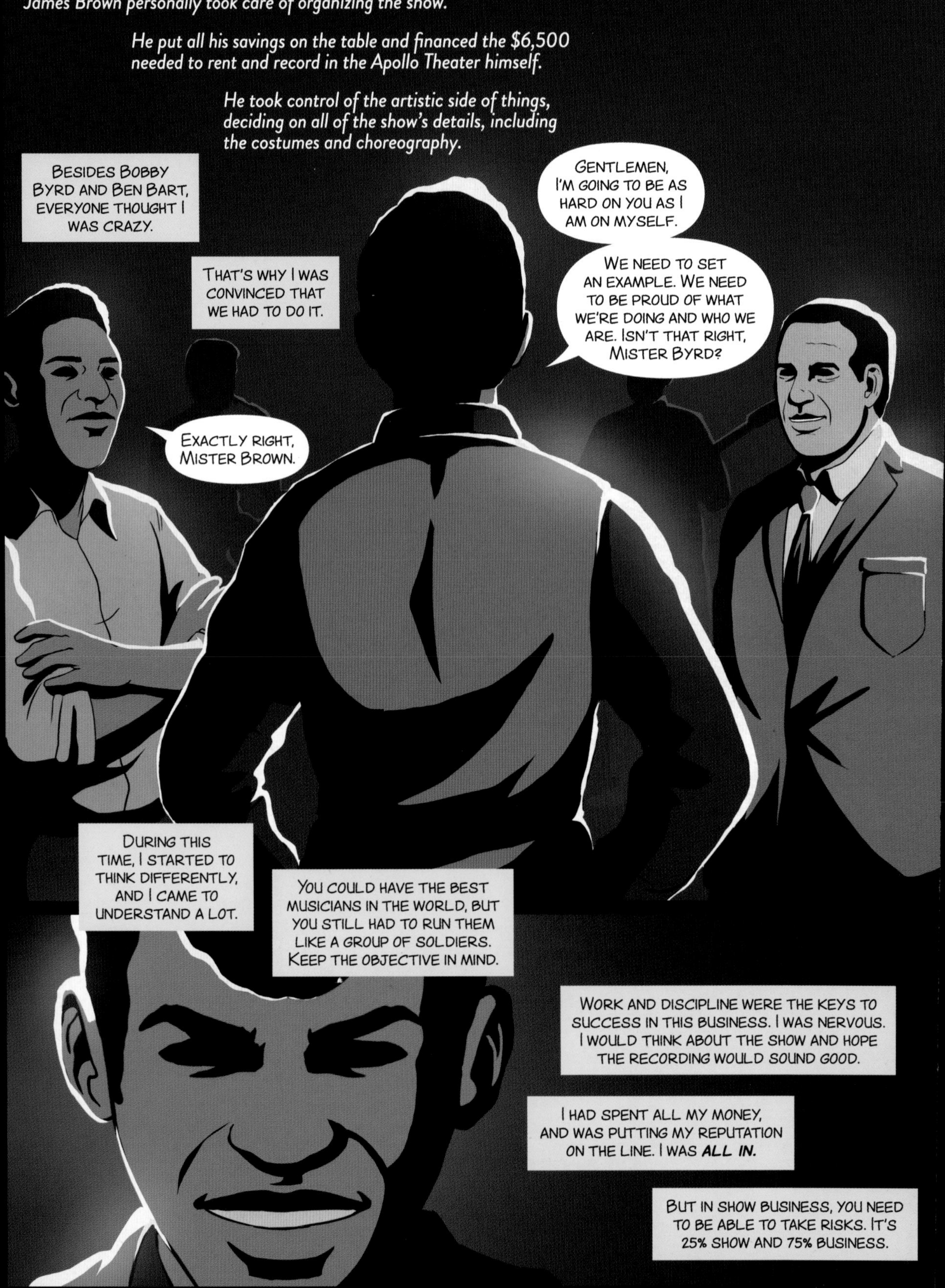
James Brown personally took care of organizing the show.
He put all his savings on the table and financed the $6,500 needed to rent and record in the Apollo Theater himself.
He took control of the artistic side of things, deciding on all of the show's details, including the costumes and choreography.
BESIDES BOBBY BYRD AND BEN BART, EVERYONE THOUGHT I WAS CRAZY.
THAT'S WHY I WAS CONVINCED THAT WE HAD TO DO IT.
GENTLEMEN, I'M GOING TO BE AS HARD ON YOU AS I AM ON MYSELF.
WE NEED TO SET AN EXAMPLE. WE NEED TO BE PROUD OF WHAT WE'RE DOING AND WHO WE ARE. ISN'T THAT RIGHT, MISTER BYRD?
EXACTLY RIGHT, MISTER BROWN.
DURING THIS TIME, I STARTED TO THINK DIFFERENTLY, AND I CAME TO UNDERSTAND A LOT.
YOU COULD HAVE THE BEST MUSICIANS IN THE WORLD, BUT YOU STILL HAD TO RUN THEM LIKE A GROUP OF SOLDIERS. KEEP THE OBJECTIVE IN MIND.
WORK AND DISCIPLINE WERE THE KEYS TO SUCCESS IN THIS BUSINESS. I WAS NERVOUS. I WOULD THINK ABOUT THE SHOW AND HOPE THE RECORDING WOULD SOUND GOOD.
I HAD SPENT ALL MY MONEY, AND WAS PUTTING MY REPUTATION ON THE LINE. I WAS ***ALL IN.***
BUT IN SHOW BUSINESS, YOU NEED TO BE ABLE TO TAKE RISKS. IT'S 25% SHOW AND 75% BUSINESS.

10.24 1962 APOLLO THEATER

It was D-Day.

In the middle of the Cuban Missile Crisis, James Brown recorded his concert at the Apollo Theater. He would give four performances to an audience on the edge of their seats. The legend of the "Hardest Working Man in Show Business" began here.

James Brown came onto stage like a wild beast that you could no longer restrain. And with a torn voice he sang "Please, Please, Please." The audience loved it.

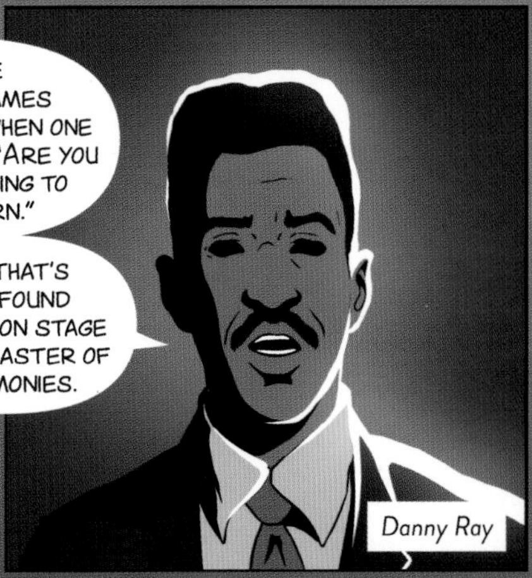
I WAS THE VALET FOR JAMES BROWN'S ROOM WHEN ONE DAY HE TOLD ME: "ARE YOU READY? IT'S GOING TO BE YOUR TURN."
AND THAT'S HOW I FOUND MYSELF ON STAGE AS THE MASTER OF CEREMONIES.
Danny Ray

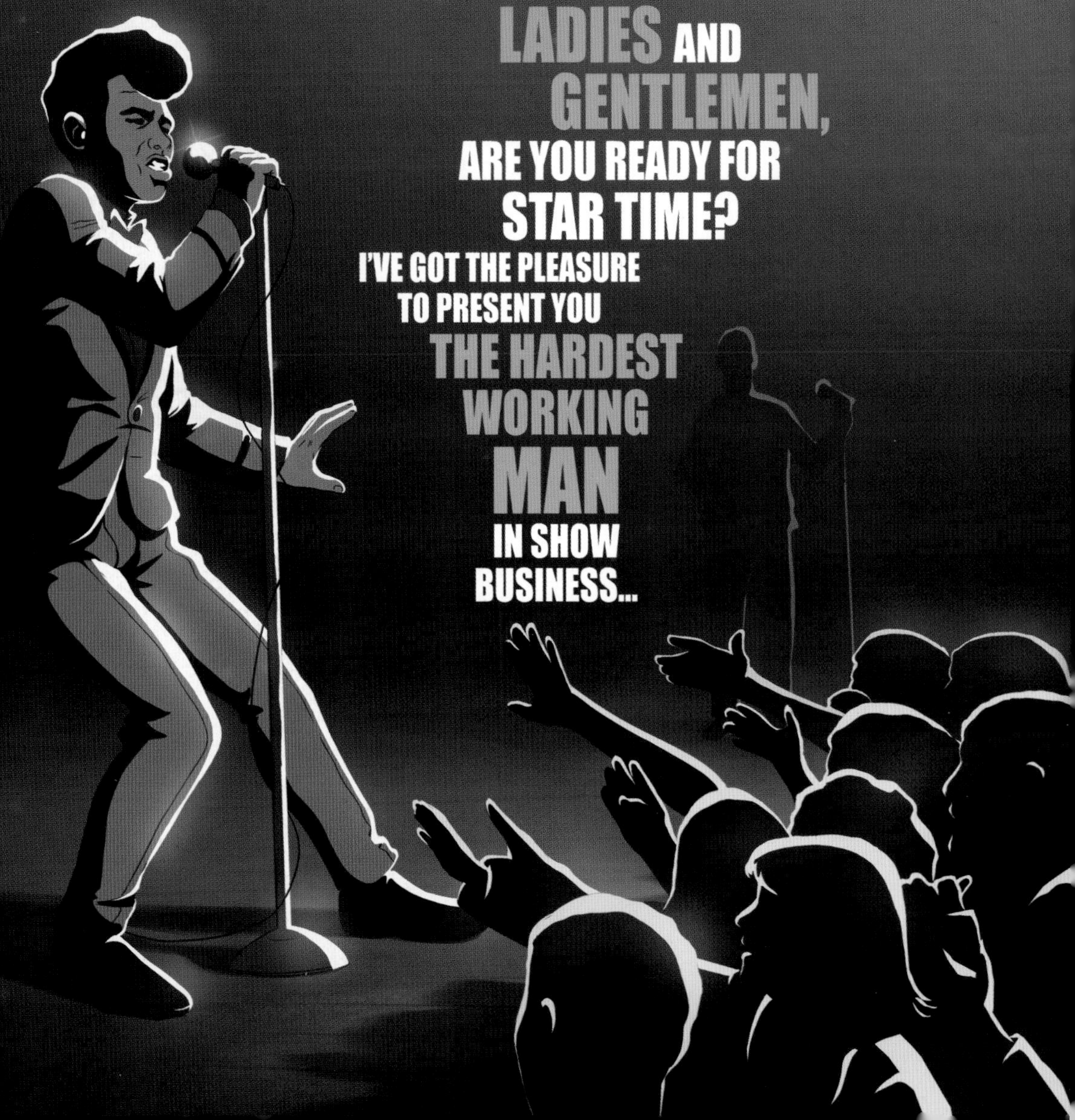
LADIES AND GENTLEMEN,
ARE YOU READY FOR STAR TIME?
I'VE GOT THE PLEASURE TO PRESENT YOU
THE HARDEST WORKING MAN
IN SHOW BUSINESS...

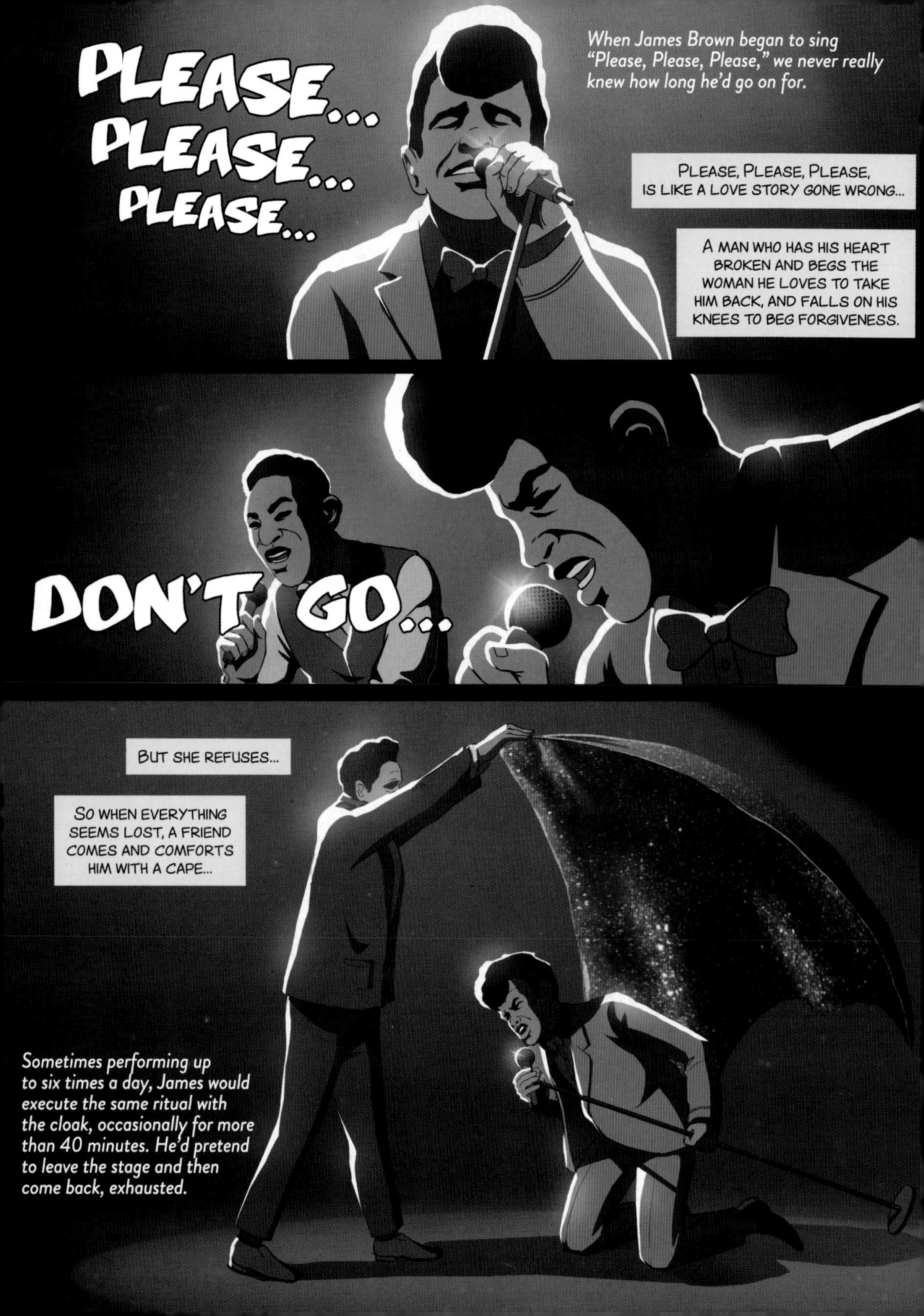

PLEASE... PLEASE... PLEASE...
When James Brown began to sing "Please, Please, Please," we never really knew how long he'd go on for.
PLEASE, PLEASE, PLEASE, IS LIKE A LOVE STORY GONE WRONG...
A MAN WHO HAS HIS HEART BROKEN AND BEGS THE WOMAN HE LOVES TO TAKE HIM BACK, AND FALLS ON HIS KNEES TO BEG FORGIVENESS.
DON'T GO...
BUT SHE REFUSES...
SO WHEN EVERYTHING SEEMS LOST, A FRIEND COMES AND COMFORTS HIM WITH A CAPE...
Sometimes performing up to six times a day, James would execute the same ritual with the cloak, occasionally for more than 40 minutes. He'd pretend to leave the stage and then come back, exhausted.

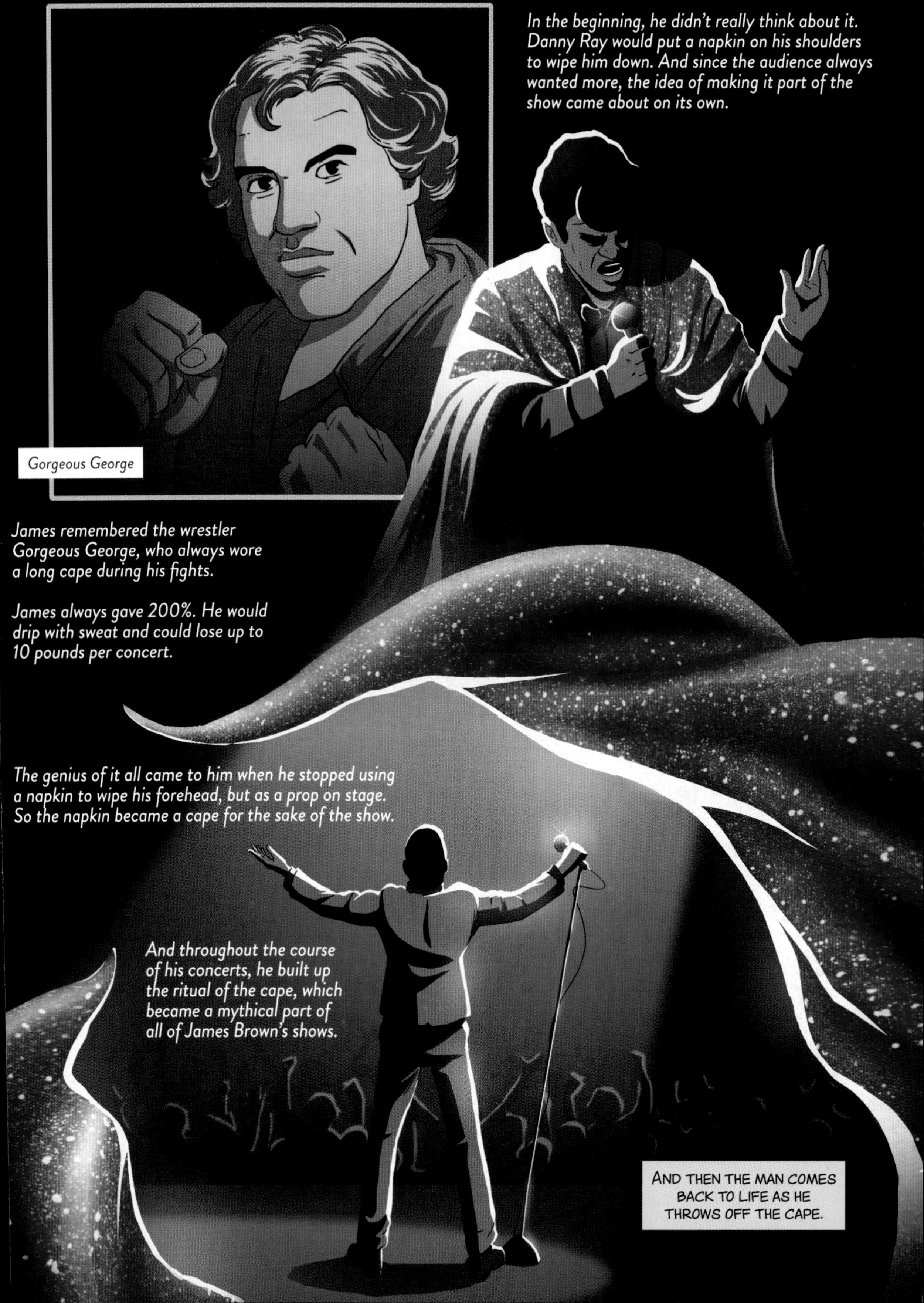
Gorgeous George
In the beginning, he didn't really think about it. Danny Ray would put a napkin on his shoulders to wipe him down. And since the audience always wanted more, the idea of making it part of the show came about on its own.
James remembered the wrestler Gorgeous George, who always wore a long cape during his fights.
James always gave 200%. He would drip with sweat and could lose up to 10 pounds per concert.
The genius of it all came to him when he stopped using a napkin to wipe his forehead, but as a prop on stage. So the napkin became a cape for the sake of the show.
And throughout the course of his concerts, he built up the ritual of the cape, which became a mythical part of all of James Brown's shows.
AND THEN THE MAN COMES BACK TO LIFE AS HE THROWS OFF THE CAPE.

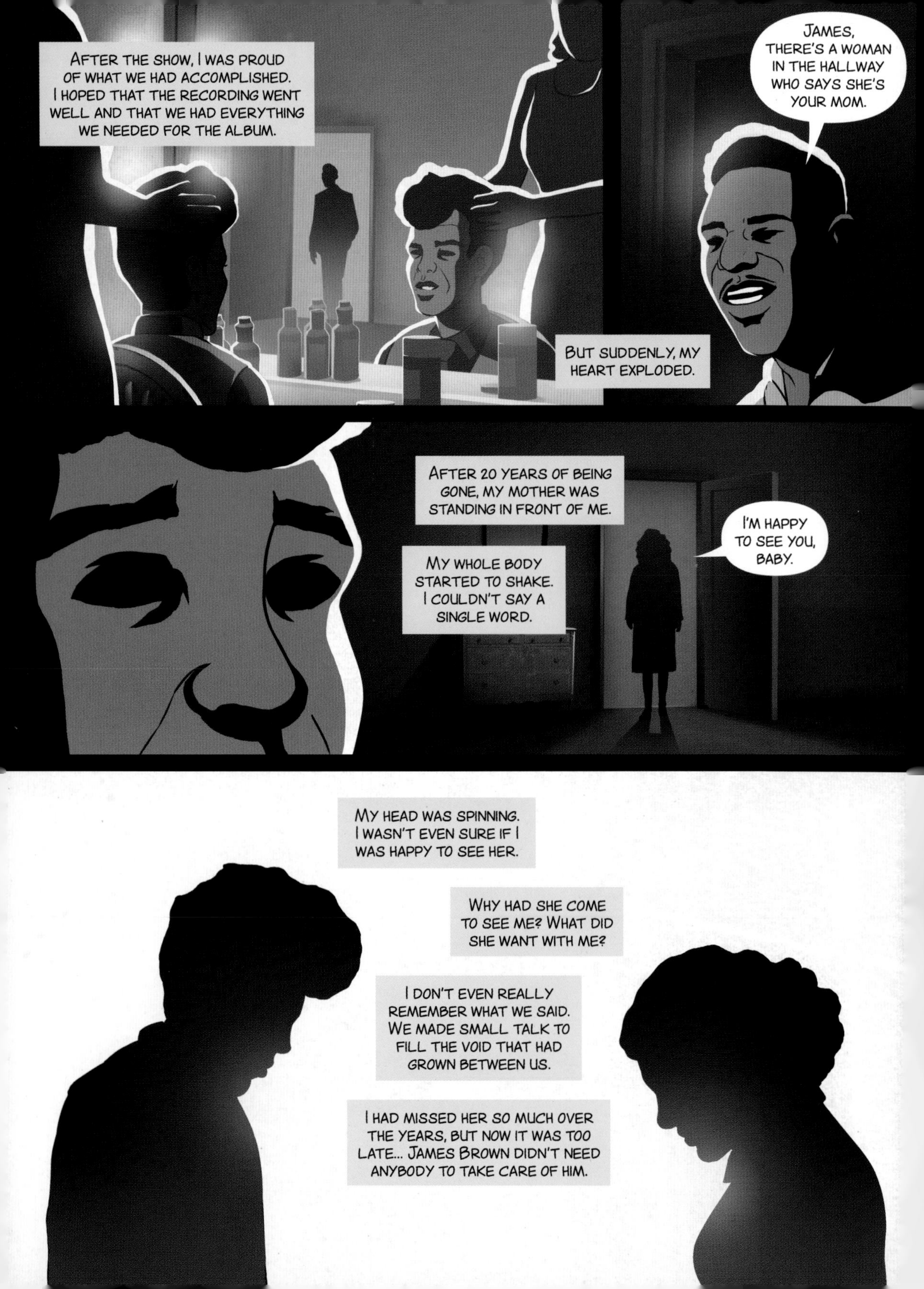

After the show, I was proud of what we had accomplished. I hoped that the recording went well and that we had everything we needed for the album.
But suddenly, my heart exploded.
James, there's a woman in the hallway who says she's your mom.
After 20 years of being gone, my mother was standing in front of me.
My whole body started to shake. I couldn't say a single word.
I'm happy to see you, baby.
My head was spinning. I wasn't even sure if I was happy to see her.
Why had she come to see me? What did she want with me?
I don't even really remember what we said. We made small talk to fill the void that had grown between us.
I had missed her so much over the years, but now it was too late... James Brown didn't need anybody to take care of him.

JANUARY 1963

The album James Brown: Live at the Apollo Volume 1 climbed to the top of the charts and sent James Brown into another dimension. White people came running to the Apollo Theater to see in real life what they heard on the record.

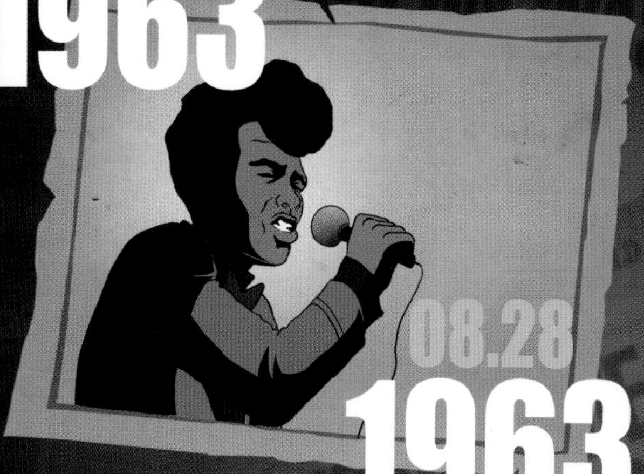

Produced by Brown and distributed by King Records, the album sold more than a million records and stayed a hit for more than 70 weeks. Today, it's considered one of the greatest live albums of all time.

08.28 1963

In front of a crowd of 250,000 people, Martin Luther King, Jr. gave his famous "I Have a Dream" speech, where he hoped for a united America free of segregation.

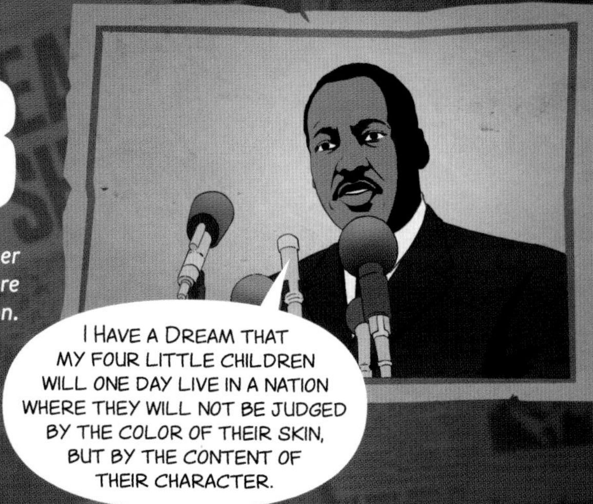
I HAVE A DREAM THAT MY FOUR LITTLE CHILDREN WILL ONE DAY LIVE IN A NATION WHERE THEY WILL NOT BE JUDGED BY THE COLOR OF THEIR SKIN, BUT BY THE CONTENT OF THEIR CHARACTER.

09.15 1963

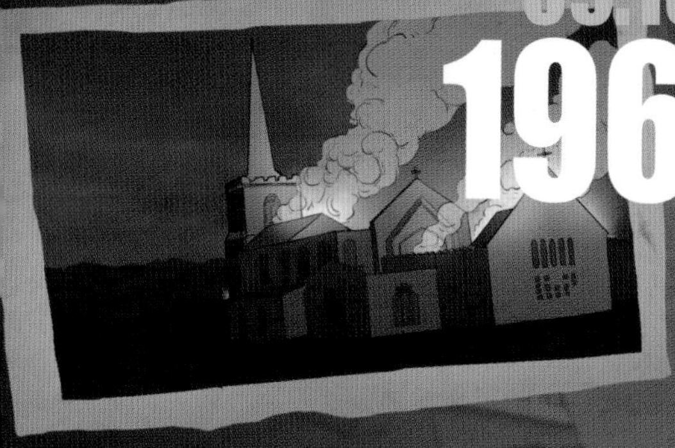

Two weeks later, after the March on Washington, the Baptist Church in Birmingham was attacked with a bomb that killed four young girls and injured twenty-two others.

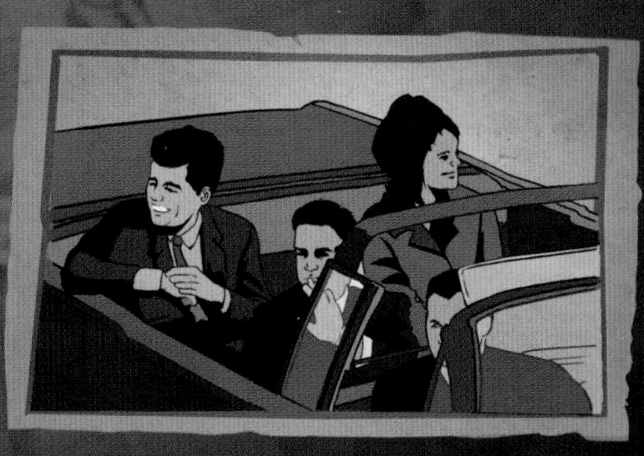

11.22 1963

John Fitzgerald Kennedy, the pioneer president of Civil Rights reform for black Americans, was assassinated in Dallas. A few months earlier, during a televised event, he had given his famous speech proposing the Civil Rights Act.

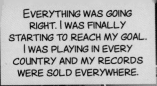

EVERYTHING WAS GOING RIGHT. I WAS FINALLY STARTING TO REACH MY GOAL. I WAS PLAYING IN EVERY COUNTRY AND MY RECORDS WERE SOLD EVERYWHERE.

James Brown was at the peak. He was everywhere and, together with Ben Bart, created "Fair Deal Productions" and started his own record label "Try Me Records."

In litigation with King Records, James Brown could only record instrumental albums.

So he decided to produce the artists of his Revue, like his friend Bobby Byrd, and the singers Yvonne Fair, Anna King, Tammi Terrel, and Vicki Anderson, who started solo careers.

Some had more luck than others in escaping their mentor's shadow.

UNFORTUNATELY, I COULDN'T AVOID CLASHING WITH SYD NATHAN, WHO COULDN'T ACCEPT THAT I WAS GOING INDEPENDENT, AND DECIDED TO FILE A COMPLAINT AGAINST ME.

Bea Ford

Joe Tex's wife, Bea Ford would have a fling with James Brown and end up pregnant. She still found time to record a duo with James, "You've Got the Power," which found little success.

Yvonne Fair

She became part of the Revue in 1962 when she recorded "I Found You" which became "I Got You (I Feel Good)" a few years later. She also released "You Can Make It If You Try," and retired pregnant by James Brown. In 1975, she returned to the stage with an album, "The Bitch is Black."

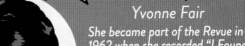

Tammi Terrell (or Tammi Montgomery)

After having a tumultuous affair with James, she left the Revue and signed with Motown, where she found enormous success with Marvin Gaye and "Ain't No Mountain High Enough." Unfortunately she died shortly thereafter, at 25, from a brain tumor.

Anna King

Anna King started singing in church at the age of 6. In the early '60s, she became part of the James Brown Revue. Replacing Tammi Terrell, she became JB's protégé. In 1964 she recorded a duo with Bobby Byrd "Baby, Baby, Baby" and Back to Soul, an album produced by James Brown on Smash. After leaving the Revue, she accompanied Duke Ellington and retired to become a pastor.

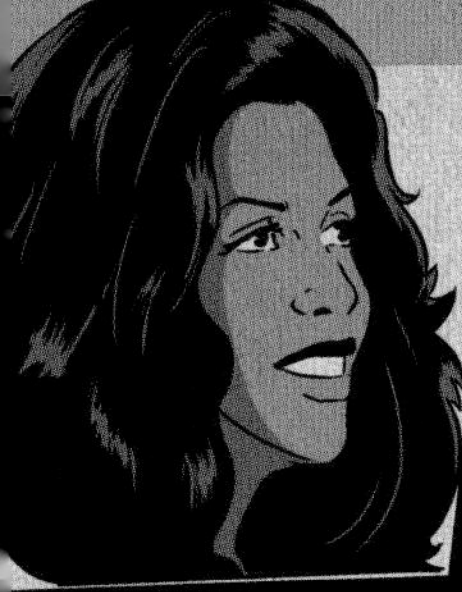

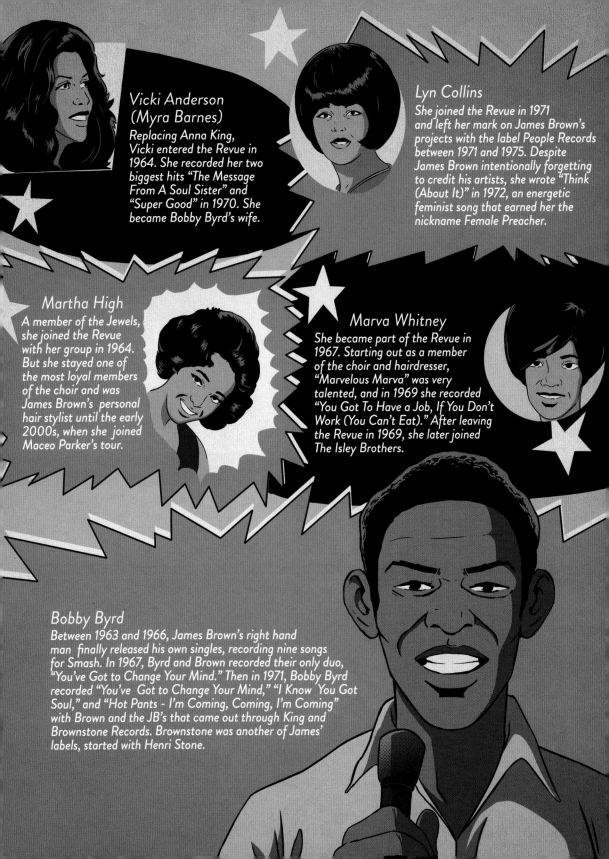

Vicki Anderson (Myra Barnes)

Replacing Anna King, Vicki entered the Revue in 1964. She recorded her two biggest hits "The Message From A Soul Sister" and "Super Good" in 1970. She became Bobby Byrd's wife.

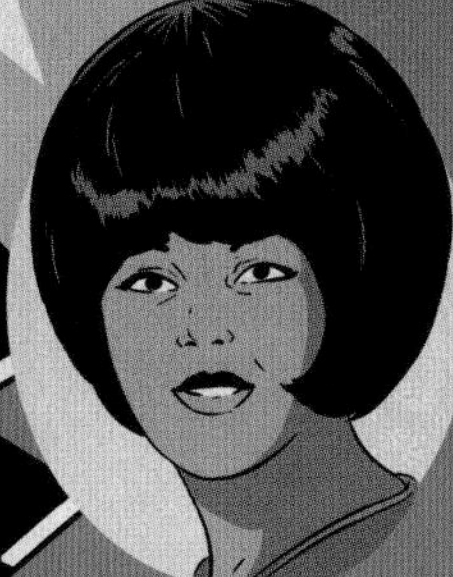

Lyn Collins

She joined the Revue in 1971 and left her mark on James Brown's projects with the label People Records between 1971 and 1975. Despite James Brown intentionally forgetting to credit his artists, she wrote "Think (About It)" in 1972, an energetic feminist song that earned her the nickname Female Preacher.

Martha High

A member of the Jewels, she joined the Revue with her group in 1964. But she stayed one of the most loyal members of the choir and was James Brown's personal hair stylist until the early 2000s, when she joined Maceo Parker's tour.

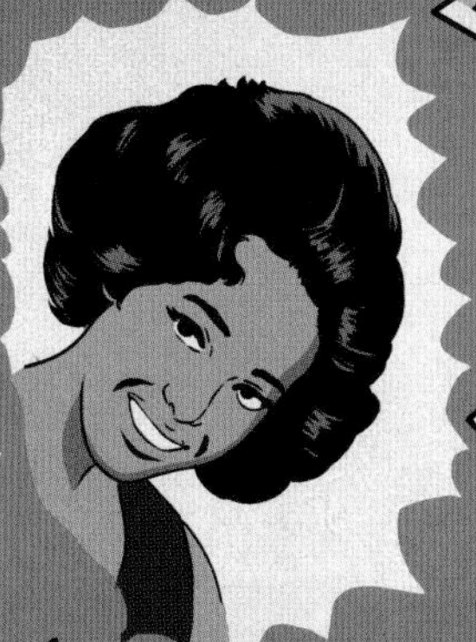

Marva Whitney

She became part of the Revue in 1967. Starting out as a member of the choir and hairdresser, "Marvelous Marva" was very talented, and in 1969 she recorded "You Got To Have a Job, If You Don't Work (You Can't Eat)." After leaving the Revue in 1969, she later joined The Isley Brothers.

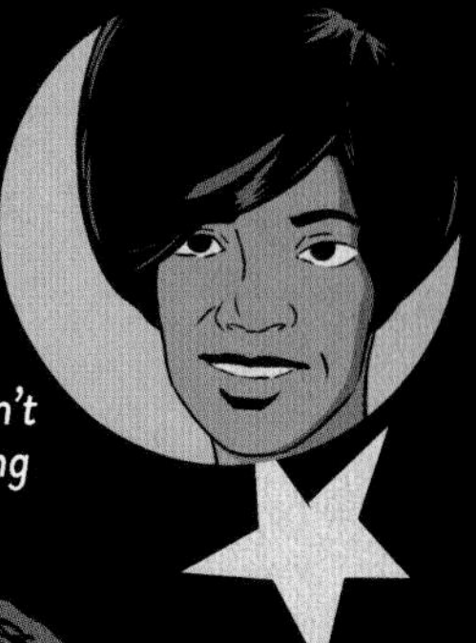

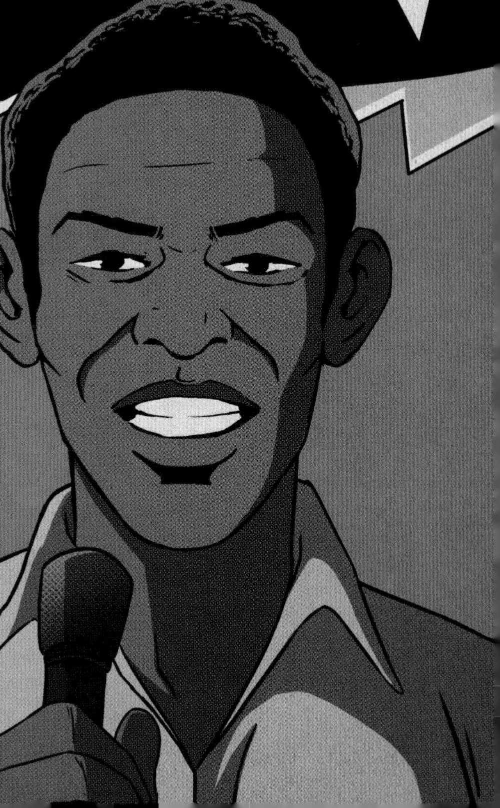

Bobby Byrd

Between 1963 and 1966, James Brown's right hand man finally released his own singles, recording nine songs for Smash. In 1967, Byrd and Brown recorded their only duo, "You've Got to Change Your Mind." Then in 1971, Bobby Byrd recorded "You've Got to Change Your Mind," "I Know You Got Soul," and "Hot Pants - I'm Coming, Coming, I'm Coming" with Brown and the JB's that came out through King and Brownstone Records. Brownstone was another of James' labels, started with Henri Stone.

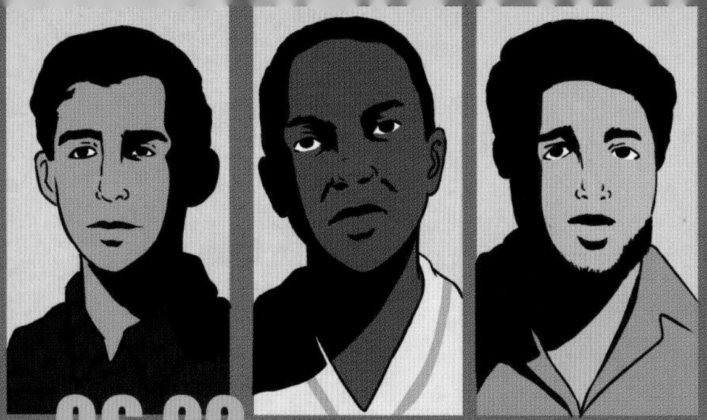

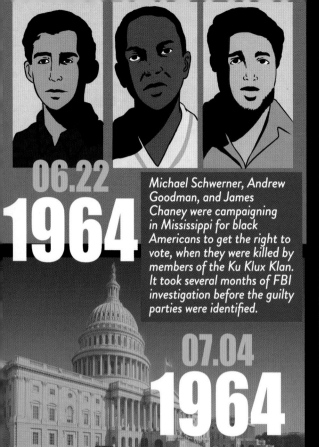

06.22 1964

Michael Schwerner, Andrew Goodman, and James Chaney were campaigning in Mississippi for black Americans to get the right to vote, when they were killed by members of the Ku Klux Klan. It took several months of FBI investigation before the guilty parties were identified.

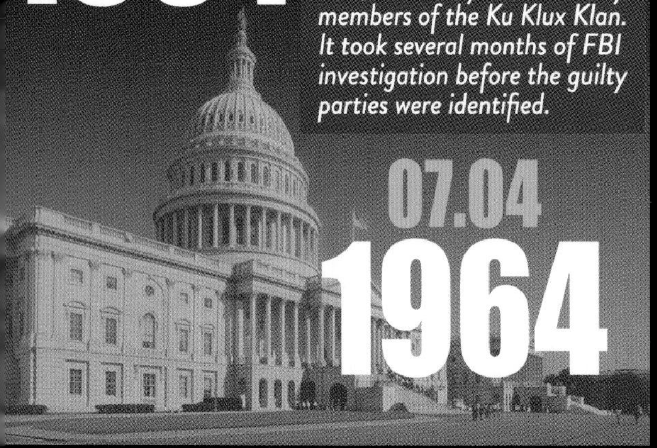

07.04 1964

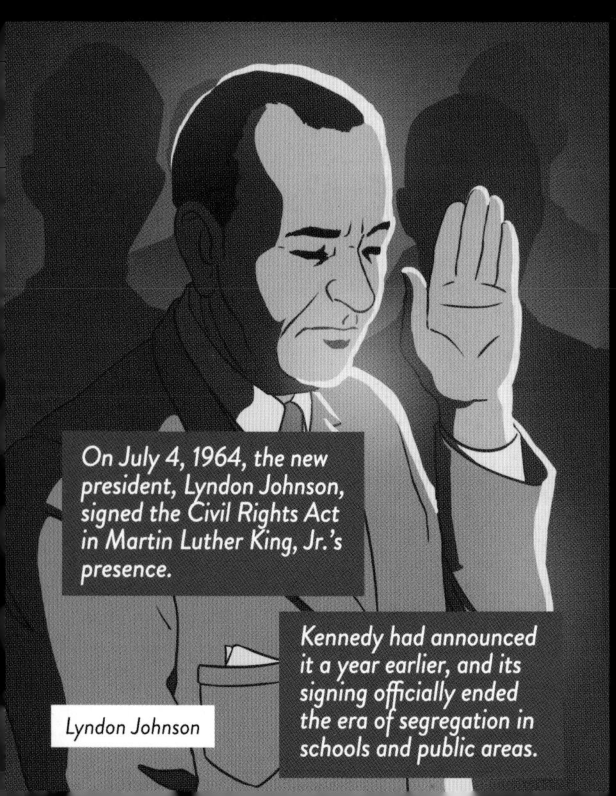

On July 4, 1964, the new president, Lyndon Johnson, signed the Civil Rights Act in Martin Luther King, Jr.'s presence.

Kennedy had announced it a year earlier, and its signing officially ended the era of segregation in schools and public areas.

Lyndon Johnson

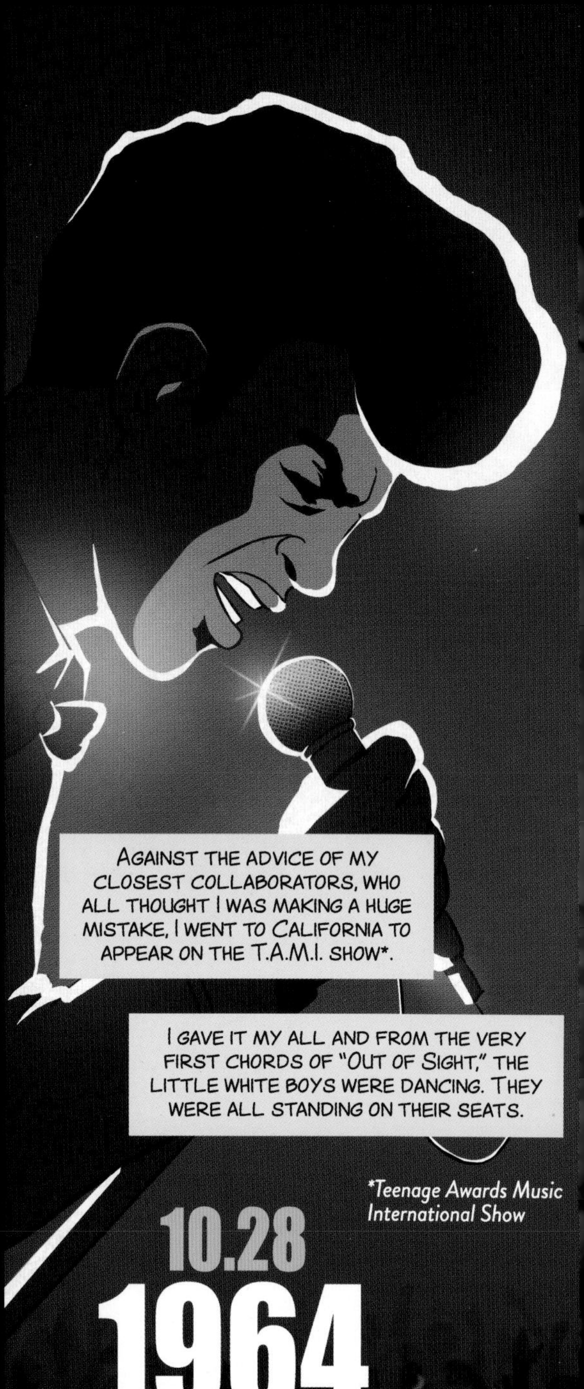

AGAINST THE ADVICE OF MY CLOSEST COLLABORATORS, WHO ALL THOUGHT I WAS MAKING A HUGE MISTAKE, I WENT TO CALIFORNIA TO APPEAR ON THE T.A.M.I. SHOW*.
I GAVE IT MY ALL AND FROM THE VERY FIRST CHORDS OF "OUT OF SIGHT," THE LITTLE WHITE BOYS WERE DANCING. THEY WERE ALL STANDING ON THEIR SEATS.

*Teenage Awards Music International Show

10.28 1964

Recorded and filmed in California during the fall of 1964 the performance James Brown gave at the T.A.M.I. Show cemented him as one of the biggest stars.

Accompanied by the Famous Flames' new lineup, James sang "Out of Sight," "Prisoner of Love," "Please, Please, Please," and "Night Train" in front of a young, excited audience, who were finally discovering what everyone had been talking about for years.

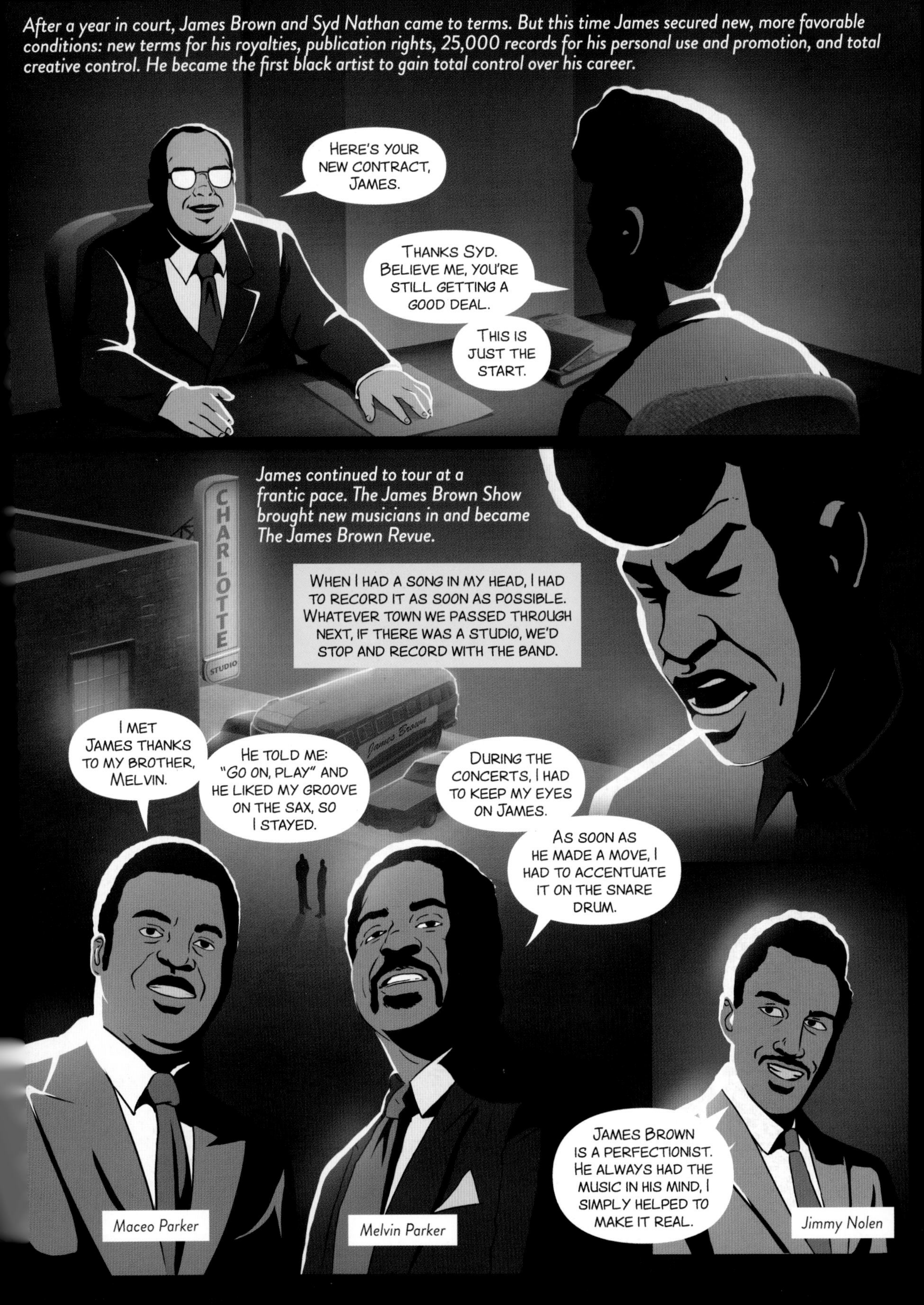
After a year in court, James Brown and Syd Nathan came to terms. But this time James secured new, more favorable conditions: new terms for his royalties, publication rights, 25,000 records for his personal use and promotion, and total creative control. He became the first black artist to gain total control over his career.
HERE'S YOUR NEW CONTRACT, JAMES.
THANKS SYD. BELIEVE ME, YOU'RE STILL GETTING A GOOD DEAL.
THIS IS JUST THE START.
James continued to tour at a frantic pace. The James Brown Show brought new musicians in and became The James Brown Revue.
CHARLOTTE
STUDIO
WHEN I HAD A SONG IN MY HEAD, I HAD TO RECORD IT AS SOON AS POSSIBLE. WHATEVER TOWN WE PASSED THROUGH NEXT, IF THERE WAS A STUDIO, WE'D STOP AND RECORD WITH THE BAND.
I MET JAMES THANKS TO MY BROTHER, MELVIN.
HE TOLD ME: "GO ON, PLAY" AND HE LIKED MY GROOVE ON THE SAX, SO I STAYED.
DURING THE CONCERTS, I HAD TO KEEP MY EYES ON JAMES.
AS SOON AS HE MADE A MOVE, I HAD TO ACCENTUATE IT ON THE SNARE DRUM.
JAMES BROWN IS A PERFECTIONIST. HE ALWAYS HAD THE MUSIC IN HIS MIND, I SIMPLY HELPED TO MAKE IT REAL.
Maceo Parker
Melvin Parker
Jimmy Nolen

In February 1965, James Brown was in the studio with his musicians. In barely an hour, he recorded "Papa's Got A Brand New Bag," one of funk's first classics.

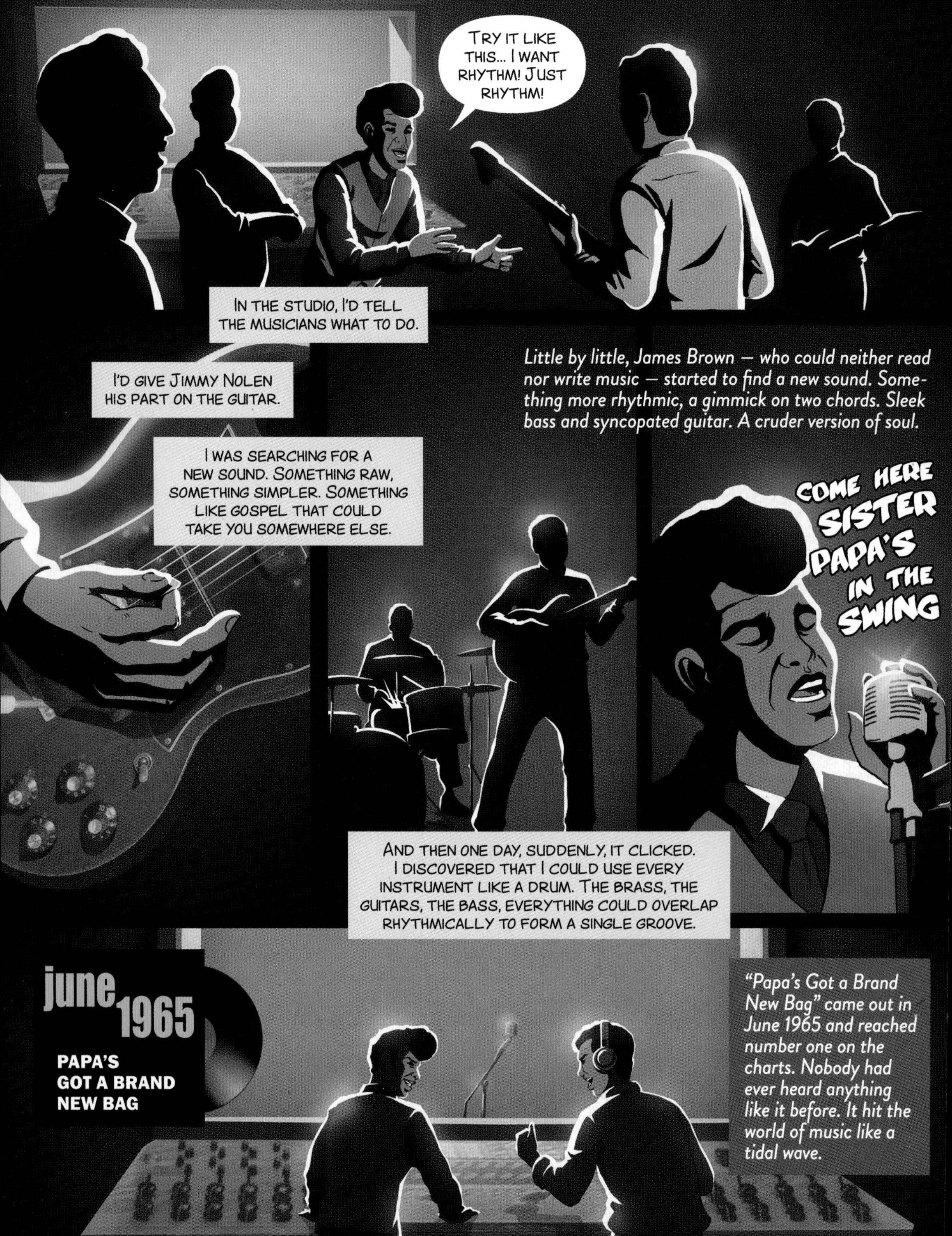
TRY IT LIKE THIS... I WANT RHYTHM! JUST RHYTHM!
IN THE STUDIO, I'D TELL THE MUSICIANS WHAT TO DO.
I'D GIVE JIMMY NOLEN HIS PART ON THE GUITAR.
I WAS SEARCHING FOR A NEW SOUND. SOMETHING RAW, SOMETHING SIMPLER. SOMETHING LIKE GOSPEL THAT COULD TAKE YOU SOMEWHERE ELSE.
Little by little, James Brown — who could neither read nor write music — started to find a new sound. Something more rhythmic, a gimmick on two chords. Sleek bass and syncopated guitar. A cruder version of soul.
COME HERE SISTER PAPA'S IN THE SWING
AND THEN ONE DAY, SUDDENLY, IT CLICKED. I DISCOVERED THAT I COULD USE EVERY INSTRUMENT LIKE A DRUM. THE BRASS, THE GUITARS, THE BASS, EVERYTHING COULD OVERLAP RHYTHMICALLY TO FORM A SINGLE GROOVE.
june 1965
PAPA'S GOT A BRAND NEW BAG
"Papa's Got a Brand New Bag" came out in June 1965 and reached number one on the charts. Nobody had ever heard anything like it before. It hit the world of music like a tidal wave.

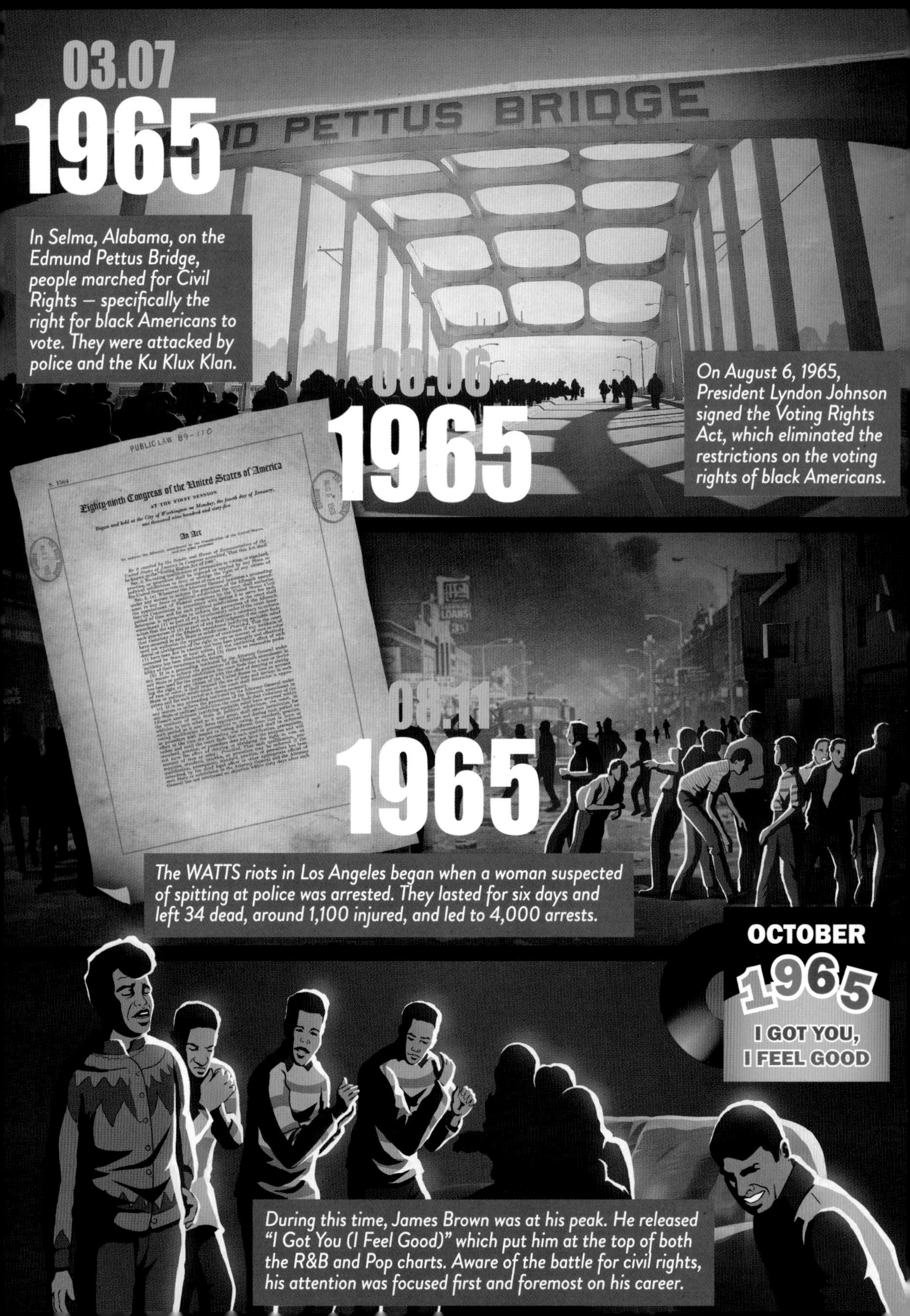

03.07
1965

ID PETTUS BRIDGE

In Selma, Alabama, on the Edmund Pettus Bridge, people marched for Civil Rights — specifically the right for black Americans to vote. They were attacked by police and the Ku Klux Klan.

08.06
1965

On August 6, 1965, President Lyndon Johnson signed the Voting Rights Act, which eliminated the restrictions on the voting rights of black Americans.

PUBLIC LAW 89-110

S. 1564

Eighty-ninth Congress of the United States of America

AT THE FIRST SESSION

Begun and held at the City of Washington on Monday, the fourth day of January, one thousand nine hundred and sixty-five

An Act

08.11
1965

The WATTS riots in Los Angeles began when a woman suspected of spitting at police was arrested. They lasted for six days and left 34 dead, around 1,100 injured, and led to 4,000 arrests.

OCTOBER
1965
I GOT YOU, I FEEL GOOD

During this time, James Brown was at his peak. He released "I Got You (I Feel Good)" which put him at the top of both the R&B and Pop charts. Aware of the battle for civil rights, his attention was focused first and foremost on his career.

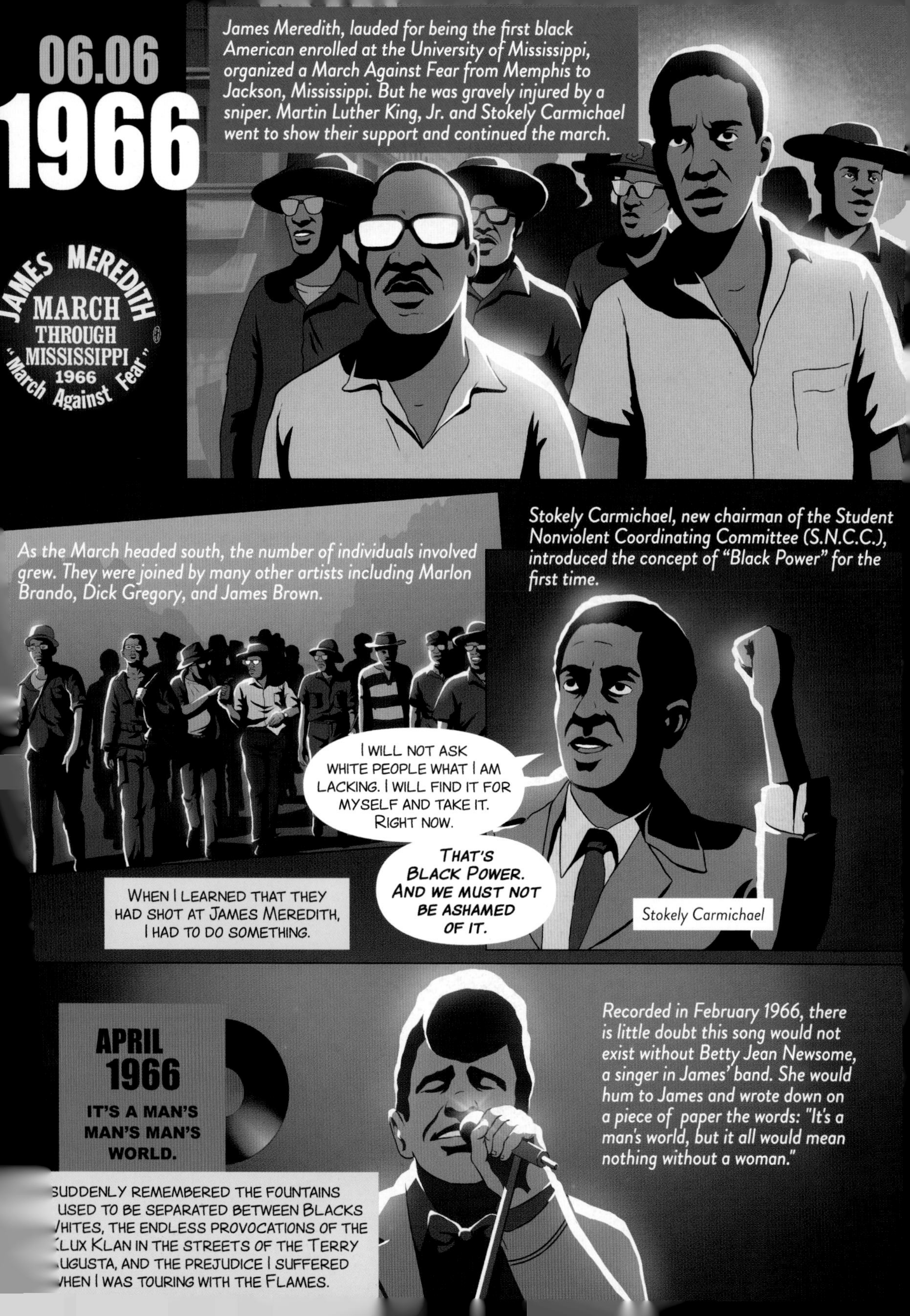
06.06
1966
James Meredith, lauded for being the first black American enrolled at the University of Mississippi, organized a March Against Fear from Memphis to Jackson, Mississippi. But he was gravely injured by a sniper. Martin Luther King, Jr. and Stokely Carmichael went to show their support and continued the march.
JAMES MEREDITH
MARCH
THROUGH
MISSISSIPPI
1966
"March Against Fear"
As the March headed south, the number of individuals involved grew. They were joined by many other artists including Marlon Brando, Dick Gregory, and James Brown.
WHEN I LEARNED THAT THEY HAD SHOT AT JAMES MEREDITH, I HAD TO DO SOMETHING.
Stokely Carmichael, new chairman of the Student Nonviolent Coordinating Committee (S.N.C.C.), introduced the concept of "Black Power" for the first time.
I WILL NOT ASK WHITE PEOPLE WHAT I AM LACKING. I WILL FIND IT FOR MYSELF AND TAKE IT. RIGHT NOW.
THAT'S BLACK POWER. AND WE MUST NOT BE ASHAMED OF IT.
Stokely Carmichael
APRIL
1966
IT'S A MAN'S MAN'S MAN'S WORLD.
Recorded in February 1966, there is little doubt this song would not exist without Betty Jean Newsome, a singer in James' band. She would hum to James and wrote down on a piece of paper the words: "It's a man's world, but it all would mean nothing without a woman."
SUDDENLY REMEMBERED THE FOUNTAINS
USED TO BE SEPARATED BETWEEN BLACKS
HITES, THE ENDLESS PROVOCATIONS OF THE
LUX KLAN IN THE STREETS OF THE TERRY
UGUSTA, AND THE PREJUDICE I SUFFERED
HEN I WAS TOURING WITH THE FLAMES.

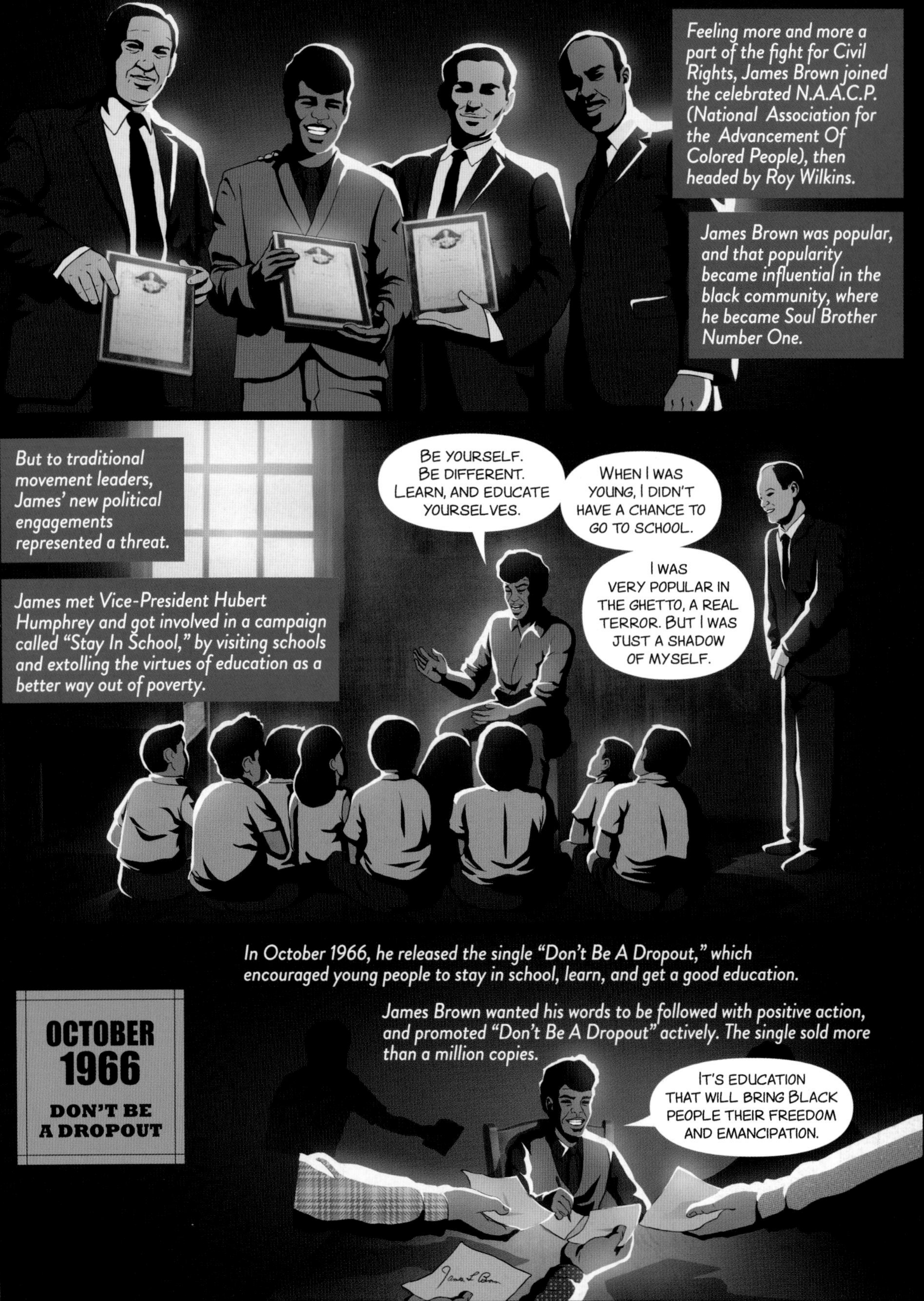

Feeling more and more a part of the fight for Civil Rights, James Brown joined the celebrated N.A.A.C.P. (National Association for the Advancement Of Colored People), then headed by Roy Wilkins.
James Brown was popular, and that popularity became influential in the black community, where he became Soul Brother Number One.
But to traditional movement leaders, James' new political engagements represented a threat.
James met Vice-President Hubert Humphrey and got involved in a campaign called "Stay In School," by visiting schools and extolling the virtues of education as a better way out of poverty.
BE YOURSELF. BE DIFFERENT. LEARN, AND EDUCATE YOURSELVES.
WHEN I WAS YOUNG, I DIDN'T HAVE A CHANCE TO GO TO SCHOOL.
I WAS VERY POPULAR IN THE GHETTO, A REAL TERROR. BUT I WAS JUST A SHADOW OF MYSELF.
In October 1966, he released the single "Don't Be A Dropout," which encouraged young people to stay in school, learn, and get a good education.
OCTOBER 1966
DON'T BE A DROPOUT
James Brown wanted his words to be followed with positive action, and promoted "Don't Be A Dropout" actively. The single sold more than a million copies.
IT'S EDUCATION THAT WILL BRING BLACK PEOPLE THEIR FREEDOM AND EMANCIPATION.

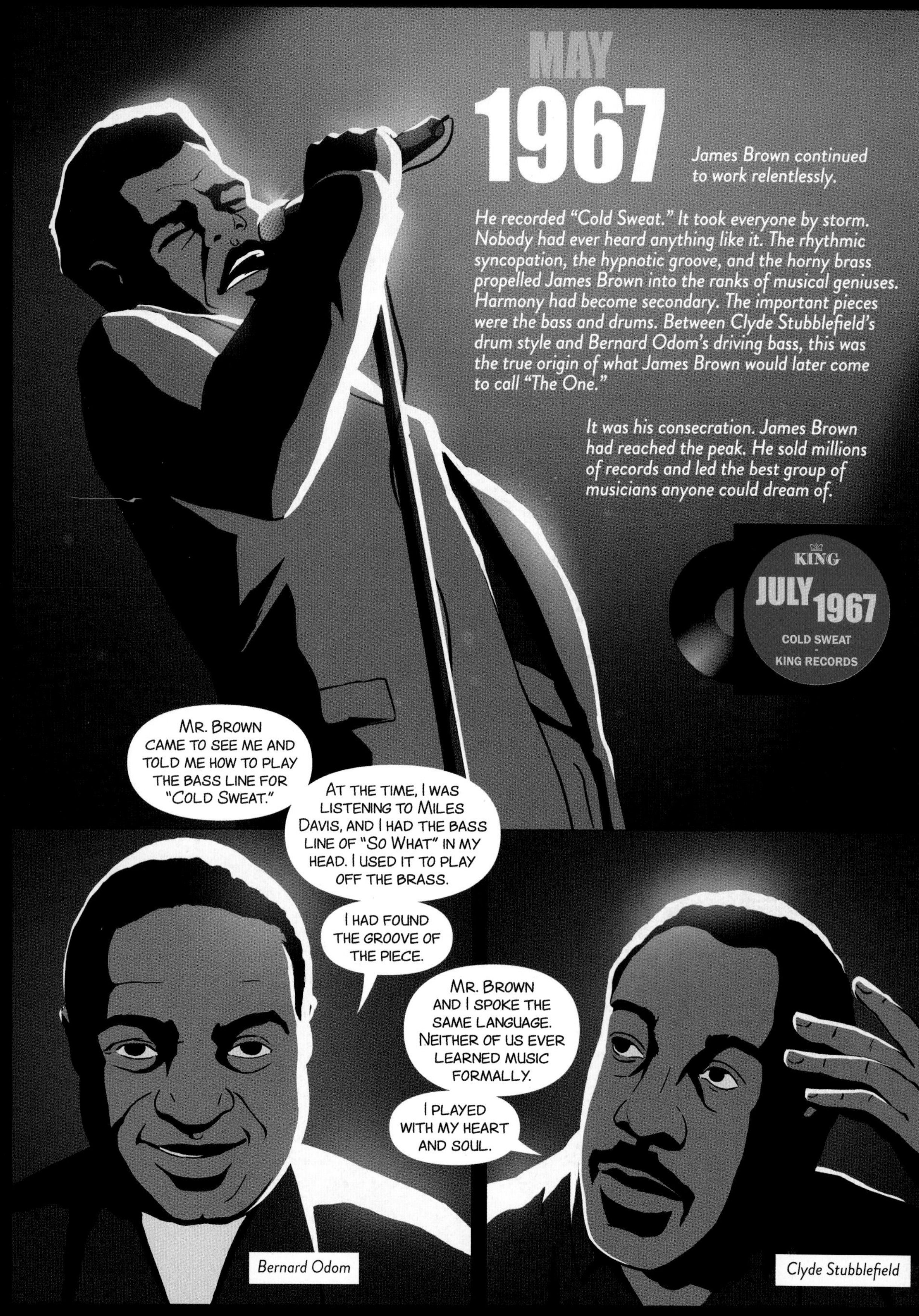
MAY
1967
James Brown continued to work relentlessly.
He recorded "Cold Sweat." It took everyone by storm. Nobody had ever heard anything like it. The rhythmic syncopation, the hypnotic groove, and the horny brass propelled James Brown into the ranks of musical geniuses. Harmony had become secondary. The important pieces were the bass and drums. Between Clyde Stubblefield's drum style and Bernard Odom's driving bass, this was the true origin of what James Brown would later come to call "The One."
It was his consecration. James Brown had reached the peak. He sold millions of records and led the best group of musicians anyone could dream of.
KING
JULY 1967
COLD SWEAT
-
KING RECORDS
MR. BROWN CAME TO SEE ME AND TOLD ME HOW TO PLAY THE BASS LINE FOR "COLD SWEAT."
AT THE TIME, I WAS LISTENING TO MILES DAVIS, AND I HAD THE BASS LINE OF "SO WHAT" IN MY HEAD. I USED IT TO PLAY OFF THE BRASS.
I HAD FOUND THE GROOVE OF THE PIECE.
MR. BROWN AND I SPOKE THE SAME LANGUAGE. NEITHER OF US EVER LEARNED MUSIC FORMALLY.
I PLAYED WITH MY HEART AND SOUL.
Bernard Odom
Clyde Stubblefield

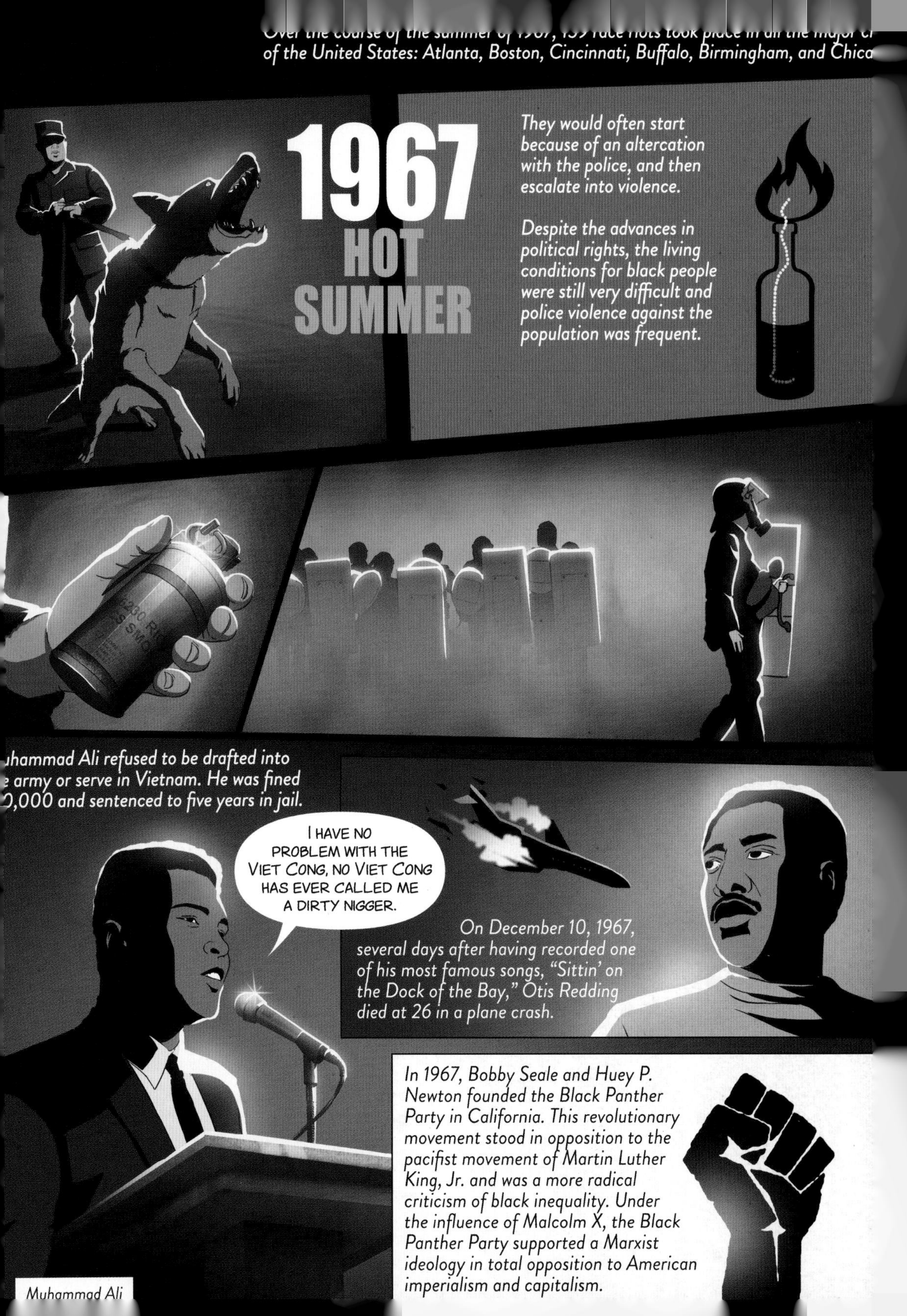
Over the course of the summer of 1967, 159 race riots took place in all the major ci
of the United States: Atlanta, Boston, Cincinnati, Buffalo, Birmingham, and Chica
1967
HOT SUMMER
They would often start because of an altercation with the police, and then escalate into violence.
Despite the advances in political rights, the living conditions for black people were still very difficult and police violence against the population was frequent.
uhammad Ali refused to be drafted into
army or serve in Vietnam. He was fined
0,000 and sentenced to five years in jail.
I HAVE NO PROBLEM WITH THE VIET CONG, NO VIET CONG HAS EVER CALLED ME A DIRTY NIGGER.
On December 10, 1967, several days after having recorded one of his most famous songs, "Sittin' on the Dock of the Bay," Otis Redding died at 26 in a plane crash.
In 1967, Bobby Seale and Huey P. Newton founded the Black Panther Party in California. This revolutionary movement stood in opposition to the pacifist movement of Martin Luther King, Jr. and was a more radical criticism of black inequality. Under the influence of Malcolm X, the Black Panther Party supported a Marxist ideology in total opposition to American imperialism and capitalism.
Muhammad Ali

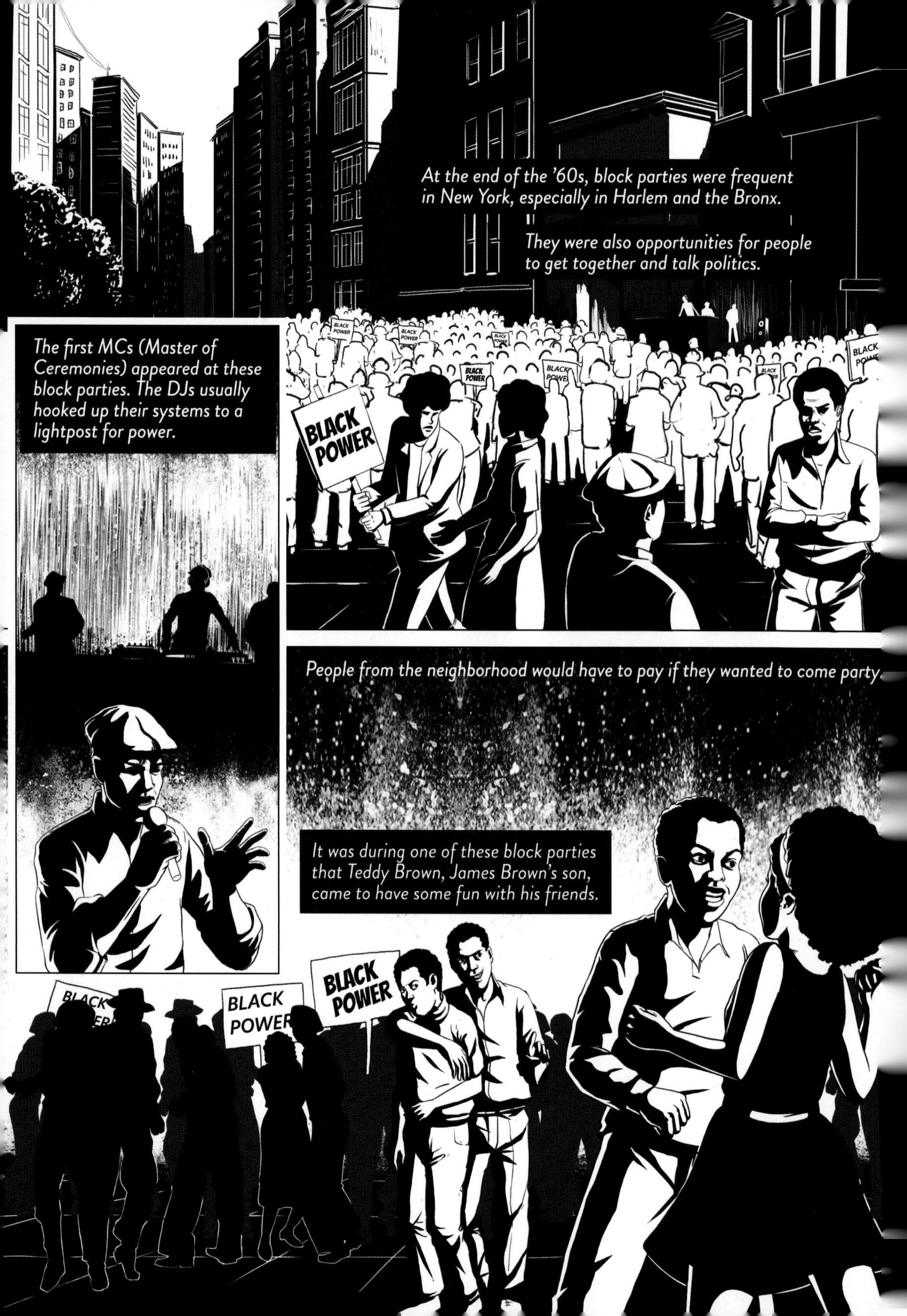
At the end of the '60s, block parties were frequent in New York, especially in Harlem and the Bronx.
They were also opportunities for people to get together and talk politics.
BLACK POWER
The first MCs (Master of Ceremonies) appeared at these block parties. The DJs usually hooked up their systems to a lightpost for power.
People from the neighborhood would have to pay if they wanted to come party.
It was during one of these block parties that Teddy Brown, James Brown's son, came to have some fun with his friends.
BLACK POWER
BLACK POWER

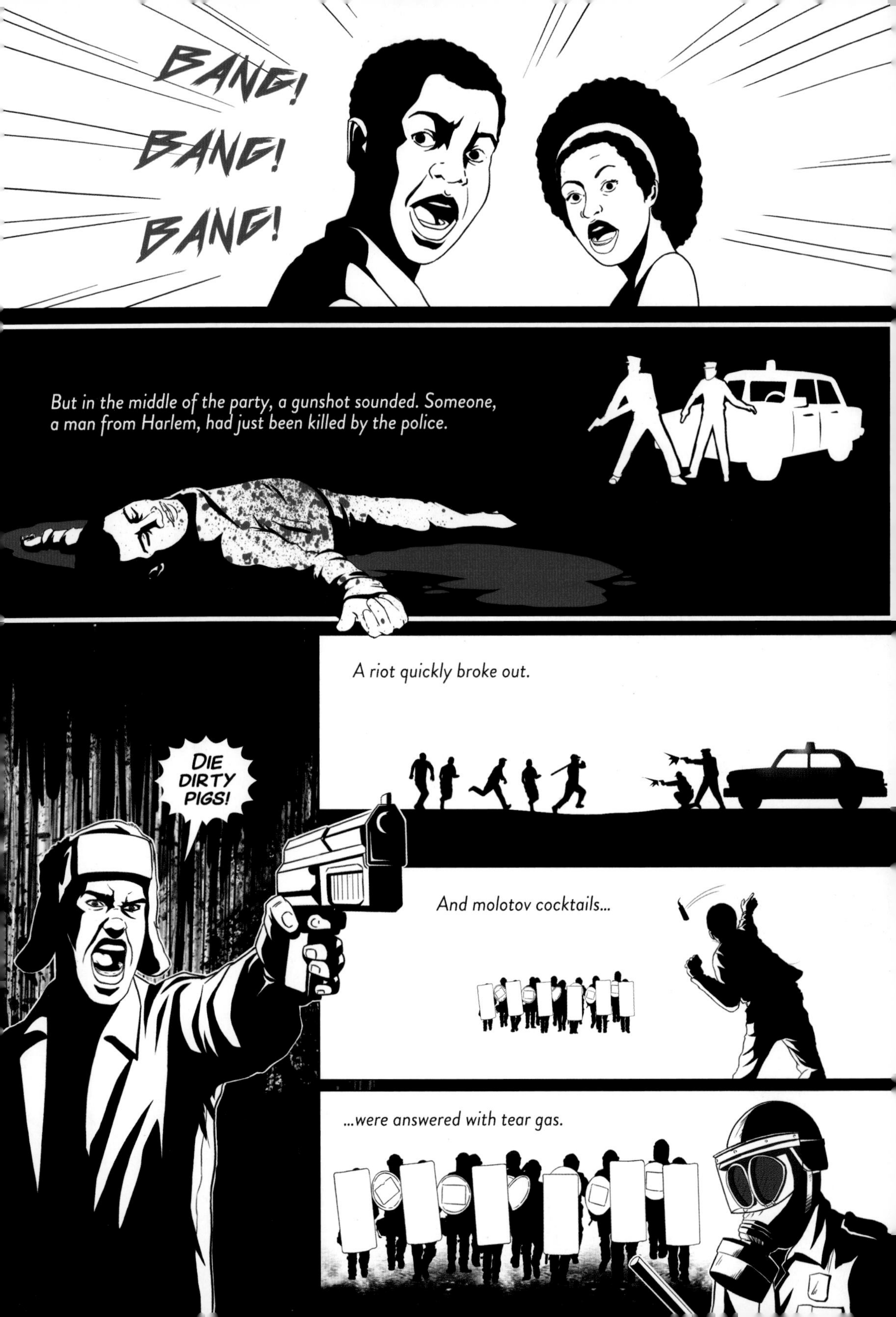
BANG!
BANG!
BANG!
But in the middle of the party, a gunshot sounded. Someone, a man from Harlem, had just been killed by the police.
A riot quickly broke out.
DIE DIRTY PIGS!
And molotov cocktails...
...were answered with tear gas.

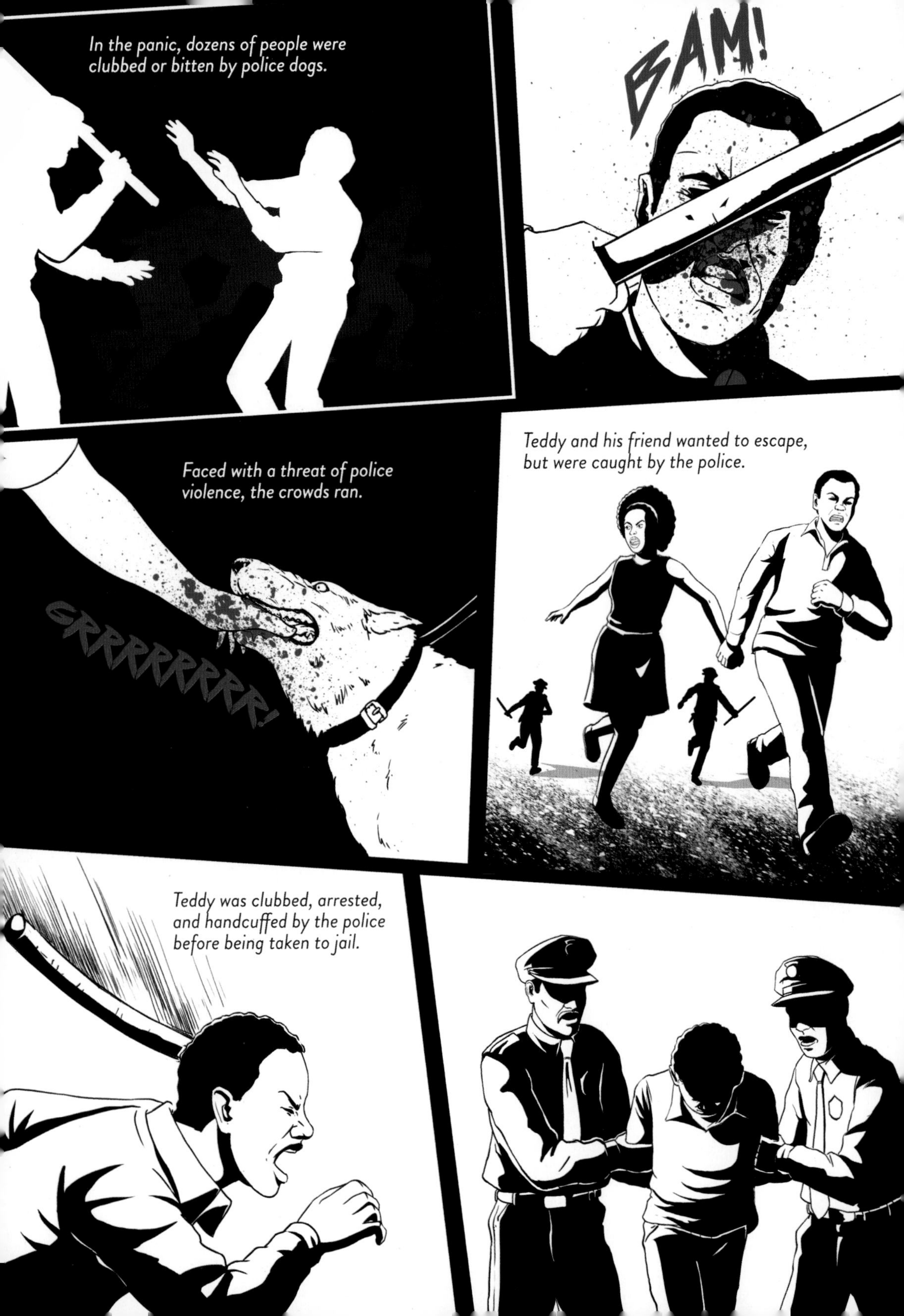
In the panic, dozens of people were clubbed or bitten by police dogs.
BAM!
Faced with a threat of police violence, the crowds ran.
GRRRRRRRR!
Teddy and his friend wanted to escape, but were caught by the police.
Teddy was clubbed, arrested, and handcuffed by the police before being taken to jail.

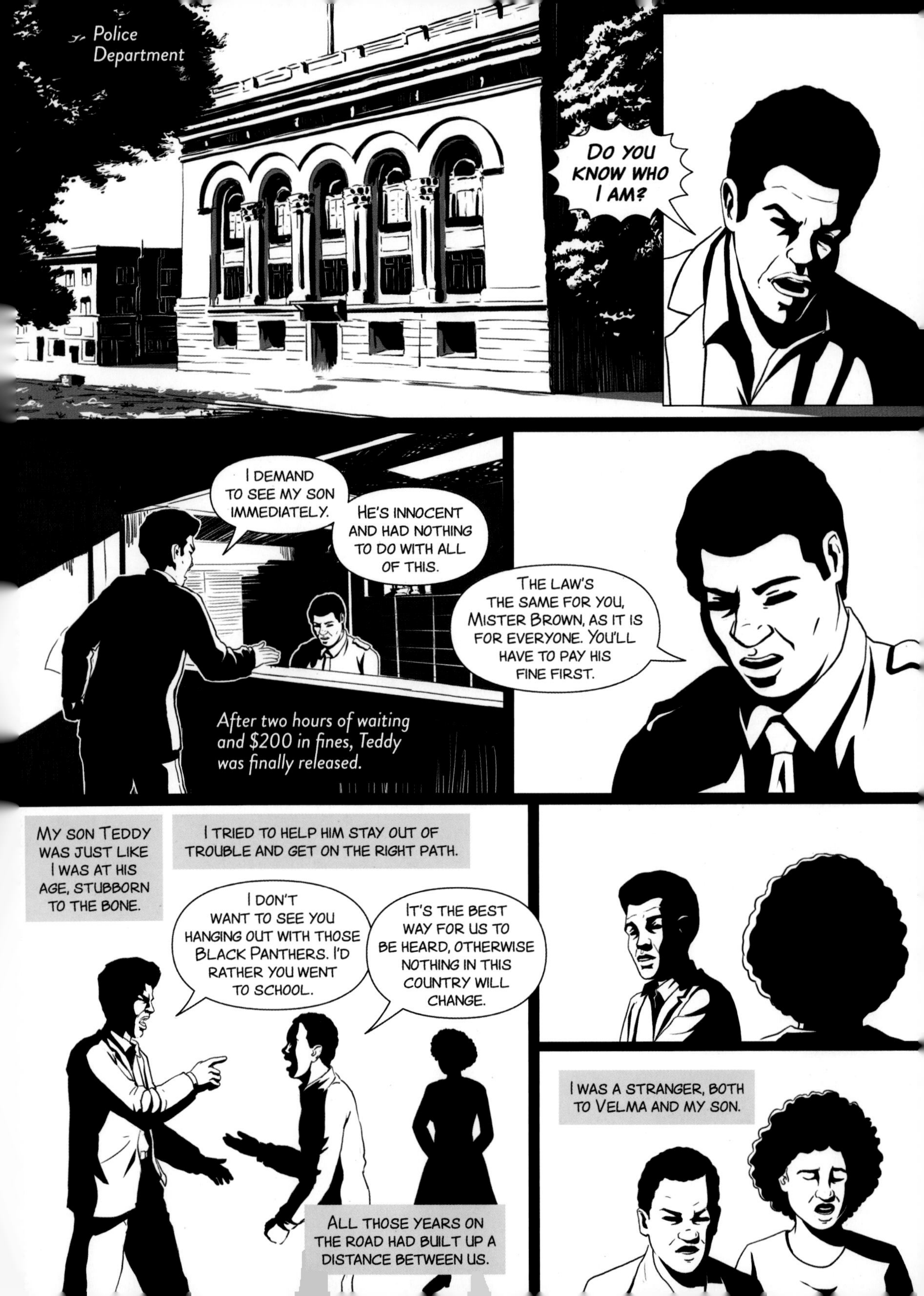
Police Department
DO YOU KNOW WHO I AM?
I DEMAND TO SEE MY SON IMMEDIATELY.
HE'S INNOCENT AND HAD NOTHING TO DO WITH ALL OF THIS.
After two hours of waiting and $200 in fines, Teddy was finally released.
THE LAW'S THE SAME FOR YOU, MISTER BROWN, AS IT IS FOR EVERYONE. YOU'LL HAVE TO PAY HIS FINE FIRST.
MY SON TEDDY WAS JUST LIKE I WAS AT HIS AGE, STUBBORN TO THE BONE.
I TRIED TO HELP HIM STAY OUT OF TROUBLE AND GET ON THE RIGHT PATH.
I DON'T WANT TO SEE YOU HANGING OUT WITH THOSE BLACK PANTHERS. I'D RATHER YOU WENT TO SCHOOL.
IT'S THE BEST WAY FOR US TO BE HEARD, OTHERWISE NOTHING IN THIS COUNTRY WILL CHANGE.
ALL THOSE YEARS ON THE ROAD HAD BUILT UP A DISTANCE BETWEEN US.
I WAS A STRANGER, BOTH TO VELMA AND MY SON.

1968

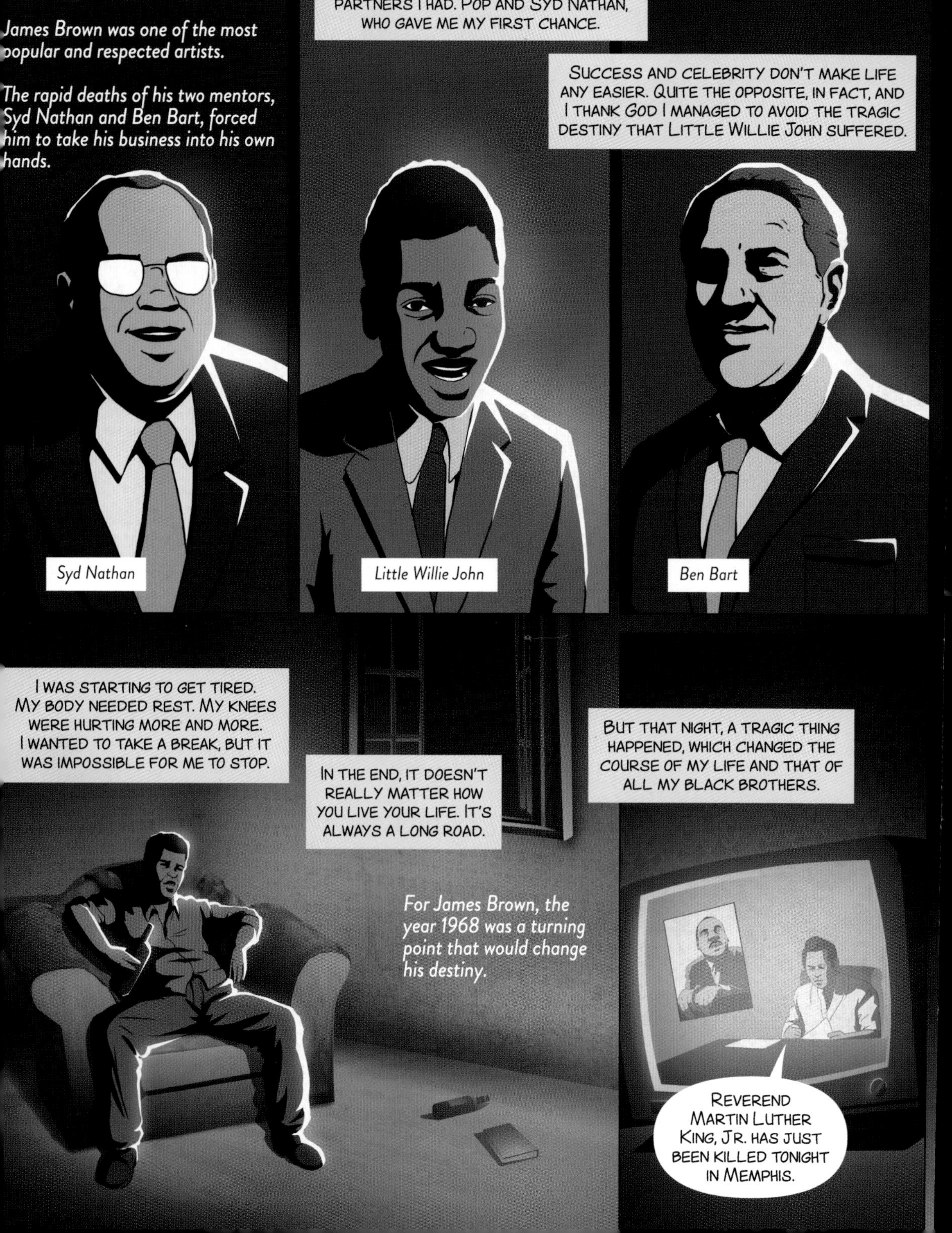
James Brown was one of the most popular and respected artists.
The rapid deaths of his two mentors, Syd Nathan and Ben Bart, forced him to take his business into his own hands.
IN 1968, I LOST THE TWO MOST IMPORTANT PARTNERS I HAD. POP AND SYD NATHAN, WHO GAVE ME MY FIRST CHANCE.
SUCCESS AND CELEBRITY DON'T MAKE LIFE ANY EASIER. QUITE THE OPPOSITE, IN FACT, AND I THANK GOD I MANAGED TO AVOID THE TRAGIC DESTINY THAT LITTLE WILLIE JOHN SUFFERED.
Syd Nathan
Little Willie John
Ben Bart
I WAS STARTING TO GET TIRED. MY BODY NEEDED REST. MY KNEES WERE HURTING MORE AND MORE. I WANTED TO TAKE A BREAK, BUT IT WAS IMPOSSIBLE FOR ME TO STOP.
IN THE END, IT DOESN'T REALLY MATTER HOW YOU LIVE YOUR LIFE. IT'S ALWAYS A LONG ROAD.
For James Brown, the year 1968 was a turning point that would change his destiny.
BUT THAT NIGHT, A TRAGIC THING HAPPENED, WHICH CHANGED THE COURSE OF MY LIFE AND THAT OF ALL MY BLACK BROTHERS.
REVEREND MARTIN LUTHER KING, JR. HAS JUST BEEN KILLED TONIGHT IN MEMPHIS.

BLACK IS
NOT A COLOR,
IT'S AN ATTITUDE
OF INDEPENDENCE,
RESPECT, AND
DIGNITY.

-4-
BLACK POWER

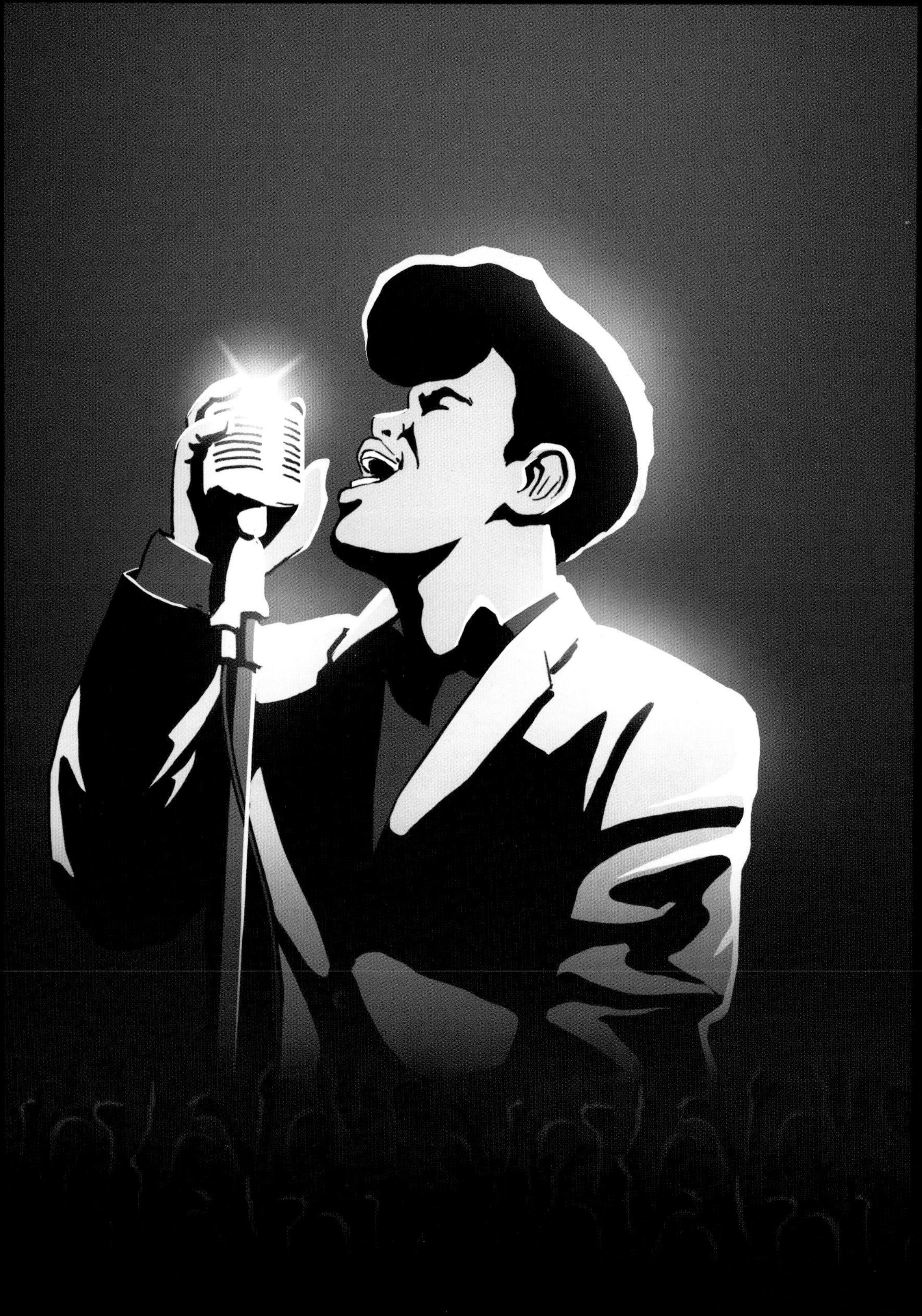

"HATE CANNOT DRIVE OUT HATE, ONLY LOVE CAN DO THAT."

Born in Atlanta in 1929, Martin Luther King, Jr. became a pastor at the age of 19 in the Baptist church in Montgomery, Alabama.

In 1955, he organized the protests to defend the rights of Rosa Parks, a seamstress, who was arrested by the police for refusing to give up her seat in a bus.

Martin Luther King, Jr. continued his fight and responded to insults with gatherings and peaceful "sit-ins" that formed the basis of his non-violent activism. It succeeded in moving the audience and changing public opinion due to the contrast with the televised images of police violence.

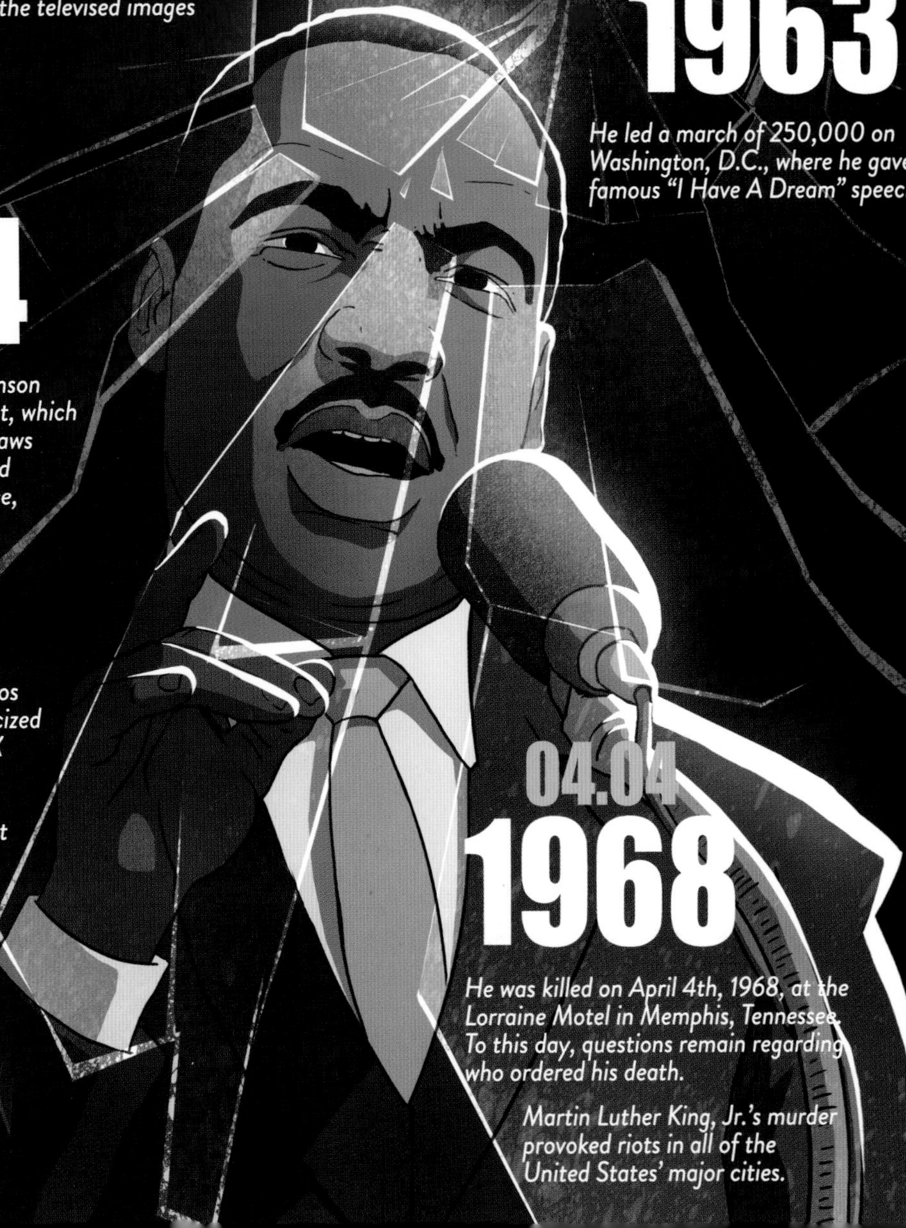

08.28 1963

He led a march of 250,000 on Washington, D.C., where he gave his famous "I Have A Dream" speech.

07.02 1964

President Lyndon B. Johnson signed the Civil Right Act, which abolished the Jim Crow laws of the South and declared discrimination due to race, religion, sex, or national origin illegal.

But the conditions of black Americans didn't change as quickly as necessary, and the ghettos continued to grow. Criticized by leaders like Malcom X or the Black Panther Party, Martin Luther King, Jr. began to protest the war in Vietnam and became involved with social welfare programs meant to combat poverty.

04.04 1968

He was killed on April 4th, 1968, at the Lorraine Motel in Memphis, Tennessee. To this day, questions remain regarding who ordered his death.

Martin Luther King, Jr.'s murder provoked riots in all of the United States' major cities.

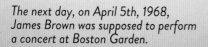

The next day, on April 5th, 1968, James Brown was supposed to perform a concert at Boston Garden.

But given the riots happening, especially in the black neighborhood of Roxbury, the mayor of Boston, Kevin White, wanted to cancel it.

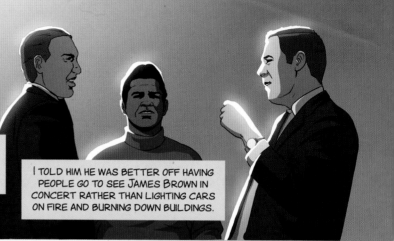

I WAS SHOCKED THAT THE MAYOR JUST WANTED TO CANCEL EVERYTHING. BUT I'M NOT ONE TO RUN AWAY FROM MY RESPONSIBILITIES.

I TOLD HIM HE WAS BETTER OFF HAVING PEOPLE GO TO SEE JAMES BROWN IN CONCERT RATHER THAN LIGHTING CARS ON FIRE AND BURNING DOWN BUILDINGS.

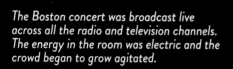

The Boston concert was broadcast live across all the radio and television channels. The energy in the room was electric and the crowd began to grow agitated.

BEFORE STARTING, I SAID A FEW WORDS IN HONOR OF THE REVEREND.

I WAS AWARE THAT AT ANY SECOND, EVERYTHING COULD POP OFF, AND THAT I COULD GET HURT, OR EVEN ASSASSINATED.

PLEASE, YOU MUST TAKE CARE NOT TO DO ANYTHING TO DISHONOR THE REVEREND'S MEMORY.

EVERYTHING WAS GOING WELL UNTIL THE SECURITY STARTED TO PUSH AWAY THE KIDS WHO JUST WANTED TO DANCE ON STAGE.

IT'S OKAY, THERE'S NO PROBLEM HERE. HE JUST WANTS TO SHAKE MY HAND.

NOW LET ME DO MY SHOW... WE'RE ALL IN THIS TOGETHER, AREN'T WE?

I ASKED THE POLICE TO STAY BACK BECAUSE I THOUGHT I COULD EARN A BIT OF RESPECT FROM MY OWN PEOPLE...

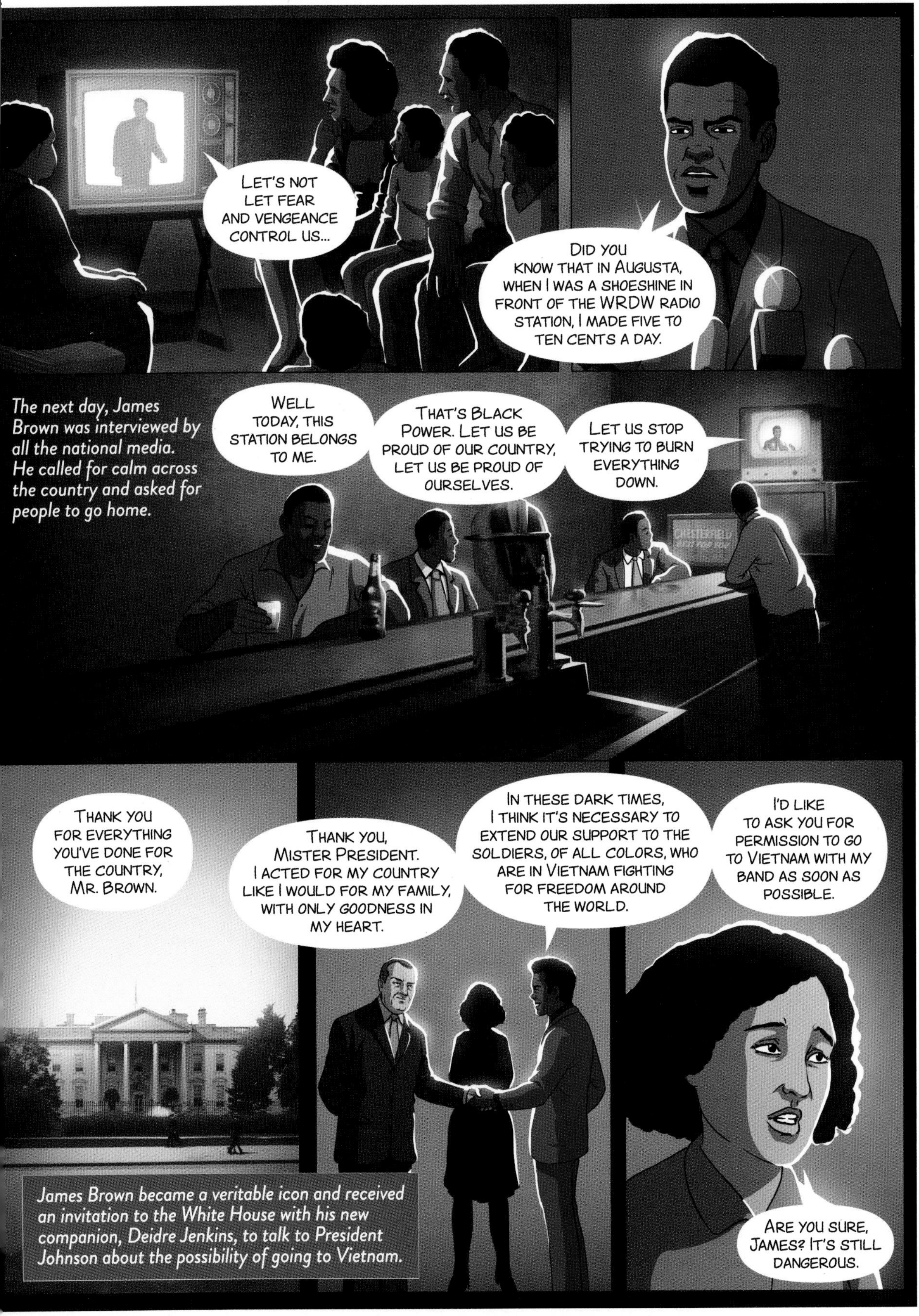
LET'S NOT LET FEAR AND VENGEANCE CONTROL US...
DID YOU KNOW THAT IN AUGUSTA, WHEN I WAS A SHOESHINE IN FRONT OF THE WRDW RADIO STATION, I MADE FIVE TO TEN CENTS A DAY.
The next day, James Brown was interviewed by all the national media. He called for calm across the country and asked for people to go home.
WELL TODAY, THIS STATION BELONGS TO ME.
THAT'S BLACK POWER. LET US BE PROUD OF OUR COUNTRY, LET US BE PROUD OF OURSELVES.
LET US STOP TRYING TO BURN EVERYTHING DOWN.
CHESTERFIELD
THANK YOU FOR EVERYTHING YOU'VE DONE FOR THE COUNTRY, MR. BROWN.
THANK YOU, MISTER PRESIDENT. I ACTED FOR MY COUNTRY LIKE I WOULD FOR MY FAMILY, WITH ONLY GOODNESS IN MY HEART.
IN THESE DARK TIMES, I THINK IT'S NECESSARY TO EXTEND OUR SUPPORT TO THE SOLDIERS, OF ALL COLORS, WHO ARE IN VIETNAM FIGHTING FOR FREEDOM AROUND THE WORLD.
I'D LIKE TO ASK YOU FOR PERMISSION TO GO TO VIETNAM WITH MY BAND AS SOON AS POSSIBLE.
James Brown became a veritable icon and received an invitation to the White House with his new companion, Deidre Jenkins, to talk to President Johnson about the possibility of going to Vietnam.
ARE YOU SURE, JAMES? IT'S STILL DANGEROUS.

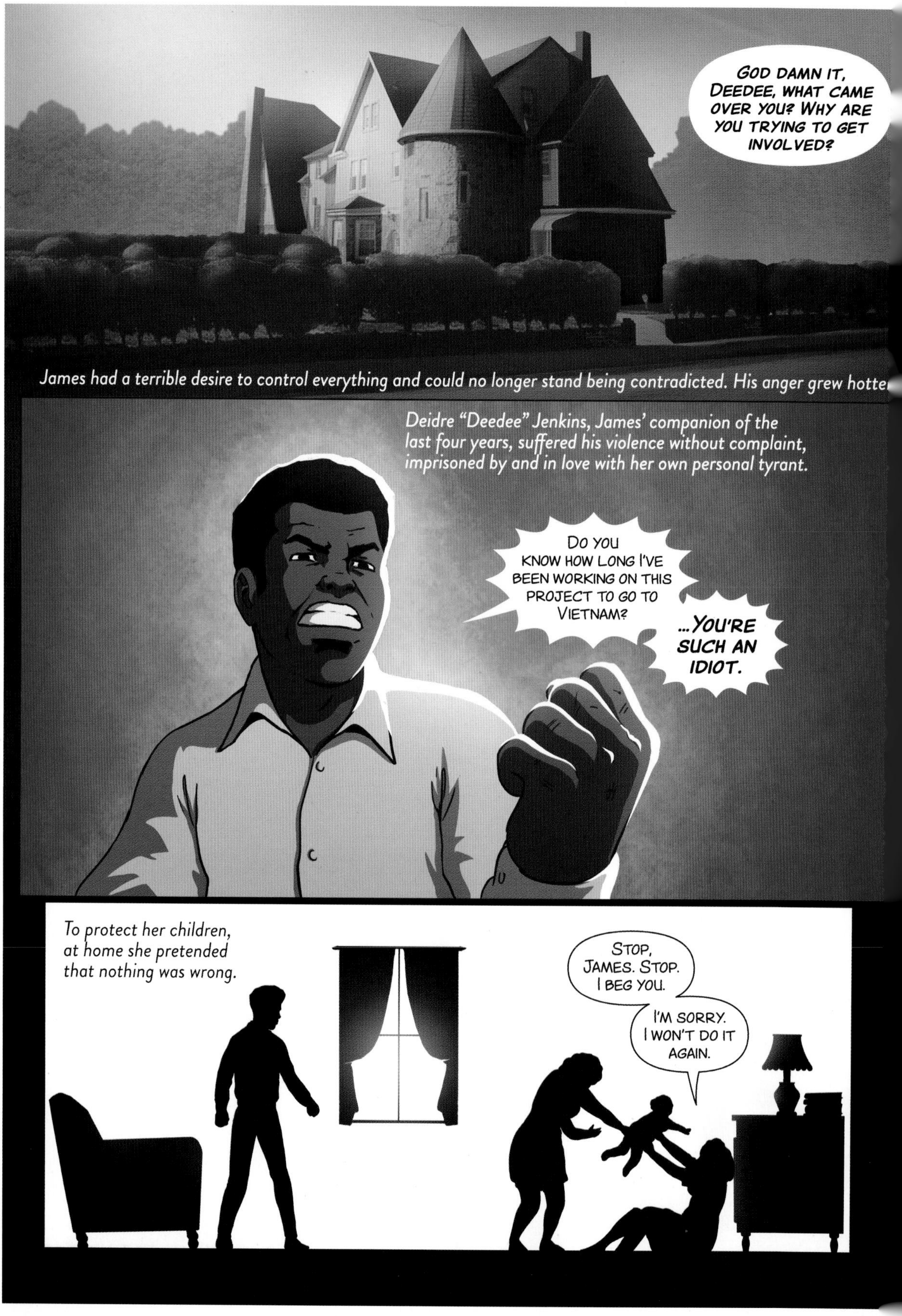
GOD DAMN IT, DEEDEE, WHAT CAME OVER YOU? WHY ARE YOU TRYING TO GET INVOLVED?
James had a terrible desire to control everything and could no longer stand being contradicted. His anger grew hotte
Deidre "Deedee" Jenkins, James' companion of the last four years, suffered his violence without complaint, imprisoned by and in love with her own personal tyrant.
DO YOU KNOW HOW LONG I'VE BEEN WORKING ON THIS PROJECT TO GO TO VIETNAM?
...YOU'RE SUCH AN IDIOT.
To protect her children, at home she pretended that nothing was wrong.
STOP, JAMES. STOP. I BEG YOU.
I'M SORRY. I WON'T DO IT AGAIN.

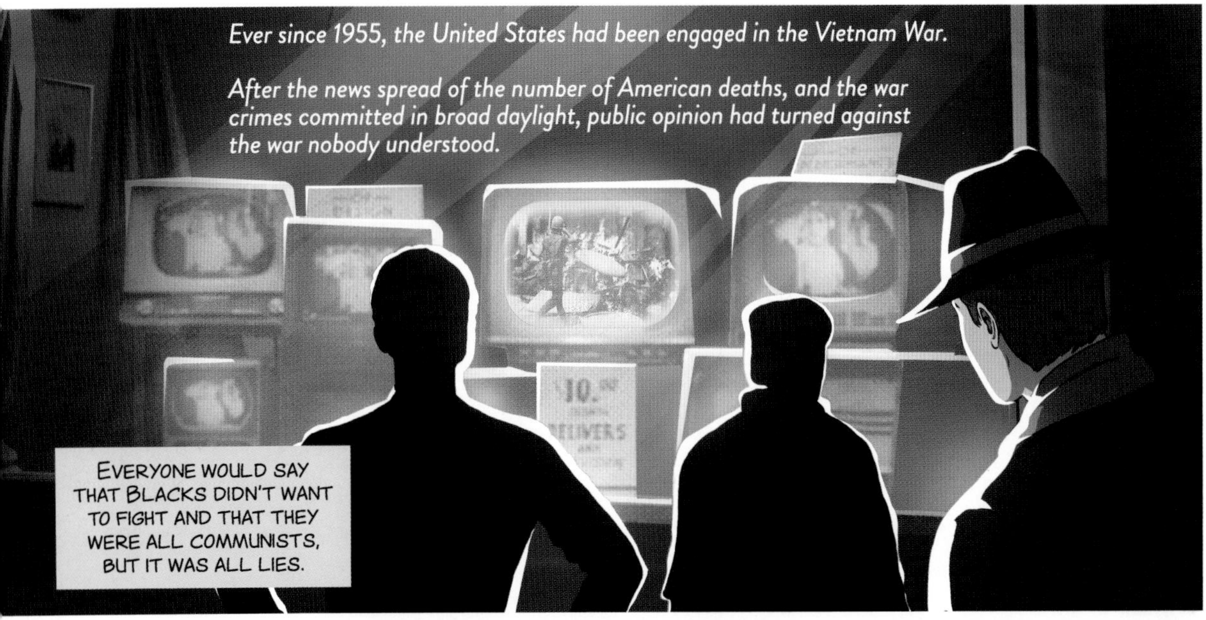
Ever since 1955, the United States had been engaged in the Vietnam War.
After the news spread of the number of American deaths, and the war crimes committed in broad daylight, public opinion had turned against the war nobody understood.
EVERYONE WOULD SAY THAT BLACKS DIDN'T WANT TO FIGHT AND THAT THEY WERE ALL COMMUNISTS, BUT IT WAS ALL LIES.

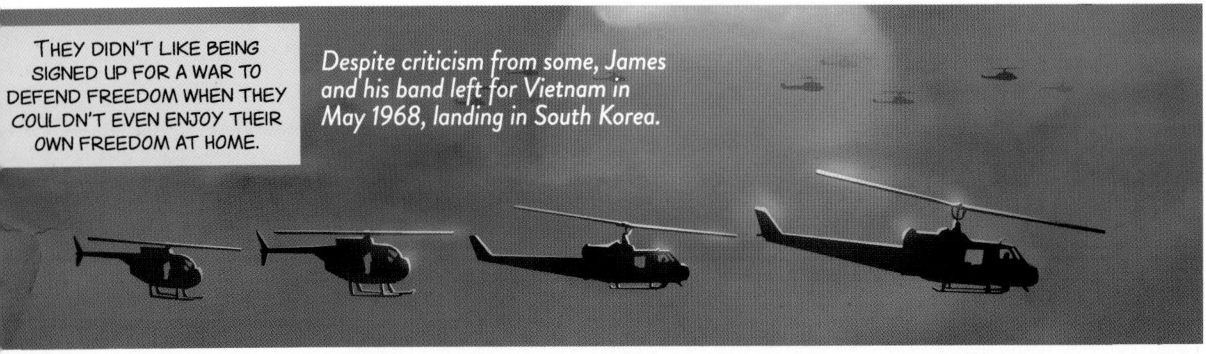
THEY DIDN'T LIKE BEING SIGNED UP FOR A WAR TO DEFEND FREEDOM WHEN THEY COULDN'T EVEN ENJOY THEIR OWN FREEDOM AT HOME.
Despite criticism from some, James and his band left for Vietnam in May 1968, landing in South Korea.

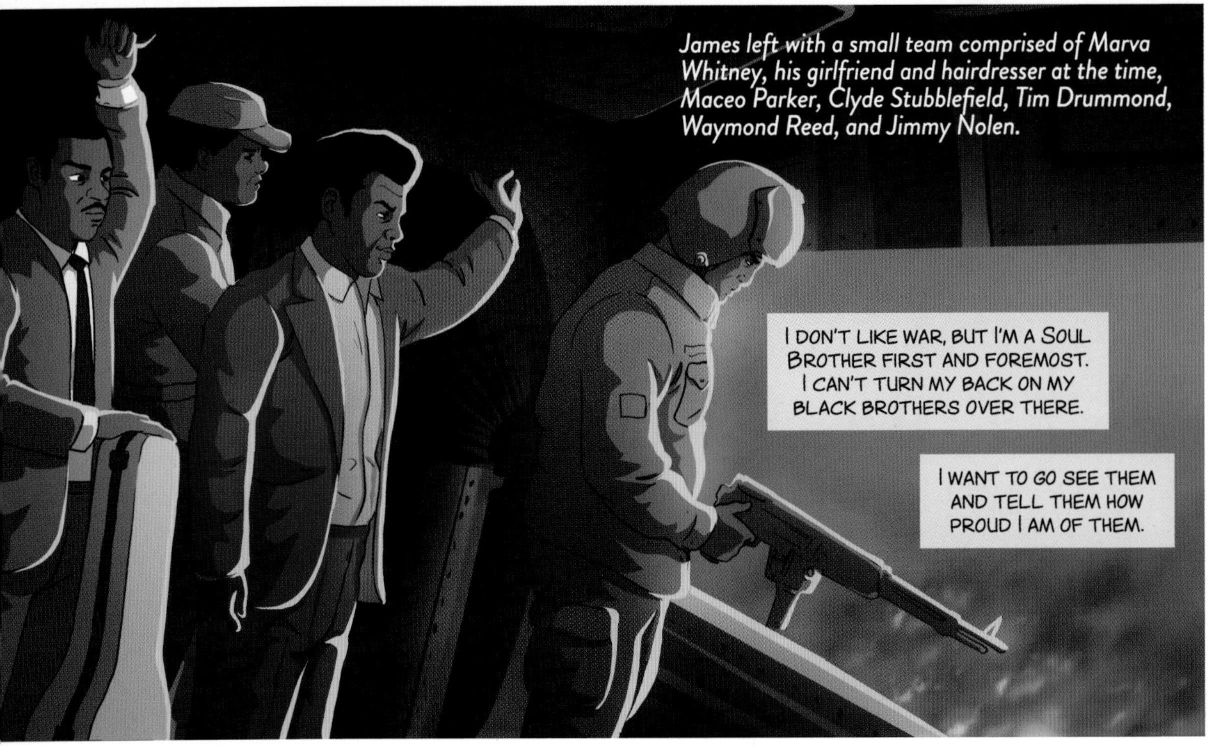
James left with a small team comprised of Marva Whitney, his girlfriend and hairdresser at the time, Maceo Parker, Clyde Stubblefield, Tim Drummond, Waymond Reed, and Jimmy Nolen.
I DON'T LIKE WAR, BUT I'M A SOUL BROTHER FIRST AND FOREMOST. I CAN'T TURN MY BACK ON MY BLACK BROTHERS OVER THERE.
I WANT TO GO SEE THEM AND TELL THEM HOW PROUD I AM OF THEM.

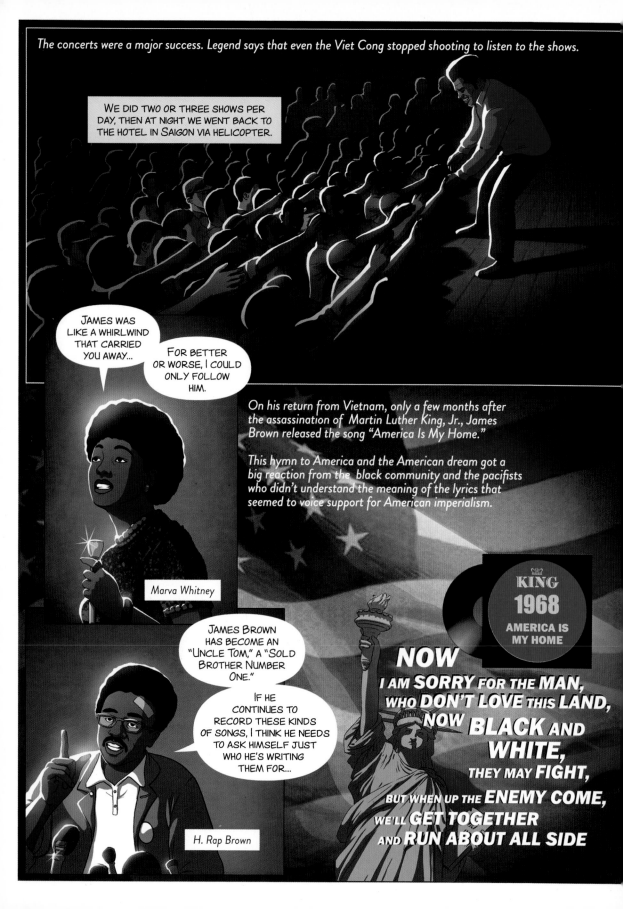

The concerts were a major success. Legend says that even the Viet Cong stopped shooting to listen to the shows.

WE DID TWO OR THREE SHOWS PER DAY, THEN AT NIGHT WE WENT BACK TO THE HOTEL IN SAIGON VIA HELICOPTER.

JAMES WAS LIKE A WHIRLWIND THAT CARRIED YOU AWAY...

FOR BETTER OR WORSE, I COULD ONLY FOLLOW HIM.

Marva Whitney

On his return from Vietnam, only a few months after the assassination of Martin Luther King, Jr., James Brown released the song "America Is My Home."

This hymn to America and the American dream got a big reaction from the black community and the pacifists who didn't understand the meaning of the lyrics that seemed to voice support for American imperialism.

KING
1968
AMERICA IS MY HOME

JAMES BROWN HAS BECOME AN "UNCLE TOM," A "SOLD BROTHER NUMBER ONE."

IF HE CONTINUES TO RECORD THESE KINDS OF SONGS, I THINK HE NEEDS TO ASK HIMSELF JUST WHO HE'S WRITING THEM FOR...

H. Rap Brown

NOW I AM SORRY FOR THE MAN, WHO DON'T LOVE THIS LAND, NOW BLACK AND WHITE, THEY MAY FIGHT, BUT WHEN UP THE ENEMY COME, WE'LL GET TOGETHER AND RUN ABOUT ALL SIDE

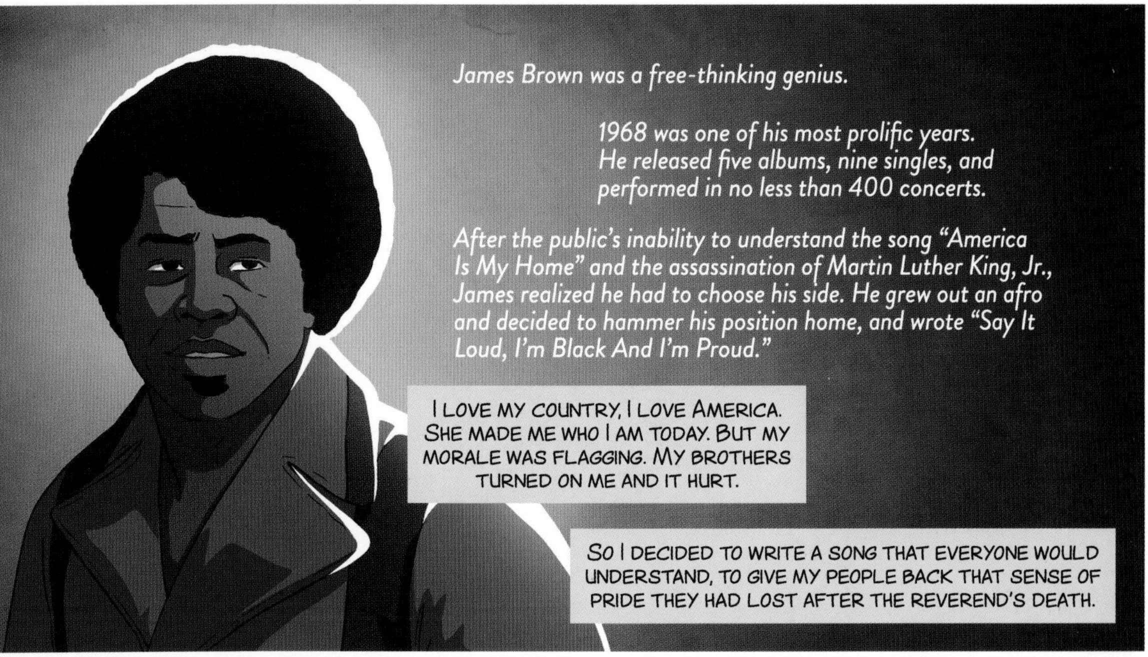
James Brown was a free-thinking genius.
1968 was one of his most prolific years. He released five albums, nine singles, and performed in no less than 400 concerts.
After the public's inability to understand the song "America Is My Home" and the assassination of Martin Luther King, Jr., James realized he had to choose his side. He grew out an afro and decided to hammer his position home, and wrote "Say It Loud, I'm Black And I'm Proud."
I LOVE MY COUNTRY, I LOVE AMERICA. SHE MADE ME WHO I AM TODAY. BUT MY MORALE WAS FLAGGING. MY BROTHERS TURNED ON ME AND IT HURT.
SO I DECIDED TO WRITE A SONG THAT EVERYONE WOULD UNDERSTAND, TO GIVE MY PEOPLE BACK THAT SENSE OF PRIDE THEY HAD LOST AFTER THE REVEREND'S DEATH.

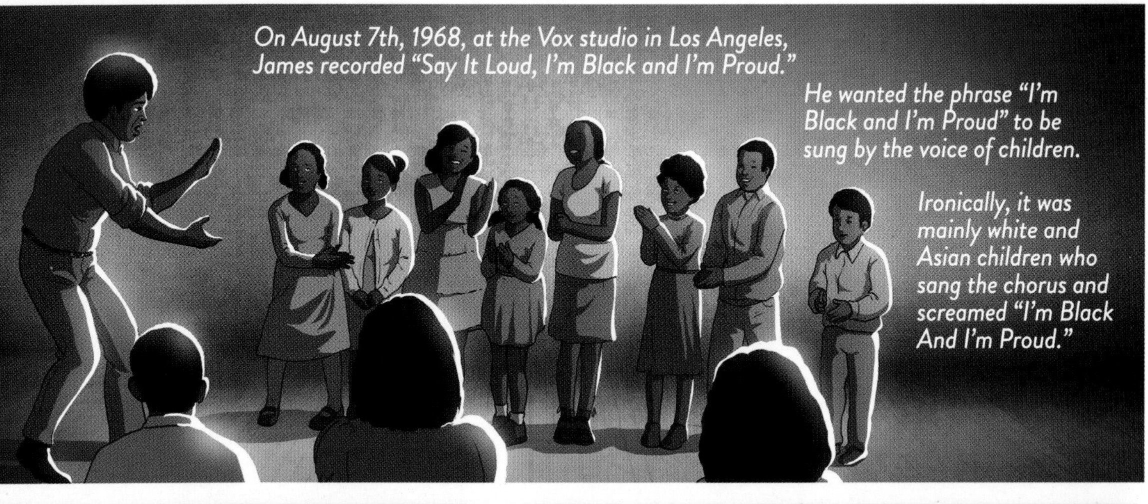
On August 7th, 1968, at the Vox studio in Los Angeles, James recorded "Say It Loud, I'm Black and I'm Proud."
He wanted the phrase "I'm Black and I'm Proud" to be sung by the voice of children.
Ironically, it was mainly white and Asian children who sang the chorus and screamed "I'm Black And I'm Proud."

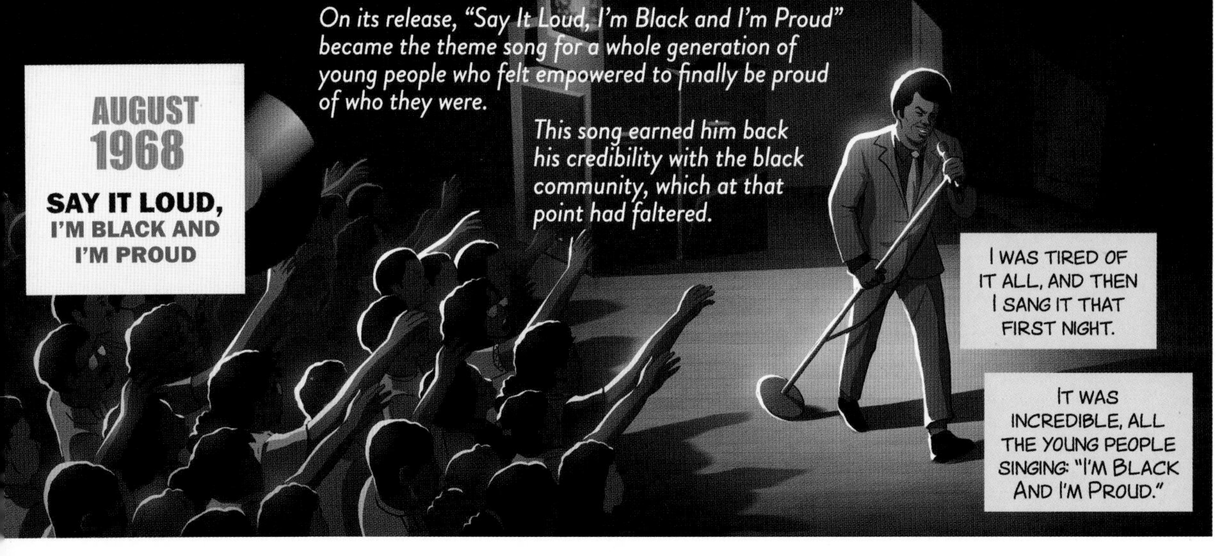
AUGUST 1968
SAY IT LOUD, I'M BLACK AND I'M PROUD
On its release, "Say It Loud, I'm Black and I'm Proud" became the theme song for a whole generation of young people who felt empowered to finally be proud of who they were.
This song earned him back his credibility with the black community, which at that point had faltered.
I WAS TIRED OF IT ALL, AND THEN I SANG IT THAT FIRST NIGHT.
IT WAS INCREDIBLE, ALL THE YOUNG PEOPLE SINGING: "I'M BLACK AND I'M PROUD."

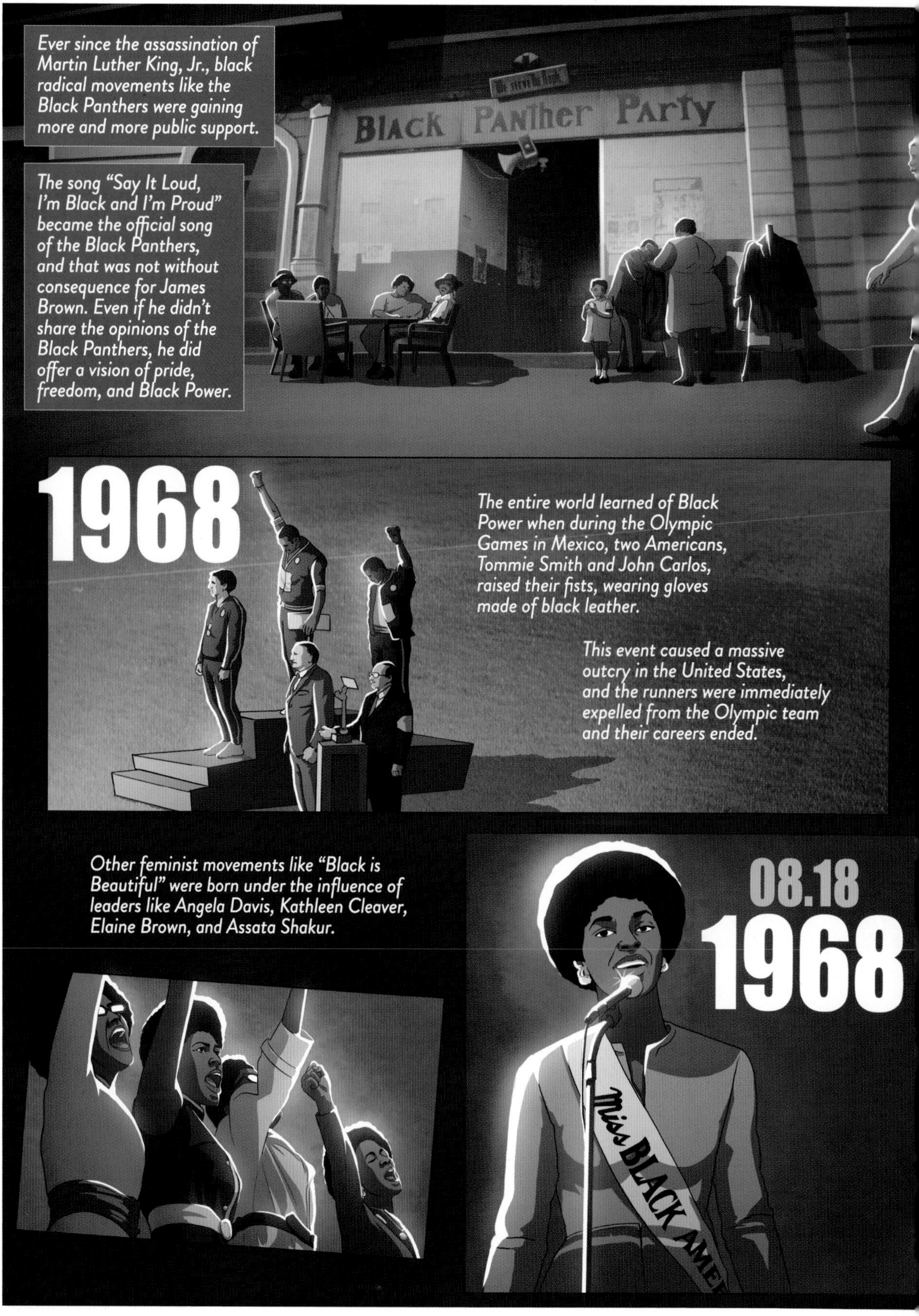
Ever since the assassination of Martin Luther King, Jr., black radical movements like the Black Panthers were gaining more and more public support.
BLACK PANTHER PARTY
The song "Say It Loud, I'm Black and I'm Proud" became the official song of the Black Panthers, and that was not without consequence for James Brown. Even if he didn't share the opinions of the Black Panthers, he did offer a vision of pride, freedom, and Black Power.
1968
The entire world learned of Black Power when during the Olympic Games in Mexico, two Americans, Tommie Smith and John Carlos, raised their fists, wearing gloves made of black leather.
This event caused a massive outcry in the United States, and the runners were immediately expelled from the Olympic team and their careers ended.
Other feminist movements like "Black is Beautiful" were born under the influence of leaders like Angela Davis, Kathleen Cleaver, Elaine Brown, and Assata Shakur.
08.18
1968
Miss BLACK AME

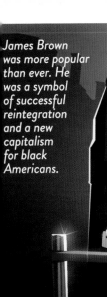

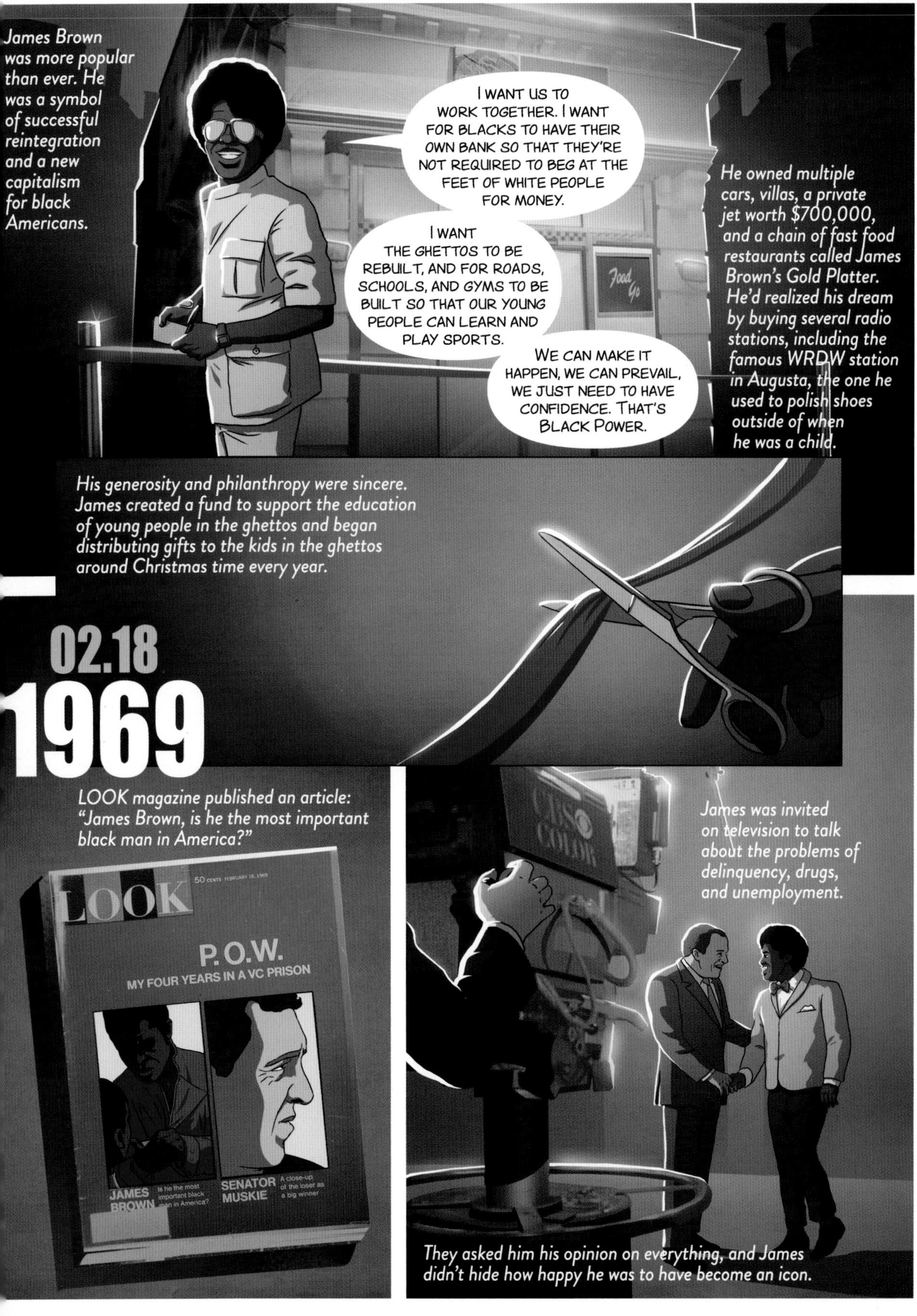

James Brown was more popular than ever. He was a symbol of successful reintegration and a new capitalism for black Americans.
I WANT US TO WORK TOGETHER. I WANT FOR BLACKS TO HAVE THEIR OWN BANK SO THAT THEY'RE NOT REQUIRED TO BEG AT THE FEET OF WHITE PEOPLE FOR MONEY.
I WANT THE GHETTOS TO BE REBUILT, AND FOR ROADS, SCHOOLS, AND GYMS TO BE BUILT SO THAT OUR YOUNG PEOPLE CAN LEARN AND PLAY SPORTS.
WE CAN MAKE IT HAPPEN, WE CAN PREVAIL, WE JUST NEED TO HAVE CONFIDENCE. THAT'S BLACK POWER.
He owned multiple cars, villas, a private jet worth $700,000, and a chain of fast food restaurants called James Brown's Gold Platter. He'd realized his dream by buying several radio stations, including the famous WRDW station in Augusta, the one he used to polish shoes outside of when he was a child.
His generosity and philanthropy were sincere. James created a fund to support the education of young people in the ghettos and began distributing gifts to the kids in the ghettos around Christmas time every year.
02.18
1969
LOOK magazine published an article: "James Brown, is he the most important black man in America?"
LOOK
50 CENTS · FEBRUARY 18, 1969
P.O.W.
MY FOUR YEARS IN A VC PRISON
JAMES BROWN
Is he the most important black man in America?
SENATOR MUSKIE
A close-up of the loser as a big winner
CBS COLOR
James was invited on television to talk about the problems of delinquency, drugs, and unemployment.
They asked him his opinion on everything, and James didn't hide how happy he was to have become an icon.

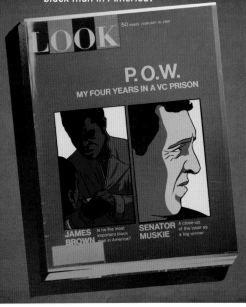

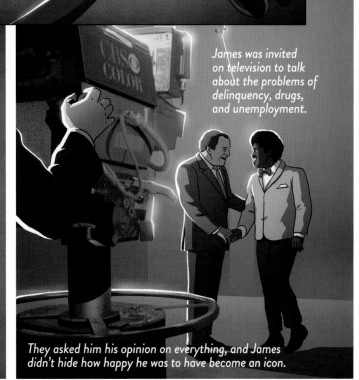

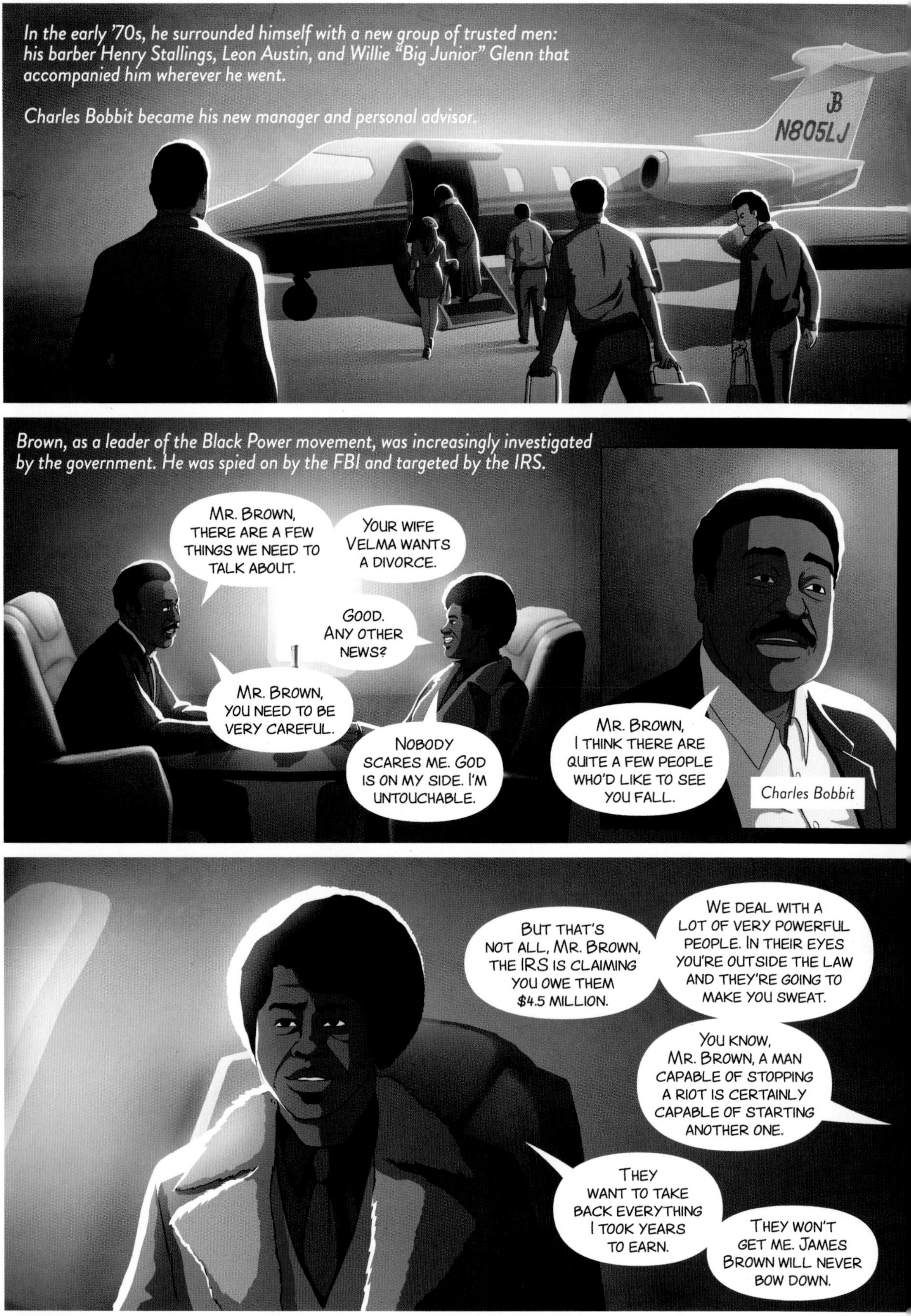
In the early '70s, he surrounded himself with a new group of trusted men: his barber Henry Stallings, Leon Austin, and Willie "Big Junior" Glenn that accompanied him wherever he went.
Charles Bobbit became his new manager and personal advisor.
JB
N805LJ
Brown, as a leader of the Black Power movement, was increasingly investigated by the government. He was spied on by the FBI and targeted by the IRS.
MR. BROWN, THERE ARE A FEW THINGS WE NEED TO TALK ABOUT.
YOUR WIFE VELMA WANTS A DIVORCE.
GOOD. ANY OTHER NEWS?
MR. BROWN, YOU NEED TO BE VERY CAREFUL.
NOBODY SCARES ME. GOD IS ON MY SIDE. I'M UNTOUCHABLE.
MR. BROWN, I THINK THERE ARE QUITE A FEW PEOPLE WHO'D LIKE TO SEE YOU FALL.
Charles Bobbit
BUT THAT'S NOT ALL, MR. BROWN, THE IRS IS CLAIMING YOU OWE THEM $4.5 MILLION.
WE DEAL WITH A LOT OF VERY POWERFUL PEOPLE. IN THEIR EYES YOU'RE OUTSIDE THE LAW AND THEY'RE GOING TO MAKE YOU SWEAT.
YOU KNOW, MR. BROWN, A MAN CAPABLE OF STOPPING A RIOT IS CERTAINLY CAPABLE OF STARTING ANOTHER ONE.
THEY WANT TO TAKE BACK EVERYTHING I TOOK YEARS TO EARN.
THEY WON'T GET ME. JAMES BROWN WILL NEVER BOW DOWN.

THE DRUMMER GIVE SOME

...om then on, James Brown ...ntrolled the entire chain ...production of his records, ...m their actual recording ...their distribution to their ...omotion. And he continued ...his path.

He rehearsed every day, sometimes even the night after a concert.

Everything was planned down to the smallest detail for the concert to be perfect.

The boss' orders, when he said "Hit Me," "Good God," or "Give the Drummer Some," indicated a change to the piece, either a break or a solo which could go on for hours.

> WHEN YOU REHEARSE WITH JAMES, EVERYTHING YOU PREPARED BEFORE-HAND IS NO GOOD.

> WE WOULD WAIT FOR HIS INSTRUCTIONS AND PLAY THE RHYTHMS FOR HOURS UNTIL HE'D FINALLY SAY: "NOW THAT'S FUNKY."

> IN GENERAL, WE HAD TO TAKE EVERYTHING FROM THE TOP, AND SINCE NOTHING WAS WRITTEN DOWN, YOU HAD TO REMEMBER ALL OF IT.

Fred Wesley

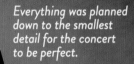

MARCH 1970 FUNKY DRUMMER

"Funky Drummer" was recorded on November 20th, 1969, in Cincinnati, and was released as a single at King Records in March 1970.

Clyde Stubblefield's drum riff became one of the most sampled rhythms in hip hop.

> I HATE THAT SONG. WE RECORDED IT REALLY LATE ONE NIGHT. IT WAS PROBABLY AROUND MIDNIGHT, AND ALL I WANTED TO DO WAS GO TO SLEEP.

> JAMES SAID: "GO ON CLYDE, DROP A BEAT." SO I DID, AND THEN IT ALL CAME TOGETHER IN LESS THAN FIVE MINUTES.

Clyde Stubblefield

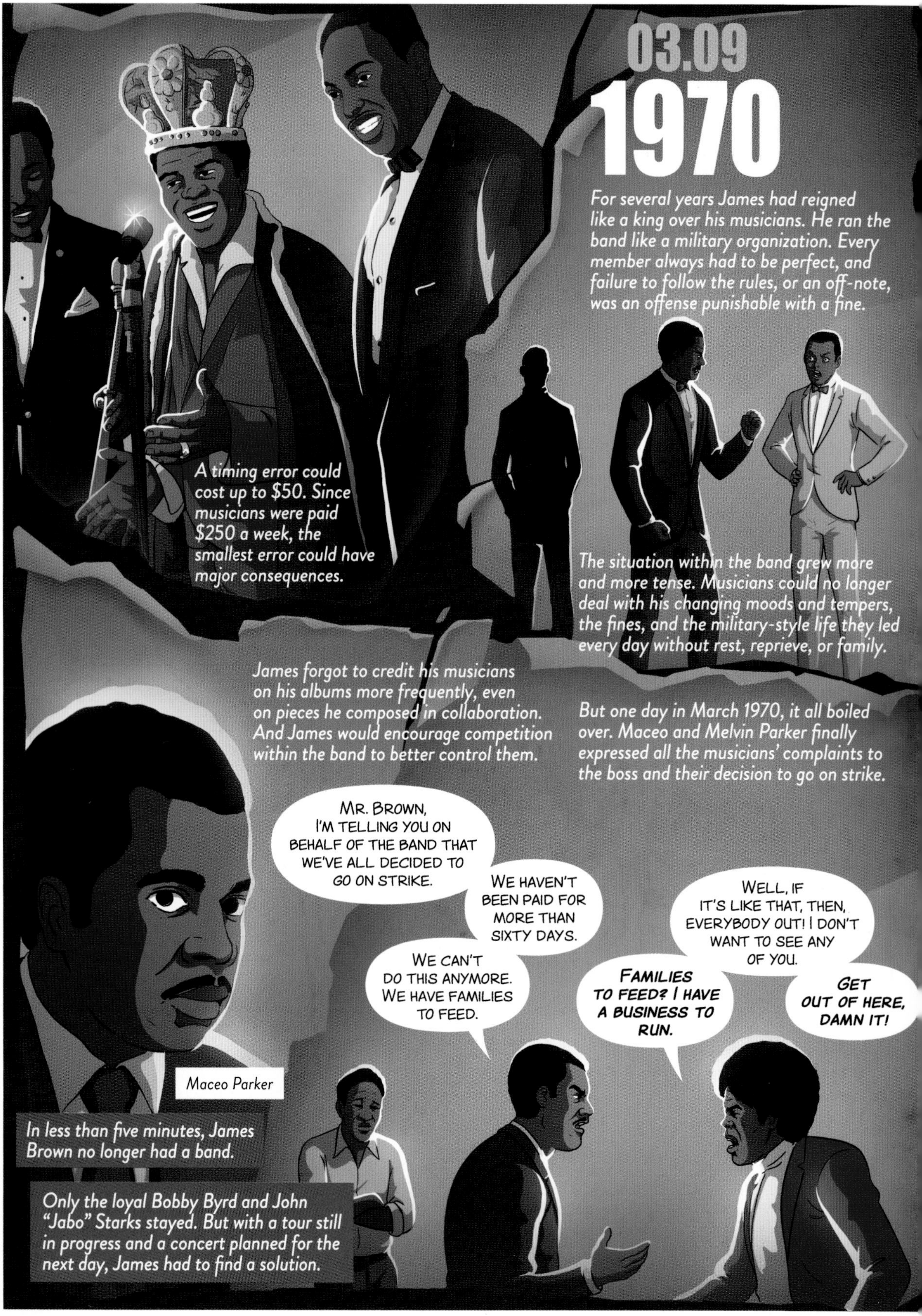

03.09
1970
For several years James had reigned like a king over his musicians. He ran the band like a military organization. Every member always had to be perfect, and failure to follow the rules, or an off-note, was an offense punishable with a fine.
A timing error could cost up to $50. Since musicians were paid $250 a week, the smallest error could have major consequences.
The situation within the band grew more and more tense. Musicians could no longer deal with his changing moods and tempers, the fines, and the military-style life they led every day without rest, reprieve, or family.
James forgot to credit his musicians on his albums more frequently, even on pieces he composed in collaboration. And James would encourage competition within the band to better control them.
But one day in March 1970, it all boiled over. Maceo and Melvin Parker finally expressed all the musicians' complaints to the boss and their decision to go on strike.
MR. BROWN, I'M TELLING YOU ON BEHALF OF THE BAND THAT WE'VE ALL DECIDED TO GO ON STRIKE.
WE HAVEN'T BEEN PAID FOR MORE THAN SIXTY DAYS.
WE CAN'T DO THIS ANYMORE. WE HAVE FAMILIES TO FEED.
WELL, IF IT'S LIKE THAT, THEN, EVERYBODY OUT! I DON'T WANT TO SEE ANY OF YOU.
FAMILIES TO FEED? I HAVE A BUSINESS TO RUN.
GET OUT OF HERE, DAMN IT!
Maceo Parker
In less than five minutes, James Brown no longer had a band.
Only the loyal Bobby Byrd and John "Jabo" Starks stayed. But with a tour still in progress and a concert planned for the next day, James had to find a solution.

So he asked Bobby Byrd to take his private jet and go to Cincinnati to get The Pacesetters.

The band in which William "Bootsy" Collins played bass and Phelps "Catfish" Collins played guitar.

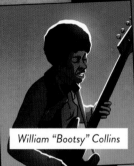
William "Bootsy" Collins

Phelps "Catfish" Collins

They'd been to King Records from time to time and James and Bobby had already noticed them.

That night, without even a single rehearsal, the Collins brothers and the other members of the Pacesetters got on stage in Colombus, Georgia like nothing had happened.

Maceo Parker, Fred Wesley, and all the other musicians watched from the wings of the concert, stunned to see James with another band.

IN SHOW BUSINESS, YOU HAVE TO BE PREPARED FOR CHANGE. WHAT COUNTS IS YOUR ABILITY TO LEAD YOUR TEAM TO VICTORY.

MUSIC IS A BUSINESS BEFORE ANYTHING ELSE. IT'S A WAY TO MAKE MONEY...

THE PEOPLE WHO WANT TO WORK FOR ME BETTER HANG ON, OR ELSE THEY MAY AS WELL GO HOME.

THEY SAY I'M A WORKAHOLIC, THE HARDEST WORKING MAN IN SHOW BUSINESS. WELL, I TAKE IT AS A COMPLIMENT! WORKING HARD HAS NEVER SCARED ME, AND GOD KNOWS YOU HAVE TO WORK IF YOU WANT TO PLAY MORE THAN 350 CONCERTS PER YEAR.

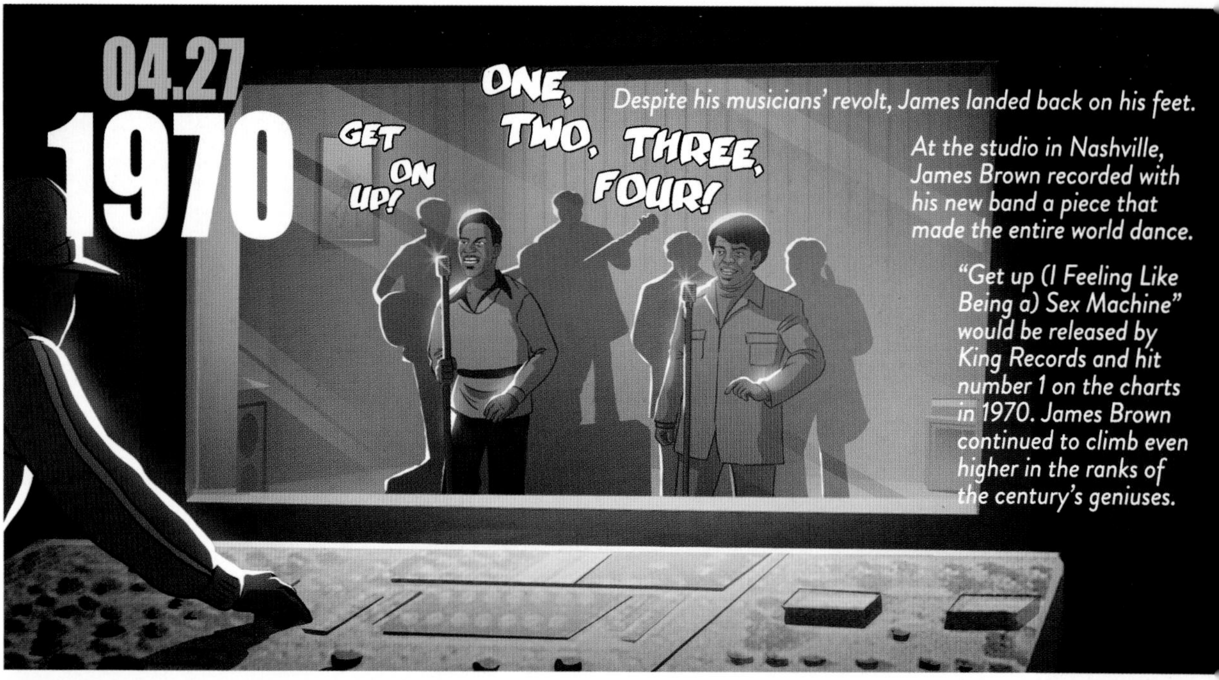
04.27
1970
GET ON UP!
ONE, TWO, THREE, FOUR!
Despite his musicians' revolt, James landed back on his feet.
At the studio in Nashville, James Brown recorded with his new band a piece that made the entire world dance.
"Get up (I Feeling Like Being a) Sex Machine" would be released by King Records and hit number 1 on the charts in 1970. James Brown continued to climb even higher in the ranks of the century's geniuses.

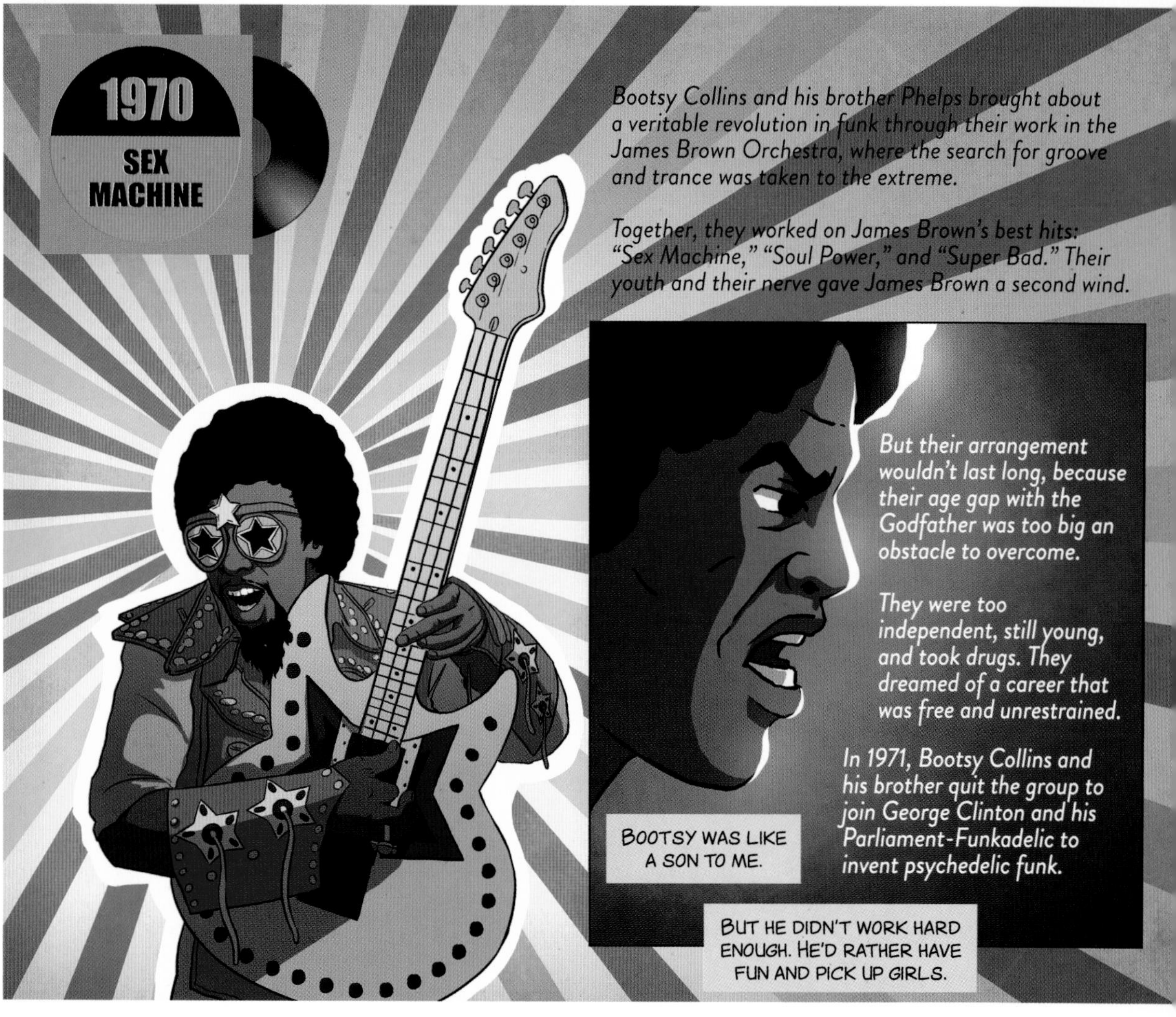
1970
SEX MACHINE
Bootsy Collins and his brother Phelps brought about a veritable revolution in funk through their work in the James Brown Orchestra, where the search for groove and trance was taken to the extreme.
Together, they worked on James Brown's best hits: "Sex Machine," "Soul Power," and "Super Bad." Their youth and their nerve gave James Brown a second wind.
But their arrangement wouldn't last long, because their age gap with the Godfather was too big an obstacle to overcome.
They were too independent, still young, and took drugs. They dreamed of a career that was free and unrestrained.
In 1971, Bootsy Collins and his brother quit the group to join George Clinton and his Parliament-Funkadelic to invent psychedelic funk.
BOOTSY WAS LIKE A SON TO ME.
BUT HE DIDN'T WORK HARD ENOUGH. HE'D RATHER HAVE FUN AND PICK UP GIRLS.

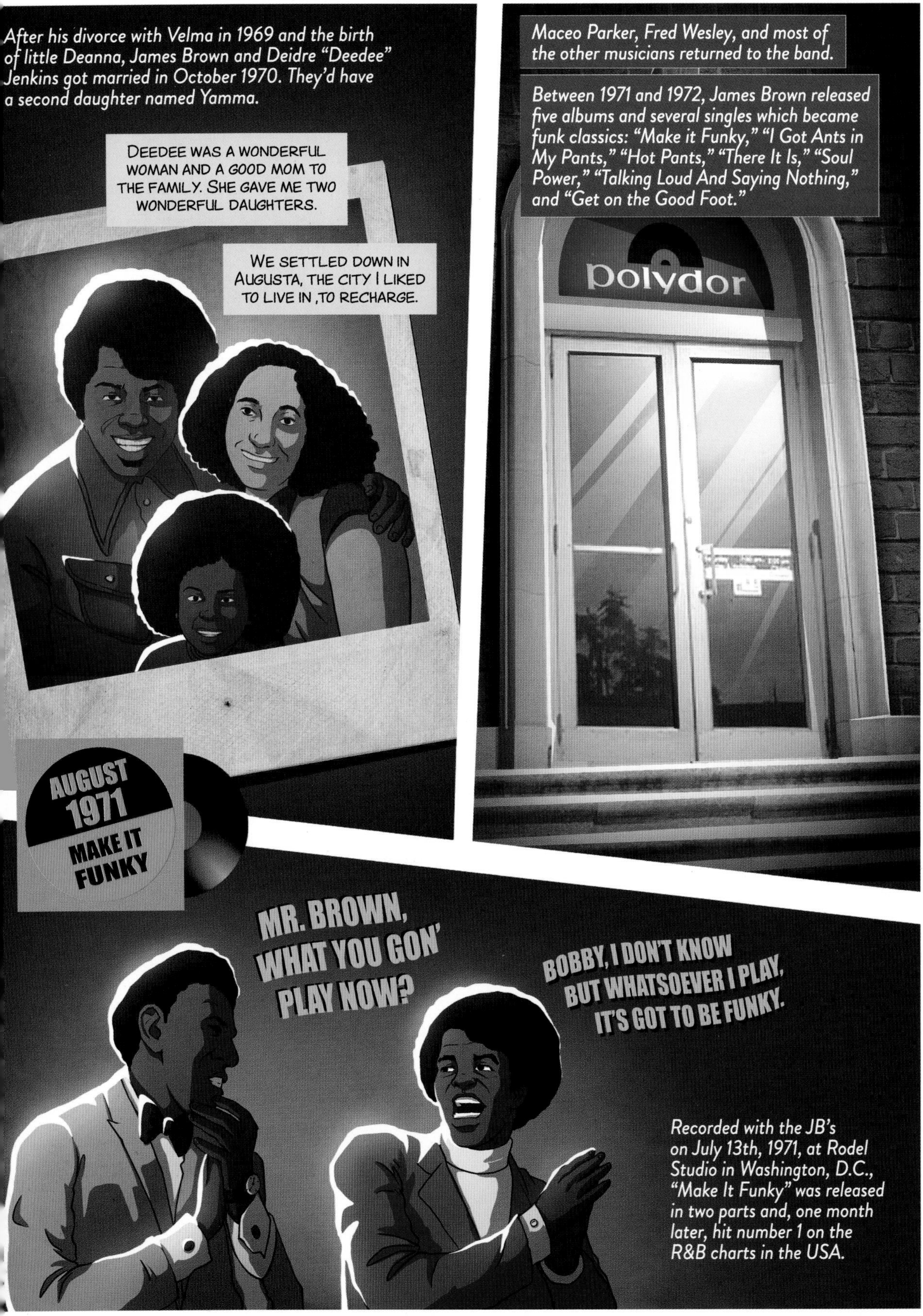
After his divorce with Velma in 1969 and the birth of little Deanna, James Brown and Deidre "Deedee" Jenkins got married in October 1970. They'd have a second daughter named Yamma.
DEEDEE WAS A WONDERFUL WOMAN AND A GOOD MOM TO THE FAMILY. SHE GAVE ME TWO WONDERFUL DAUGHTERS.
WE SETTLED DOWN IN AUGUSTA, THE CITY I LIKED TO LIVE IN ,TO RECHARGE.
Maceo Parker, Fred Wesley, and most of the other musicians returned to the band.
Between 1971 and 1972, James Brown released five albums and several singles which became funk classics: "Make it Funky," "I Got Ants in My Pants," "Hot Pants," "There It Is," "Soul Power," "Talking Loud And Saying Nothing," and "Get on the Good Foot."
polydor
AUGUST 1971
MAKE IT FUNKY
MR. BROWN, WHAT YOU GON' PLAY NOW?
BOBBY, I DON'T KNOW BUT WHATSOEVER I PLAY, IT'S GOT TO BE FUNKY.
Recorded with the JB's on July 13th, 1971, at Rodel Studio in Washington, D.C., "Make It Funky" was released in two parts and, one month later, hit number 1 on the R&B charts in the USA.

FAITH IS THE
ONLY SONG THAT
HAS DRIVEN ME
AND PUSHED ME
TO CONTINUE.

-5-
THE PAYBACK

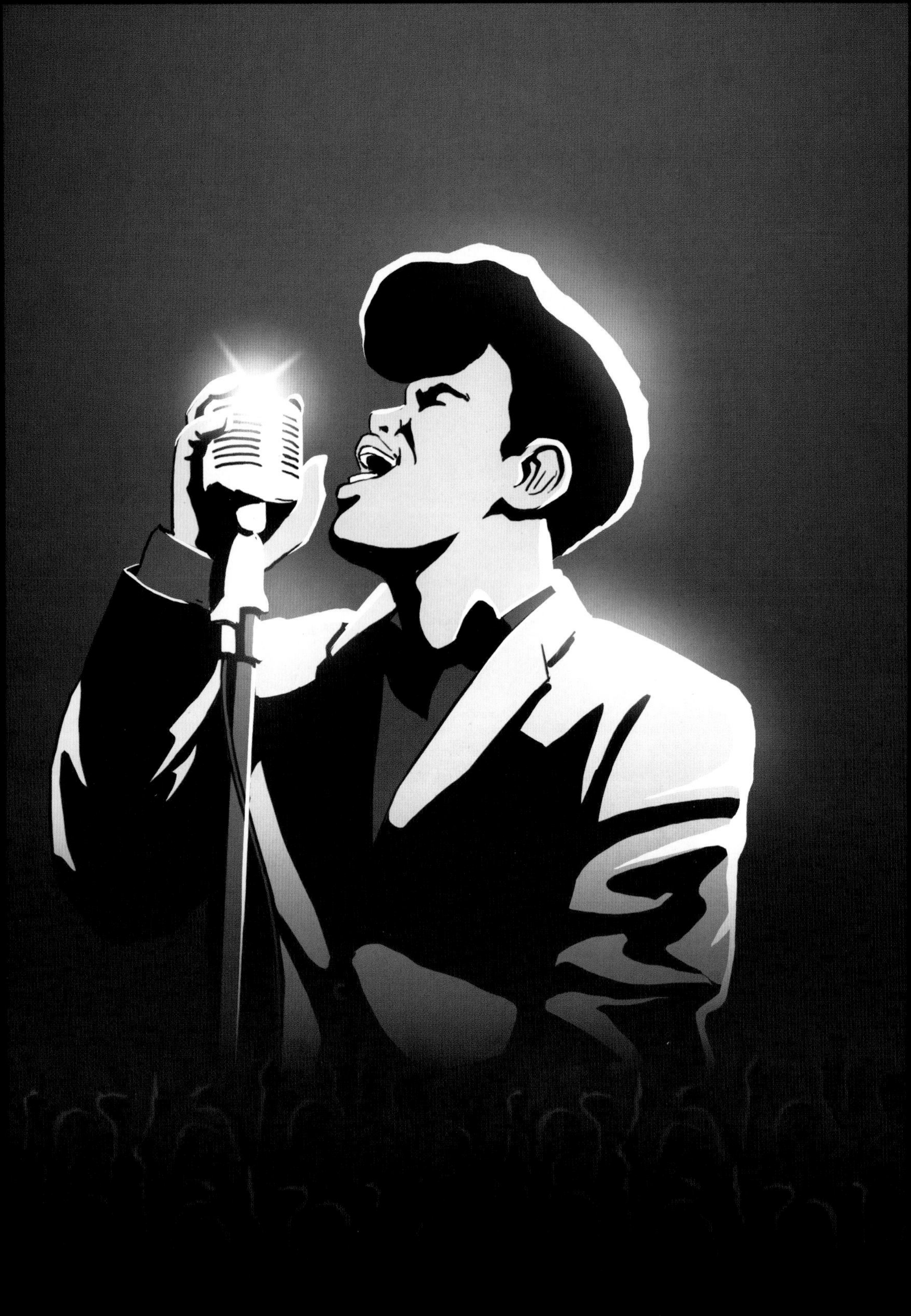

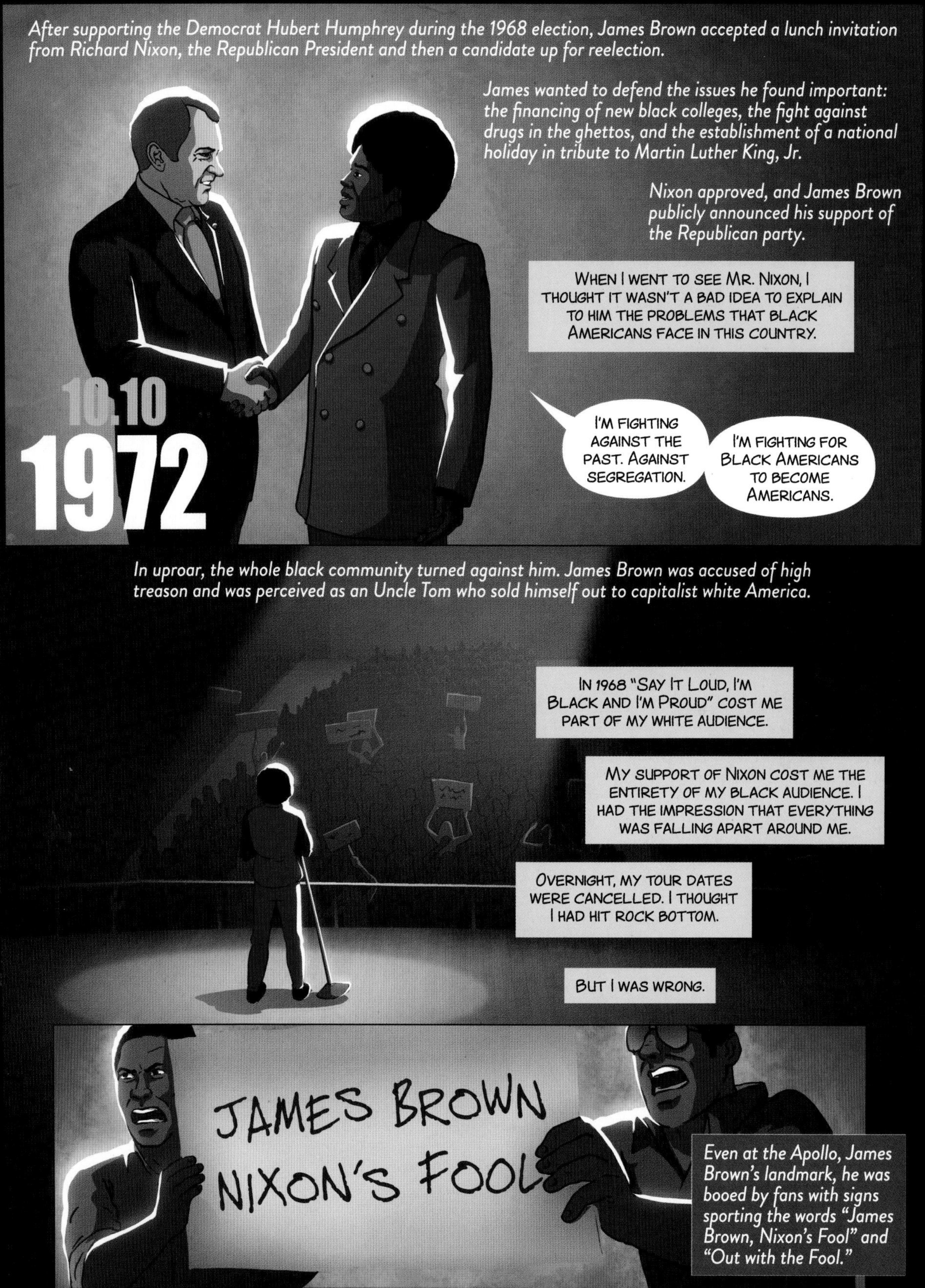
After supporting the Democrat Hubert Humphrey during the 1968 election, James Brown accepted a lunch invitation from Richard Nixon, the Republican President and then a candidate up for reelection.
James wanted to defend the issues he found important: the financing of new black colleges, the fight against drugs in the ghettos, and the establishment of a national holiday in tribute to Martin Luther King, Jr.
Nixon approved, and James Brown publicly announced his support of the Republican party.
WHEN I WENT TO SEE MR. NIXON, I THOUGHT IT WASN'T A BAD IDEA TO EXPLAIN TO HIM THE PROBLEMS THAT BLACK AMERICANS FACE IN THIS COUNTRY.
10.10
1972
I'M FIGHTING AGAINST THE PAST. AGAINST SEGREGATION.
I'M FIGHTING FOR BLACK AMERICANS TO BECOME AMERICANS.
In uproar, the whole black community turned against him. James Brown was accused of high treason and was perceived as an Uncle Tom who sold himself out to capitalist white America.
IN 1968 "SAY IT LOUD, I'M BLACK AND I'M PROUD" COST ME PART OF MY WHITE AUDIENCE.
MY SUPPORT OF NIXON COST ME THE ENTIRETY OF MY BLACK AUDIENCE. I HAD THE IMPRESSION THAT EVERYTHING WAS FALLING APART AROUND ME.
OVERNIGHT, MY TOUR DATES WERE CANCELLED. I THOUGHT I HAD HIT ROCK BOTTOM.
BUT I WAS WRONG.
JAMES BROWN
NIXON'S FOOL
Even at the Apollo, James Brown's landmark, he was booed by fans with signs sporting the words "James Brown, Nixon's Fool" and "Out with the Fool."

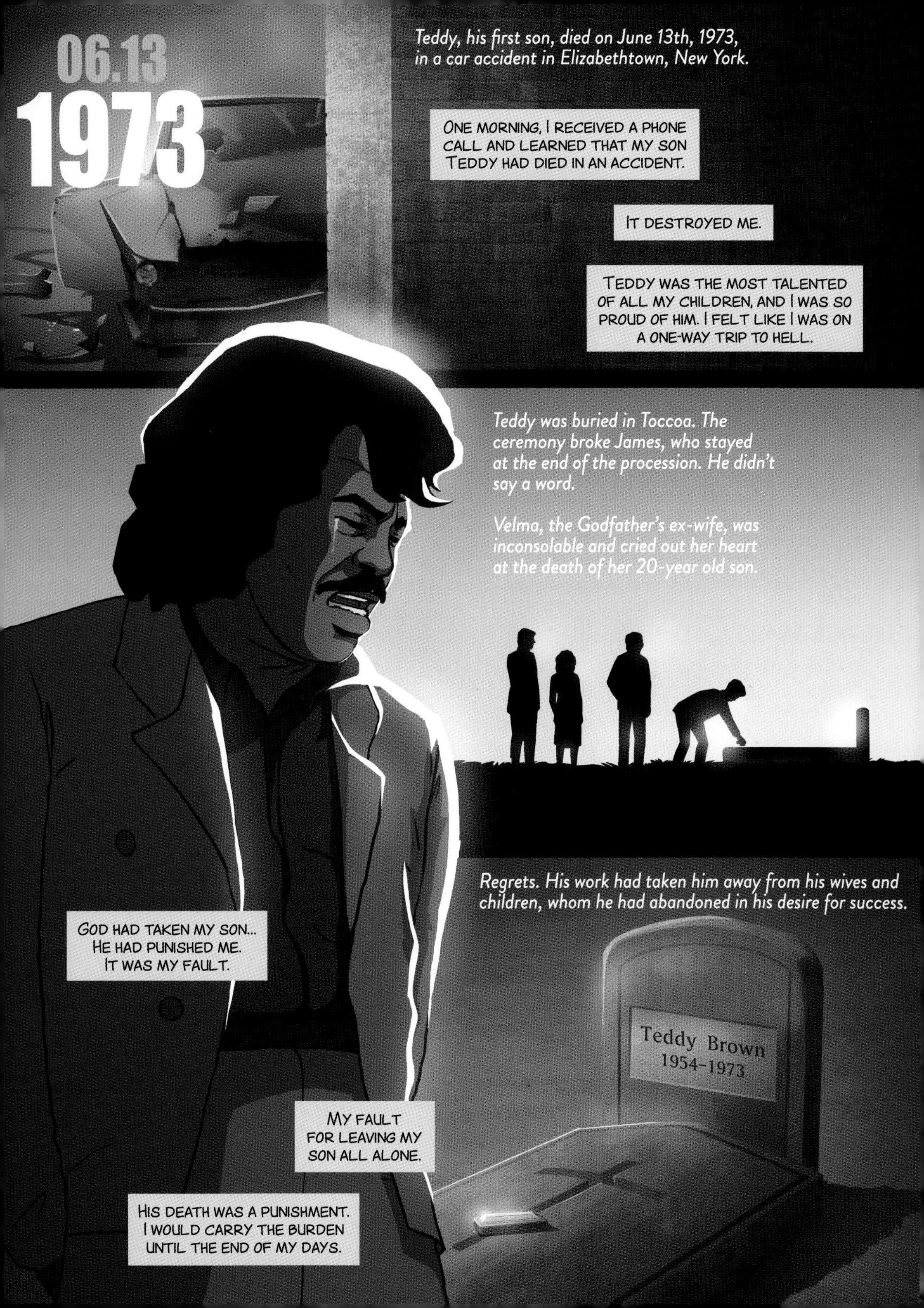
06.13
1973
Teddy, his first son, died on June 13th, 1973, in a car accident in Elizabethtown, New York.
ONE MORNING, I RECEIVED A PHONE CALL AND LEARNED THAT MY SON TEDDY HAD DIED IN AN ACCIDENT.
IT DESTROYED ME.
TEDDY WAS THE MOST TALENTED OF ALL MY CHILDREN, AND I WAS SO PROUD OF HIM. I FELT LIKE I WAS ON A ONE-WAY TRIP TO HELL.
Teddy was buried in Toccoa. The ceremony broke James, who stayed at the end of the procession. He didn't say a word.
Velma, the Godfather's ex-wife, was inconsolable and cried out her heart at the death of her 20-year old son.
Regrets. His work had taken him away from his wives and children, whom he had abandoned in his desire for success.
GOD HAD TAKEN MY SON... HE HAD PUNISHED ME. IT WAS MY FAULT.
Teddy Brown
1954–1973
MY FAULT FOR LEAVING MY SON ALL ALONE.
HIS DEATH WAS A PUNISHMENT. I WOULD CARRY THE BURDEN UNTIL THE END OF MY DAYS.

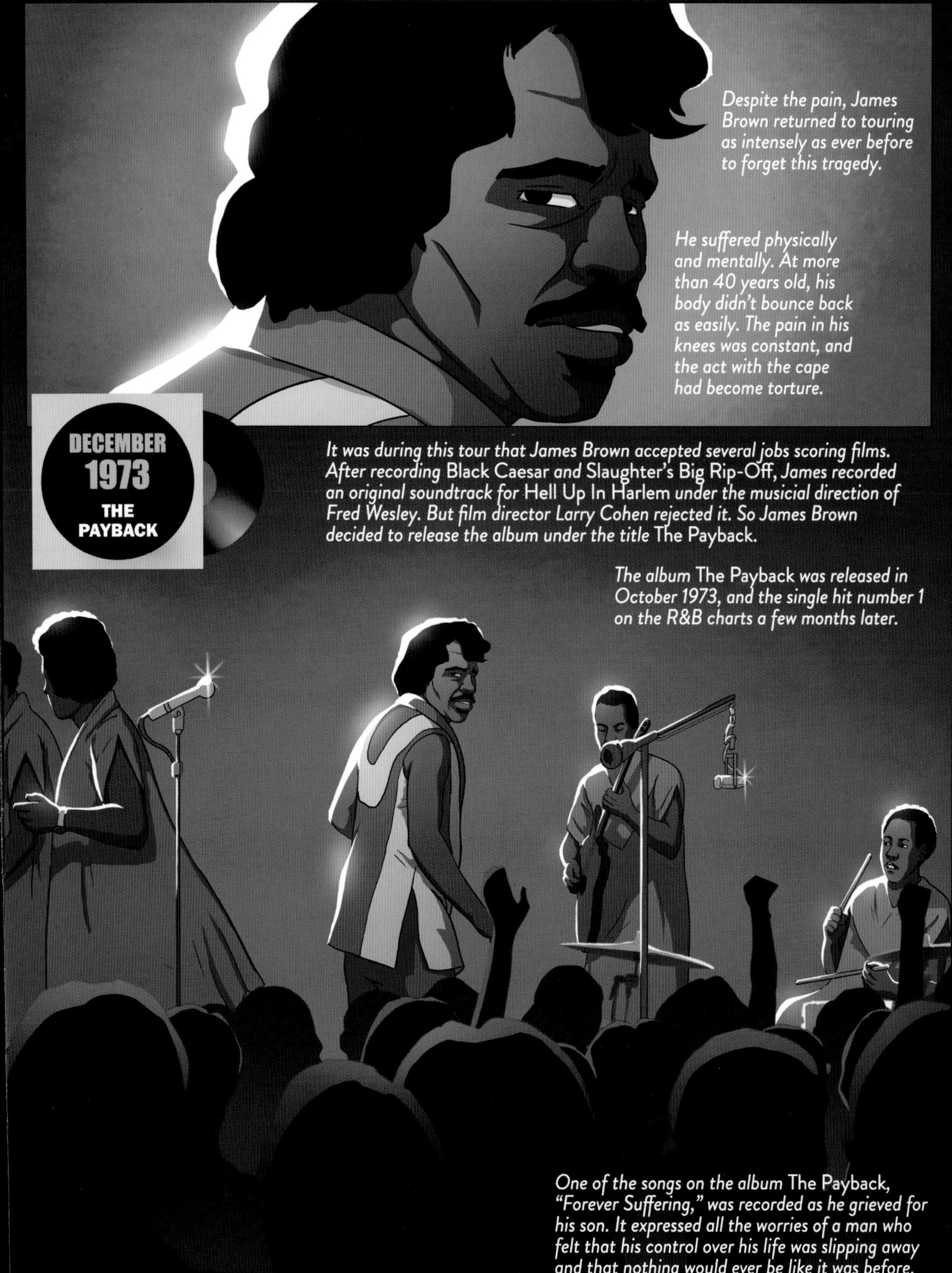
Despite the pain, James Brown returned to touring as intensely as ever before to forget this tragedy.
He suffered physically and mentally. At more than 40 years old, his body didn't bounce back as easily. The pain in his knees was constant, and the act with the cape had become torture.
DECEMBER 1973 THE PAYBACK
It was during this tour that James Brown accepted several jobs scoring films. After recording Black Caesar and Slaughter's Big Rip-Off, James recorded an original soundtrack for Hell Up In Harlem under the musicial direction of Fred Wesley. But film director Larry Cohen rejected it. So James Brown decided to release the album under the title The Payback.
The album The Payback was released in October 1973, and the single hit number 1 on the R&B charts a few months later.
One of the songs on the album The Payback, "Forever Suffering," was recorded as he grieved for his son. It expressed all the worries of a man who felt that his control over his life was slipping away and that nothing would ever be like it was before.

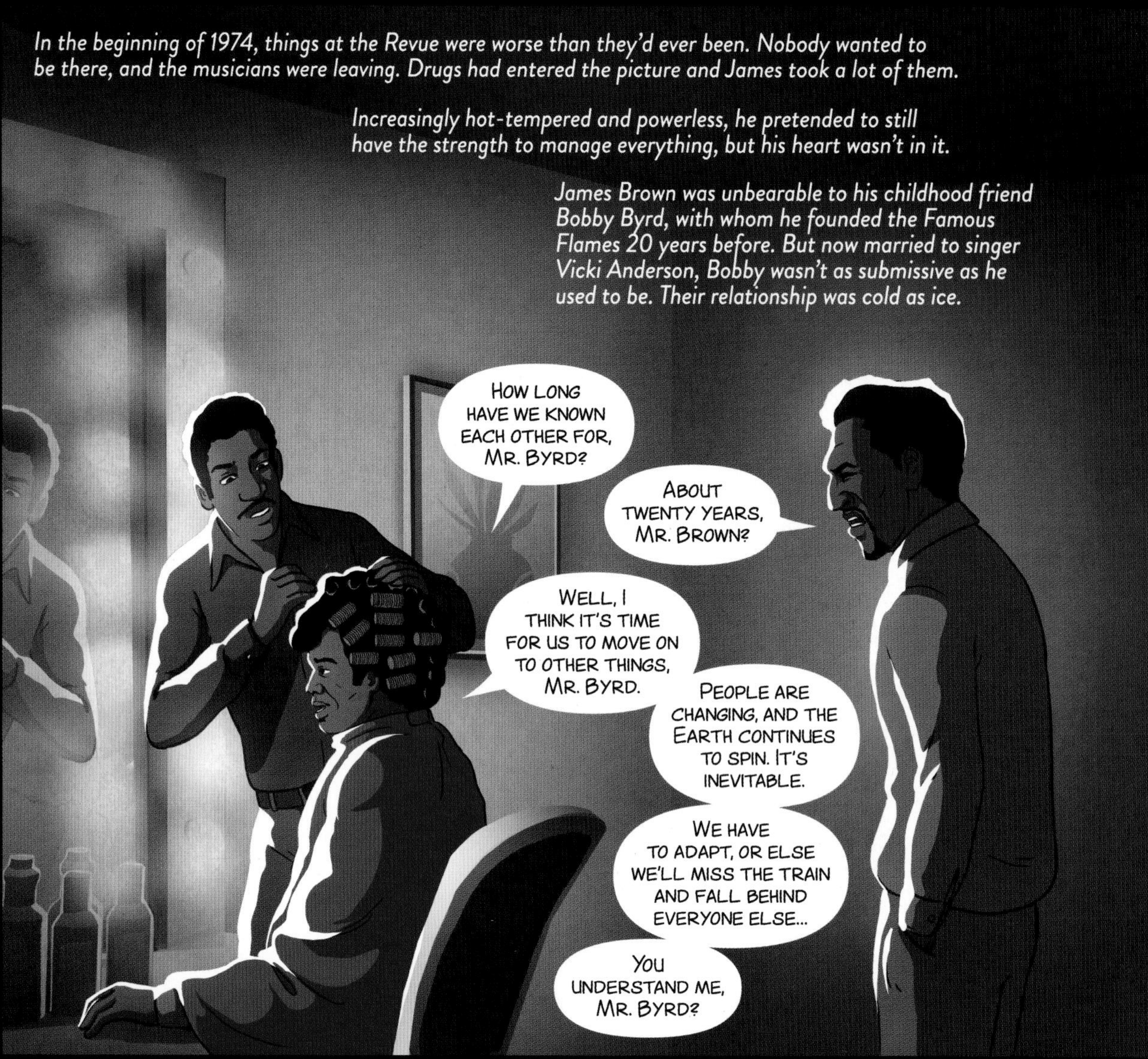
In the beginning of 1974, things at the Revue were worse than they'd ever been. Nobody wanted to be there, and the musicians were leaving. Drugs had entered the picture and James took a lot of them.
Increasingly hot-tempered and powerless, he pretended to still have the strength to manage everything, but his heart wasn't in it.
James Brown was unbearable to his childhood friend Bobby Byrd, with whom he founded the Famous Flames 20 years before. But now married to singer Vicki Anderson, Bobby wasn't as submissive as he used to be. Their relationship was cold as ice.
HOW LONG HAVE WE KNOWN EACH OTHER FOR, MR. BYRD?
ABOUT TWENTY YEARS, MR. BROWN?
WELL, I THINK IT'S TIME FOR US TO MOVE ON TO OTHER THINGS, MR. BYRD.
PEOPLE ARE CHANGING, AND THE EARTH CONTINUES TO SPIN. IT'S INEVITABLE.
WE HAVE TO ADAPT, OR ELSE WE'LL MISS THE TRAIN AND FALL BEHIND EVERYONE ELSE...
YOU UNDERSTAND ME, MR. BYRD?

James Brown fired him bluntly and without explanation. Bobby Byrd didn't fight it, likely tired by all the years of loyalty and submission, tolerating James' anger and humiliation. He decided to leave for his own good, too.

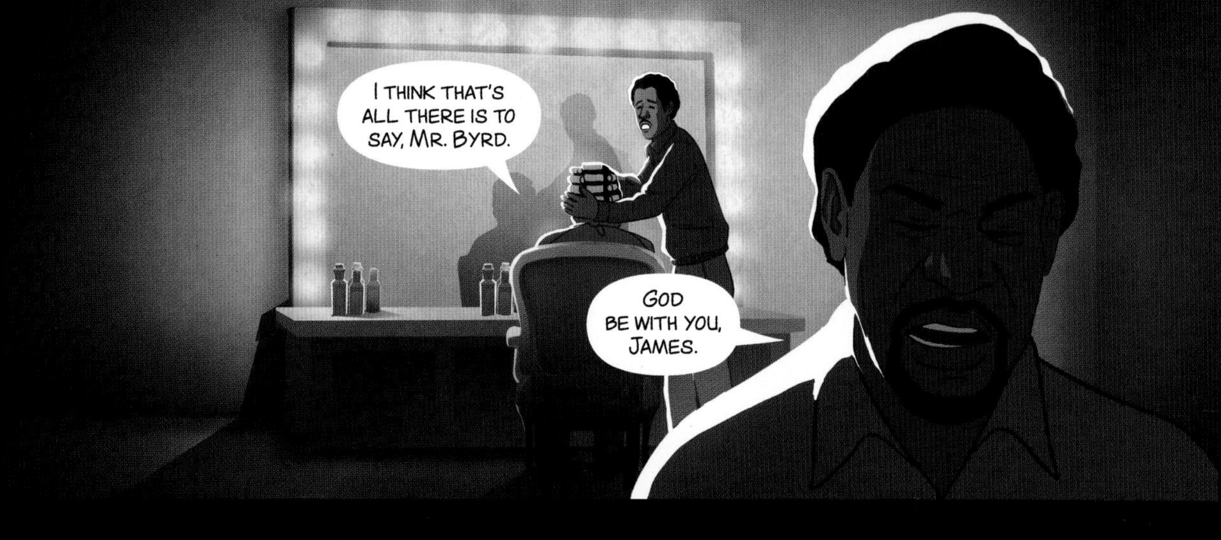
I THINK THAT'S ALL THERE IS TO SAY, MR. BYRD.
GOD BE WITH YOU, JAMES.

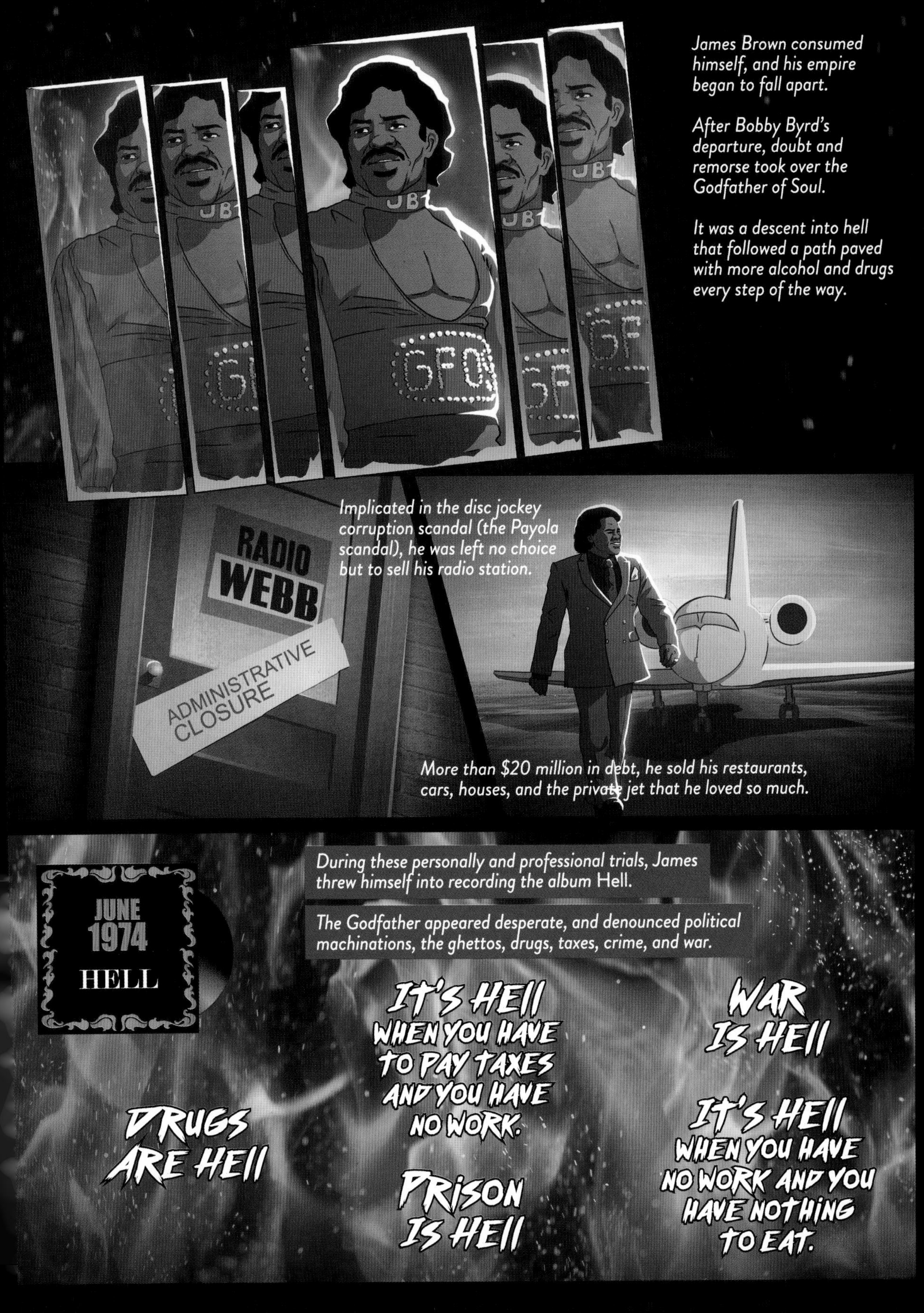

James Brown consumed himself, and his empire began to fall apart.
After Bobby Byrd's departure, doubt and remorse took over the Godfather of Soul.
It was a descent into hell that followed a path paved with more alcohol and drugs every step of the way.
JB
GFOS
RADIO WEBB
ADMINISTRATIVE CLOSURE
Implicated in the disc jockey corruption scandal (the Payola scandal), he was left no choice but to sell his radio station.
More than $20 million in debt, he sold his restaurants, cars, houses, and the private jet that he loved so much.
JUNE 1974
HELL
During these personally and professional trials, James threw himself into recording the album Hell.
The Godfather appeared desperate, and denounced political machinations, the ghettos, drugs, taxes, crime, and war.
IT'S HELL WHEN YOU HAVE TO PAY TAXES AND YOU HAVE NO WORK.
WAR IS HELL
DRUGS ARE HELL
IT'S HELL WHEN YOU HAVE NO WORK AND YOU HAVE NOTHING TO EAT.
PRISON IS HELL

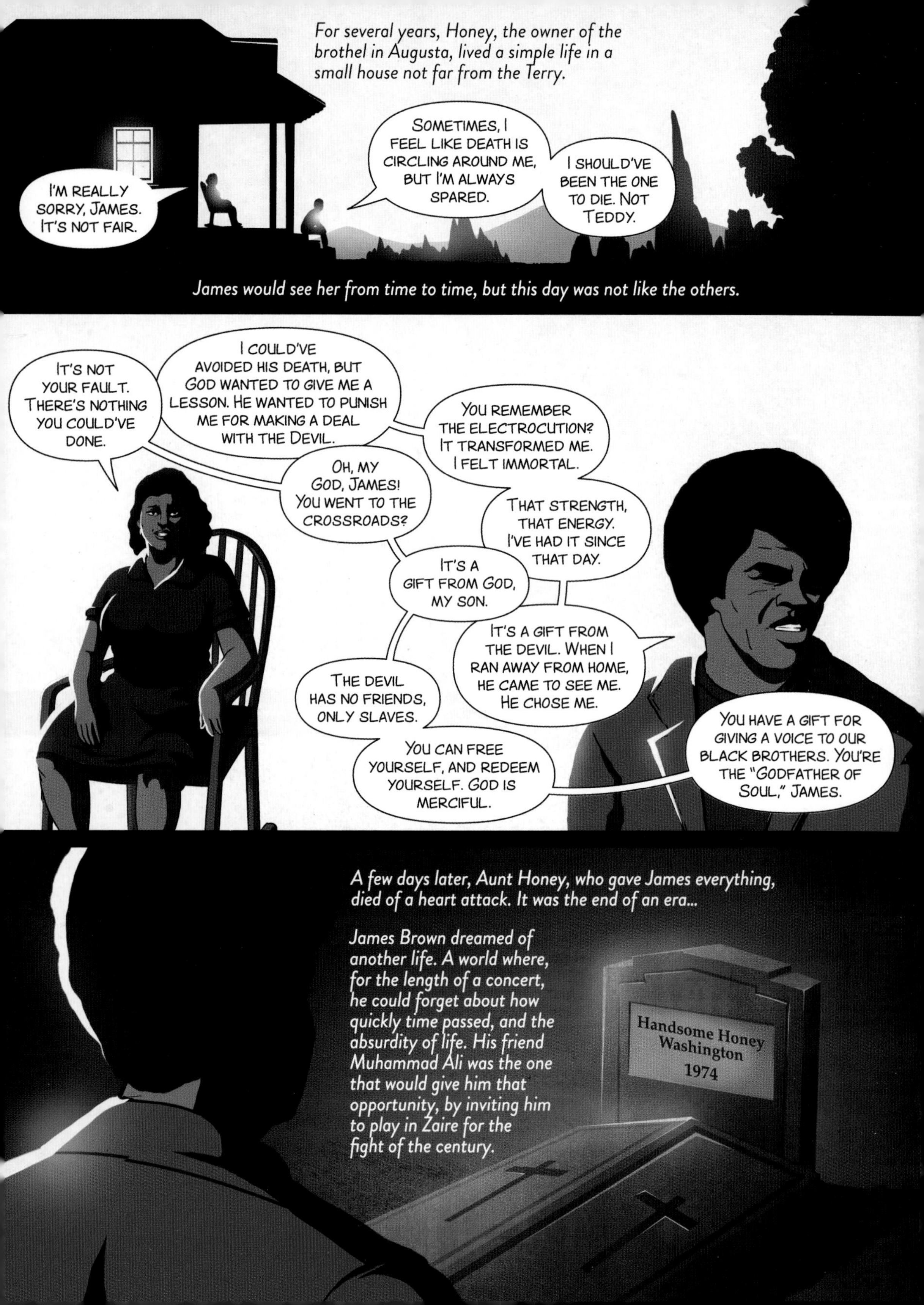
For several years, Honey, the owner of the brothel in Augusta, lived a simple life in a small house not far from the Terry.
I'M REALLY SORRY, JAMES. IT'S NOT FAIR.
SOMETIMES, I FEEL LIKE DEATH IS CIRCLING AROUND ME, BUT I'M ALWAYS SPARED.
I SHOULD'VE BEEN THE ONE TO DIE. NOT TEDDY.
James would see her from time to time, but this day was not like the others.
IT'S NOT YOUR FAULT. THERE'S NOTHING YOU COULD'VE DONE.
I COULD'VE AVOIDED HIS DEATH, BUT GOD WANTED TO GIVE ME A LESSON. HE WANTED TO PUNISH ME FOR MAKING A DEAL WITH THE DEVIL.
OH, MY GOD, JAMES! YOU WENT TO THE CROSSROADS?
YOU REMEMBER THE ELECTROCUTION? IT TRANSFORMED ME. I FELT IMMORTAL.
THAT STRENGTH, THAT ENERGY. I'VE HAD IT SINCE THAT DAY.
IT'S A GIFT FROM GOD, MY SON.
IT'S A GIFT FROM THE DEVIL. WHEN I RAN AWAY FROM HOME, HE CAME TO SEE ME. HE CHOSE ME.
THE DEVIL HAS NO FRIENDS, ONLY SLAVES.
YOU CAN FREE YOURSELF, AND REDEEM YOURSELF. GOD IS MERCIFUL.
YOU HAVE A GIFT FOR GIVING A VOICE TO OUR BLACK BROTHERS. YOU'RE THE "GODFATHER OF SOUL," JAMES.
A few days later, Aunt Honey, who gave James everything, died of a heart attack. It was the end of an era...
James Brown dreamed of another life. A world where, for the length of a concert, he could forget about how quickly time passed, and the absurdity of life. His friend Muhammad Ali was the one that would give him that opportunity, by inviting him to play in Zaire for the fight of the century.
Handsome Honey Washington 1974

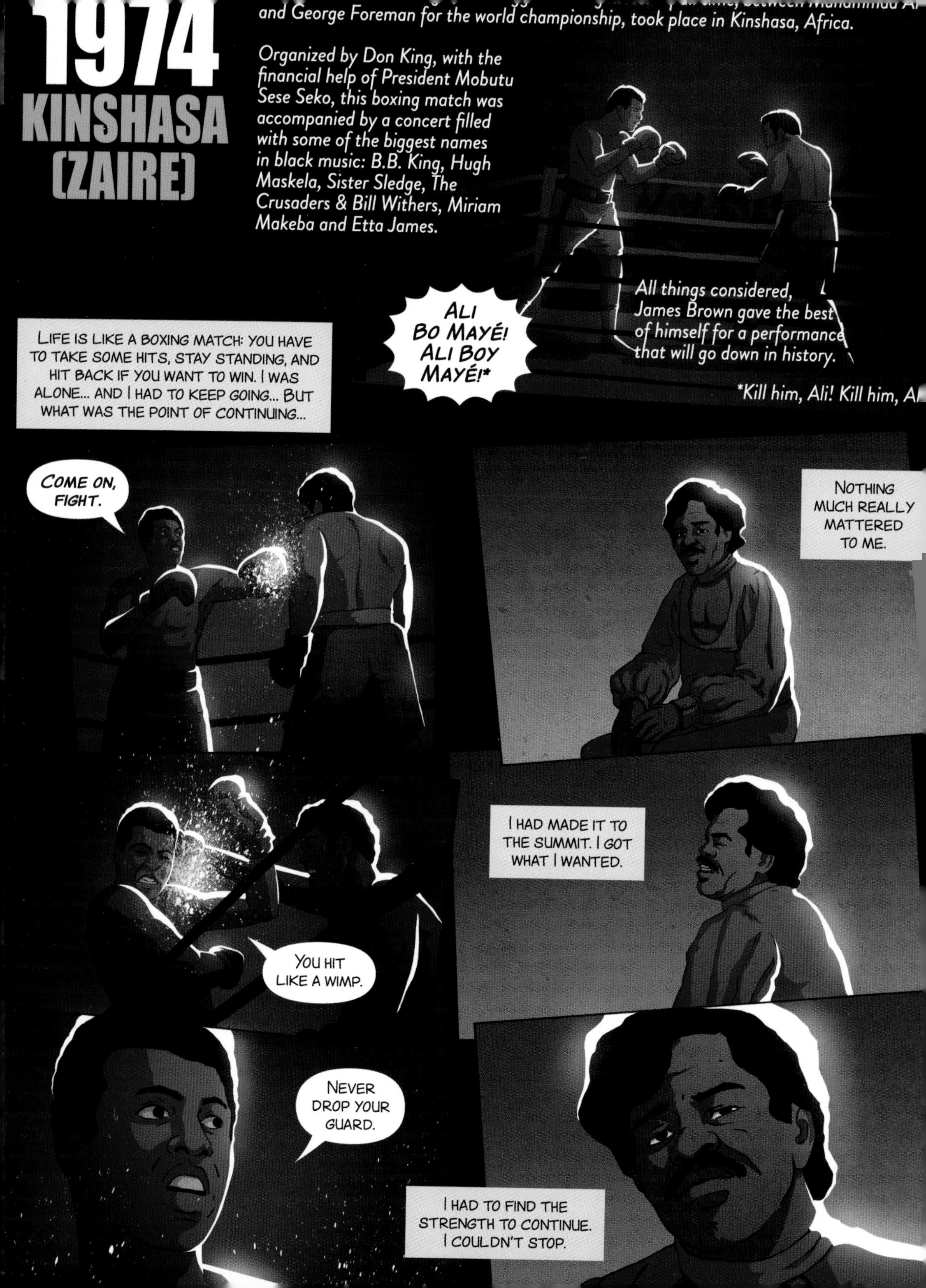
1974
KINSHASA (ZAIRE)
and George Foreman for the world championship, took place in Kinshasa, Africa.
Organized by Don King, with the financial help of President Mobutu Sese Seko, this boxing match was accompanied by a concert filled with some of the biggest names in black music: B.B. King, Hugh Maskela, Sister Sledge, The Crusaders & Bill Withers, Miriam Makeba and Etta James.
All things considered, James Brown gave the best of himself for a performance that will go down in history.
ALI BO MAYÉ! ALI BOY MAYÉ!*
*Kill him, Ali! Kill him,
LIFE IS LIKE A BOXING MATCH: YOU HAVE TO TAKE SOME HITS, STAY STANDING, AND HIT BACK IF YOU WANT TO WIN. I WAS ALONE... AND I HAD TO KEEP GOING... BUT WHAT WAS THE POINT OF CONTINUING...
COME ON, FIGHT.
NOTHING MUCH REALLY MATTERED TO ME.
I HAD MADE IT TO THE SUMMIT. I GOT WHAT I WANTED.
YOU HIT LIKE A WIMP.
NEVER DROP YOUR GUARD.
I HAD TO FIND THE STRENGTH TO CONTINUE. I COULDN'T STOP.

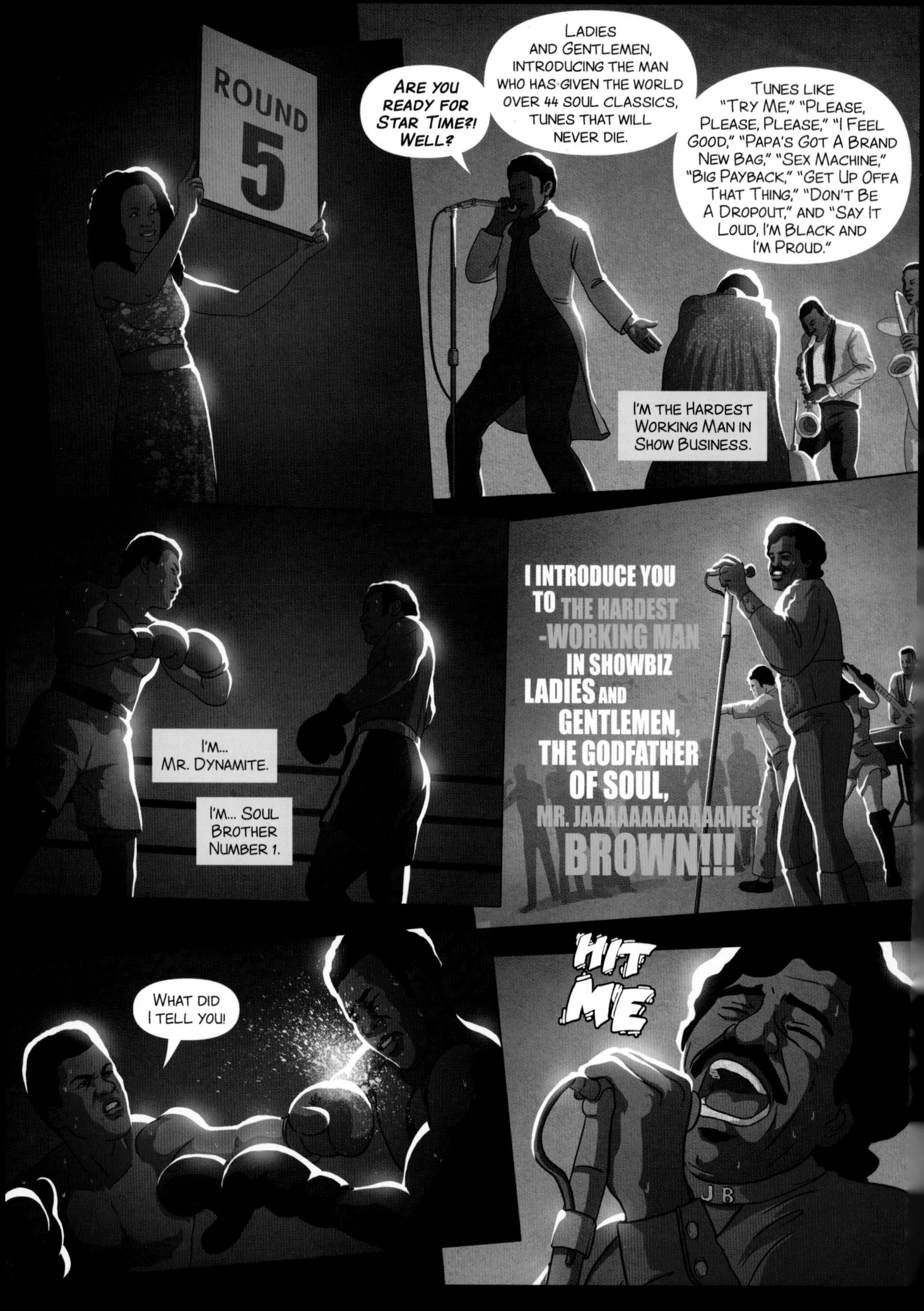
ROUND 5
ARE YOU READY FOR STAR TIME?! WELL?
LADIES AND GENTLEMEN, INTRODUCING THE MAN WHO HAS GIVEN THE WORLD OVER 44 SOUL CLASSICS, TUNES THAT WILL NEVER DIE.
TUNES LIKE "TRY ME," "PLEASE, PLEASE, PLEASE," "I FEEL GOOD," "PAPA'S GOT A BRAND NEW BAG," "SEX MACHINE," "BIG PAYBACK," "GET UP OFFA THAT THING," "DON'T BE A DROPOUT," AND "SAY IT LOUD, I'M BLACK AND I'M PROUD."
I'M THE HARDEST WORKING MAN IN SHOW BUSINESS.
I'M... MR. DYNAMITE.
I'M... SOUL BROTHER NUMBER 1.
I INTRODUCE YOU TO THE HARDEST -WORKING MAN IN SHOWBIZ LADIES AND GENTLEMEN, THE GODFATHER OF SOUL, MR. JAAAAAAAAAAAMES BROWN!!!
WHAT DID I TELL YOU!
HIT ME
JB

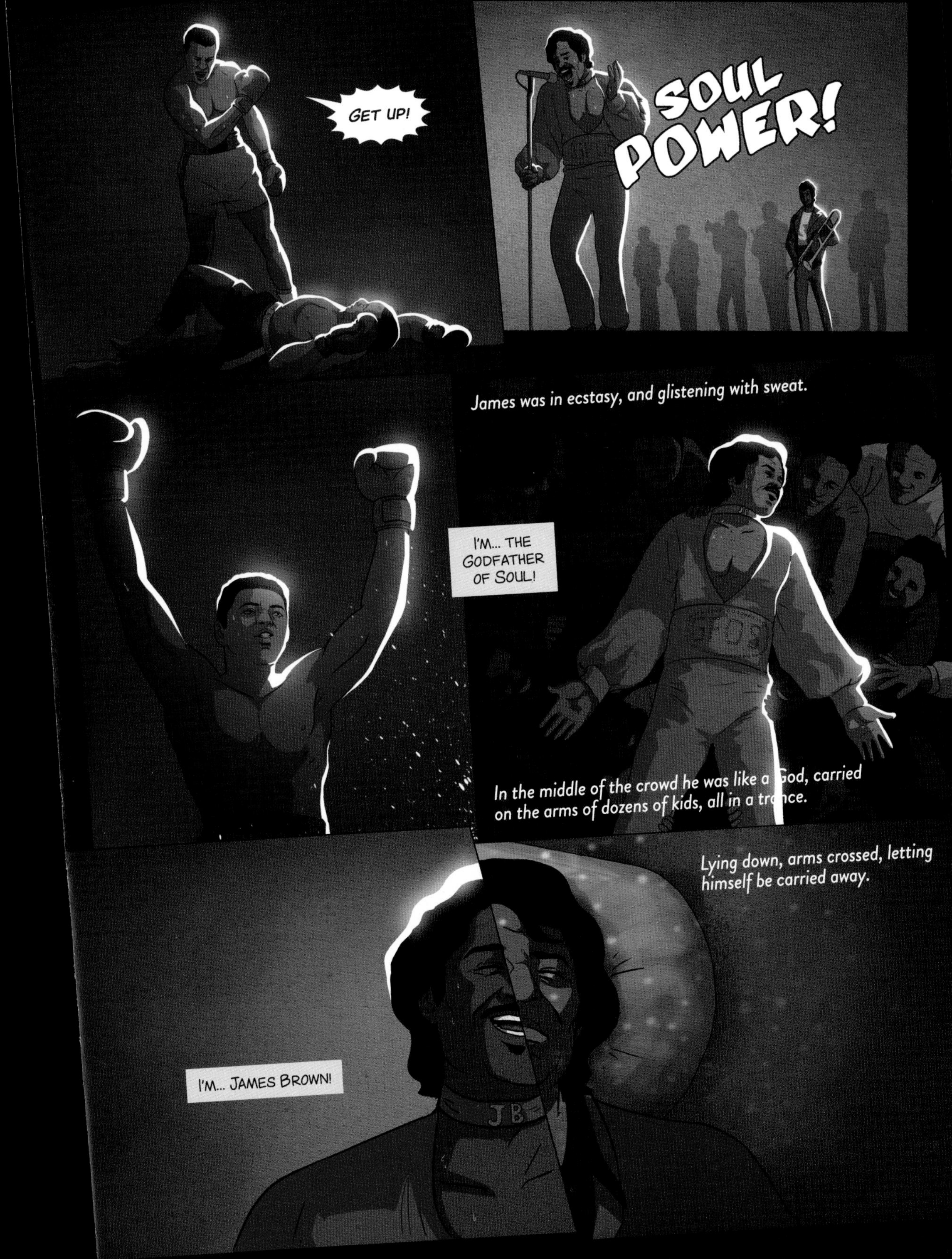
GET UP!
SOUL POWER!
James was in ecstasy, and glistening with sweat.
I'M... THE GODFATHER OF SOUL!
In the middle of the crowd he was like a God, carried on the arms of dozens of kids, all in a trance.
Lying down, arms crossed, letting himself be carried away.
I'M... JAMES BROWN!

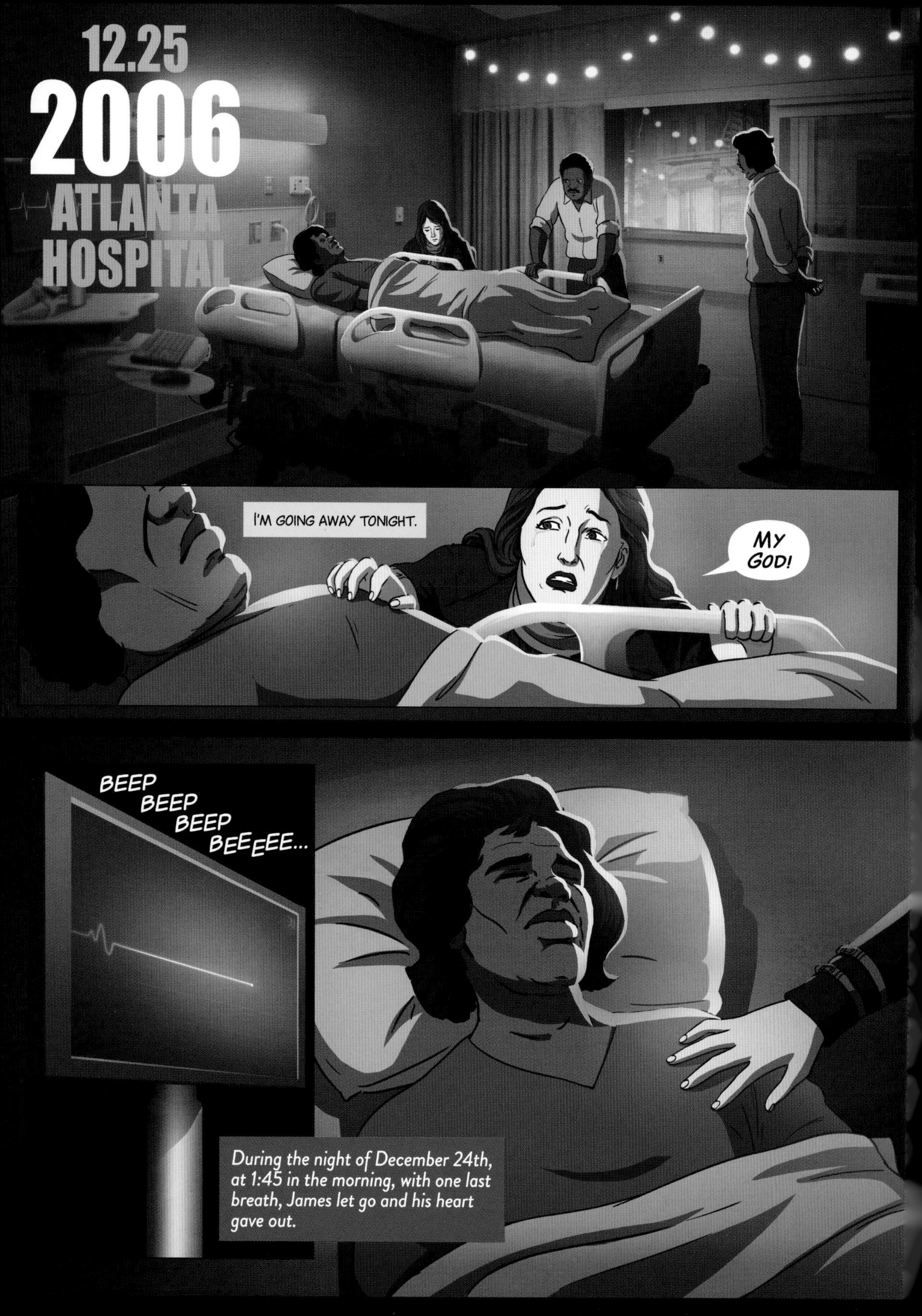
12.25
2006
ATLANTA
HOSPITAL
I'M GOING AWAY TONIGHT.
MY GOD!
BEEP
BEEP
BEEP
BEEEEE...
During the night of December 24th, at 1:45 in the morning, with one last breath, James let go and his heart gave out.

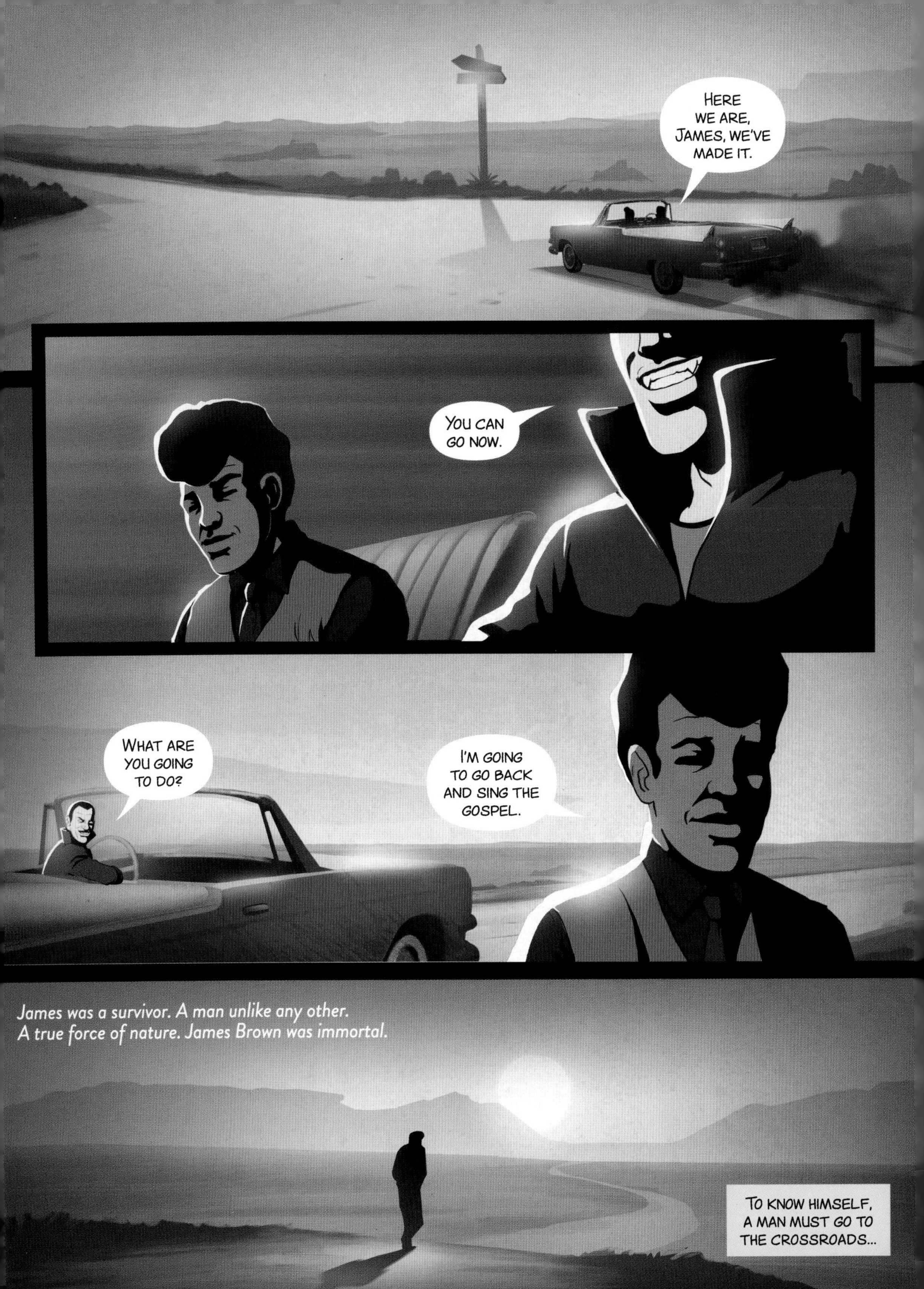
HERE WE ARE, JAMES, WE'VE MADE IT.
YOU CAN GO NOW.
WHAT ARE YOU GOING TO DO?
I'M GOING TO GO BACK AND SING THE GOSPEL.
James was a survivor. A man unlike any other. A true force of nature. James Brown was immortal.
TO KNOW HIMSELF, A MAN MUST GO TO THE CROSSROADS...

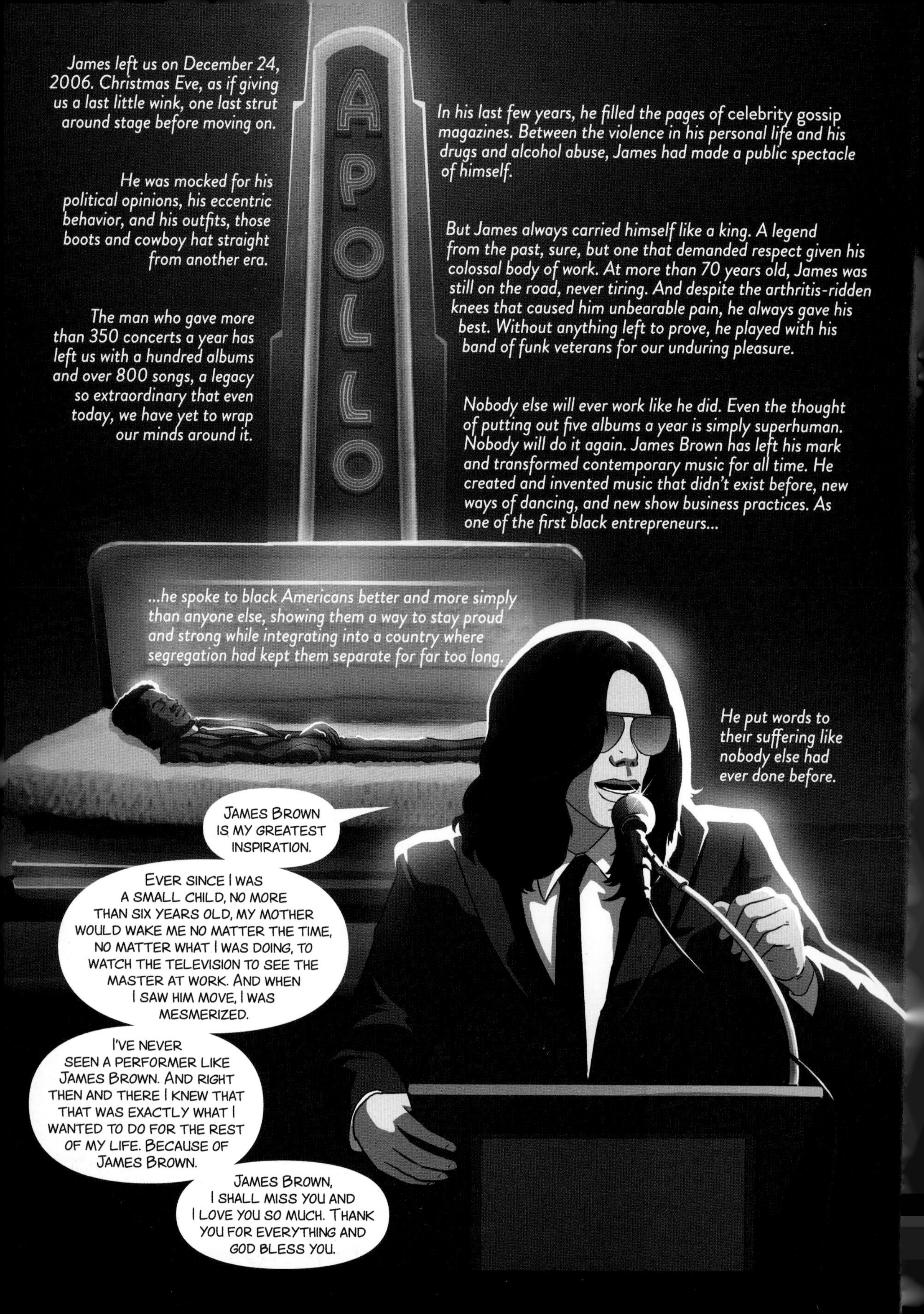
James left us on December 24, 2006. Christmas Eve, as if giving us a last little wink, one last strut around stage before moving on.
APOLLO
He was mocked for his political opinions, his eccentric behavior, and his outfits, those boots and cowboy hat straight from another era.
The man who gave more than 350 concerts a year has left us with a hundred albums and over 800 songs, a legacy so extraordinary that even today, we have yet to wrap our minds around it.
In his last few years, he filled the pages of celebrity gossip magazines. Between the violence in his personal life and his drugs and alcohol abuse, James had made a public spectacle of himself.
But James always carried himself like a king. A legend from the past, sure, but one that demanded respect given his colossal body of work. At more than 70 years old, James was still on the road, never tiring. And despite the arthritis-ridden knees that caused him unbearable pain, he always gave his best. Without anything left to prove, he played with his band of funk veterans for our unduring pleasure.
Nobody else will ever work like he did. Even the thought of putting out five albums a year is simply superhuman. Nobody will do it again. James Brown has left his mark and transformed contemporary music for all time. He created and invented music that didn't exist before, new ways of dancing, and new show business practices. As one of the first black entrepreneurs...
...he spoke to black Americans better and more simply than anyone else, showing them a way to stay proud and strong while integrating into a country where segregation had kept them separate for far too long.
He put words to their suffering like nobody else had ever done before.
JAMES BROWN IS MY GREATEST INSPIRATION.
EVER SINCE I WAS A SMALL CHILD, NO MORE THAN SIX YEARS OLD, MY MOTHER WOULD WAKE ME NO MATTER THE TIME, NO MATTER WHAT I WAS DOING, TO WATCH THE TELEVISION TO SEE THE MASTER AT WORK. AND WHEN I SAW HIM MOVE, I WAS MESMERIZED.
I'VE NEVER SEEN A PERFORMER LIKE JAMES BROWN. AND RIGHT THEN AND THERE I KNEW THAT THAT WAS EXACTLY WHAT I WANTED TO DO FOR THE REST OF MY LIFE. BECAUSE OF JAMES BROWN.
JAMES BROWN, I SHALL MISS YOU AND I LOVE YOU SO MUCH. THANK YOU FOR EVERYTHING AND GOD BLESS YOU.

James Brown

BLACK AND PROUD